ENGAGEMENT AND INDIFFERENCE

ENGAGEMENT AND INDIFFERENCE

Beckett and the Political

edited by
Henry Sussman and Christopher Devenney

State University of New York Press

Published by
State University of New York Press, Albany

© 2001 State University of New York

For information, address State University of New York Press
90 State Street, Suite 700, Albany, NY 12207

Production by Dana Foote
Marketing by Fran Keneston

Library of Congress Cataloging-in-Publication Data

Engagement and indifference : Beckett and the political / edited by
Henry Sussman and Christopher Devenney.
p. cm.
Based on a conference held in 1993 at SUNY/Buffalo.
Includes bibliographical references and index.
ISBN 0-7914-4765-0 (alk. paper) — ISBN 0-7914-4766-9 (pbk. : alk. paper)
1. Beckett, Samuel, 1906—Political and social views—Congresses. 2. Politics and literature—Ireland—History—20th century—Congresses. 3. Politics and literature—France—History—20th century—Congresses. 4. Politics in literature—Congresses. I. Sussman, Henry. II. Devenney, Christopher, 1961–

PR6003.E282 Z6386 2001
848′.91409—dc21
00–047011

10 9 8 7 6 5 4 3 2 1

CONTENTS

ACKNOWLEDGMENTS

The editors most gratefully acknowledge the inspiration and guidance of Raymond Federman that was pivotal to conceptualizing and organizing the 1993 SUNY/Buffalo conference on which this volume is based. Apart from gathering the brightest lights of Beckett scholarship for the conference and contributing two essential pieces that literally frame this volume, Federman made available the photograph appearing as the volume's cover art. It is of the original French cast of *Endgame* (*Fin de parti*), and it was taken in 1957.

The editors fondly remember interventions made by Richard Macksey of the Johns Hopkins University and Thomas Bishop of New York University at the 1993 conference. The written records of those interventions do not grace these pages, yet the contributions we are fortunate to present were surely inflected by Macksey's intimate juxtaposition of Beckett with the prose stylist with whom he would seem to share least, Proust, and by Bishop's filling in the unexpected steps in the translation of Beckett's late dramaturgy into the medium of video. In their conspicuous absence, these contributions nonetheless inform our volume considerably. The conference was enhanced by its setting: the Poetry and Rare Books Collection at SUNY/Buffalo. It was augmented by a display of Beckett materials mounted by the Collection in conjunction with Raymond Federman.

We are pleased to include the complete text of Christian Prigent's essay, "A Descent from Clowns," which was solicited for the 1993 conference. M. Prigent published an abbreviated version of the essay in the *Journal of Beckett Studies,* n.s. 3, no. 1 (1993).

Finally, we gratefully acknowledge San Diego State University Press for permission to reprint substantial sections of chapter six, which appeared under the present title in *Federman A to X-X-X-X: A Recyclopedic Narrative,* ed. Larry McCaffrey, Thomas Hartl, and Doug Rice (San Diego State University Press, 1998), 191–96.

INTRODUCTION

THE POLITICS OF LANGUAGE-BASED SYSTEMS

Henry Sussman

1. The case of Beckett is like no other. The author of texts and characters achieving a tone of relentless indifference and despair: how can this author bring his readers to an enlivened sense of the conditions of thought and existence in the twentieth century; how can he bring about such an intense commitment, if to nothing else than to his own self-generating discourse?

2. There are all sorts of reasons for not discussing Beckett seriously today. For one, there seem to be so many more *compelling* issues and writers. A generation of critics who twenty years ago were aware of the overall conditions of neglect and discrimination in "advanced" Western capitalist societies—and in the colonial cultures they had "annexed"—has experienced no small share of exasperation and bitterness at the aggravation of these conditions over the period in question. The theoretical high road, while asking utterly pivotal questions regarding ideal-based systems and conceptual operations, tended to bracket the conditions of subjectivity that was the framework or arena within which the impacts of hegemony, repression, discrimination, and neglect were experienced. For those whose intellectual attitudes and tactics were schooled under the high-powered conceptual responsibility demanded by deconstruction, Lacanian psychoanalysis, de Manian rhetoric, and so on, two primary alternatives for intellectual work emerged: (*a*) a pronounced veering away from conceptual models that questioned the value and significance of or neutralized existential interests and toward those that "inscribed" or "reinscribed" conditions of class and subjectivity—relating to socioeconomic standing, race, gender, and ethnicity—within the intellectual field; or (*b*) a synthesis, in which conceptual models sympathetic to concerns of subjectivity nonetheless retained the highest degree of linguistic discrimination possible. More succinctly put, in the wake of a perceived indifference on the part of rigorous theoretical discourse to compelling socioeconomic conditions, a generation of cultural interpreters felt it incumbent upon themselves either to adapt subject-driven models or to achieve some meaningful synthesis between these and their language-driven counterparts. These latter—the Derridean, de Manian, and Lacanian efforts—had in turn emerged from twentieth-century phenomenology, the

1

Henry Sussman

Frankfurt School, structuralism, self-aware criticism (e.g., Bataille, Blanchot), and even, to a degree, from logical analysis.

3. To make a "case" of Beckett, as a writer who will speak with some authority to the current splaying out of discursive activity on a continuum leading from "language-based" to "subject-based" models, this enterprise has an empiricist ring to it, no? But the impact of Beckett's quasi-systematic anomalousness is anything but empirical.

4. Language-based critical and theoretical models *never* overcome their "apprehension" of an irreducible intransience inhabiting, haunting the linguistic medium. This "feel" of an ongoing resistance or "drag" that language asserts toward the instruments and frameworks of totalization comprises an attitude that language-based models never "resolve," overcome, or reduce. What would demand the "toning down" or bracketing of this basic intransience is precisely *interest* itself, the impulse to place cultural exegesis *at the service* of something, some set of conditions, whose importance becomes acknowledged (by some community) as more compelling than the registration and elaboration of language's intransigence itself. It is some *interest,* even a discredited and neglected one, that would tell readers of culture to "direct" their illuminations toward an issue, even at the price of streamlining their remarks or applying a "point" to their conceptual "working-through." The motivation to address interests involves altruism: aesthetic and conceptual work should be *for* somebody. Particularly as the world has emerged in the last twenty years, there is a tremendous shortage of altruistic sensibility in every field and endeavor. There is nothing wrong with *interests:* we all have and assert them, knowingly or not. Underlying every consideration of interest is a Subject, whose constitution forms the interest-driven inquiry. The question is certainly not if criticism should utterly abandon the hope of doing anything beneficial in the world. But there is a parallel question: isn't it possible for some commitment, some altruism to emerge on the *far side* of the depersonalization and inhumanity that a significant body of twentieth-century artworks adopted as a milieu and prevailing tone? Beckett is an exemplary writer to which to turn with this question. The engagement that the contributors to the following volume may or may not locate on the far side of Beckett's discourse, in the tain of the Beckettian mirror, is analogous to the radical innocence, expressed in the wish that according to Walter Benjamin, brings denizens of the twentieth century to the gaming table instead of to the falling star, but that retains the innocence of wishing.

5. There is nothing wrong with letting subject-concerns contour or "drive" cultural criticism; it helps to be as explicit about this as possible if this happens to be the case.

6. We begin in a milieu of cultural criticism owing certain of its characteristics to a purported indifference on the part of language-based theoretical models to

subjects and their conditions; and with an author, Samuel Beckett, whose style and characterization, and the affective tonality pervading whose works, seem as well to be detached, "self-absorbed," indifferent. What does Beckett have to say about the interplay and potential dialogue between language- and subject-based models of theory and aesthetic production? This was the occasion for a conference, "Engagement and Indifference: Beckett and the Political," that took place in Buffalo between April 24 and 26, 1993. Although in a way befitting the considerable diversity of the intelligences of the critics and scholars who participated in the conference, this was also the occasion toward which their interventions, the essays that I have the privilege of introducing, were directed.

7. Please note that I am setting this introduction in a quasi-Wittgensteinian format and writing these remarks in a quasi-Wittgensteinian style. To the degree to which I can understand my own motives, I am adapting this posture in the interest of feigning the greatest possible detachment from the occasion and its specifics.

8. Even in the detachment of this style, I have the great pleasure of introducing what I consider to be a distinguished set of answers to the question regarding the possible sociopolitical dimension and benefits to an author who couched and contoured his artistic productions with the seeming greatest possible detachment to subjective concerns, whether experienced in a communal or individual way. The seeming indifference of Beckett's style and the inhumanity of his fictive landscape are indicative of major tenets in the overall aesthetic contract qualifying postmodernism. Even where the critics who participated in the conference and offered revised versions of their interventions in the composition of a focused volume ultimately negated the significance of the political in Beckett's fiction and drama, they held—admirably—to the question demanded by the occasion.

9. Jorge Luis Borges included among the demiurges of Tlön, his counterworld to Western conceptual models and procedures, one Ezra Buckley, "a freethinker, a fatalist and a defender of slavery" (L, 31).[1] Buckley belongs to the "secret and benevolent society" of thinkers (the philosopher Berkeley among them), who pass down the heresy of a language-informed understanding of culture, subjectivity, and experience from one generation to the next (L, 15). The details with which Borges characterizes Buckley reinforce the imperviousness of elaborated linguistic play to predetermined values of any sort, ideological biases among them. In the context of today's effort to trace out the implications of postcolonial discourse and conditions, Borges's specifications regarding Buckley seem gratuitously small-minded, if not reactionary. At the end of his career, Borges allowed himself to be decorated by General Augusto Pinochet, whose Chilean regime was manifestly totalitarian.

Borges's political compromises arose in keeping with a certain strand of modernist aestheticism that was skeptical, to say the least, regarding direct political values or implications of creative activity. The extreme Borgesian position, that the artist inhabits an indifferent "gray" zone somehow immune to political choices, even exerted a certain attraction early in the current epoch of theoretical articulation. There was so much fascination in pursuing the labyrinths of textuality that drawing value-laden political inferences seemed banal, if not dangerous. Having benefited, at the end of our millennium's final decade, from almost twenty years of solid theoretically based work in such areas as postcolonial theory and some of cultural studies, the forced neutrality of the implied Borgesian artist has become a much less satisfactory stance than before.

The wish for a disinterest within the aesthetic enterprise and its reception does not in itself militate for the kind of compromises that were tolerated if not demanded by Borges. The wish for such disinterest can also be construed as the hope for a higher justice and sensibility than would obtain from conditions of aggressive contention. Language-based conceptual systems and their subject-based counterparts both make provisions for ethics: where a subject-driven ethics gains in decisiveness, a language-driven ethics gains in finitude and differentiation. The fiction of Samuel Beckett serves as a splendid occasion for inquiring as to whether directness or deferral increases the political and ethical power of linguistic articulation.

10. Of all literary critics, Maurice Blanchot has perhaps best captured the stark environment and sense of fatal persistence that attends the writing of the "seminal" authors of European postmodernism, Kafka and Beckett, for instance. In "Literature and the Right to Death," Blanchot investigates and elaborates the sustained negation that describes language's relation to life. Writing, for Blanchot, effects a nondialectical synthesis between Being and its emptying. Persistence is one of writing's signature qualities, but writing's persistence transpires as an effect and marker of its negative relation to the trappings and assertions of life. Blanchot's rendition of writing, despite its rhetorical receptiveness to existentialism and Heideggerian phenomenology, is closely akin to the deconstructive elaboration of a medium held in contempt precisely for the morbidity it incorporates and leaves in its wake. For Blanchot, writing's persistence intimates a certain power and belligerence in the face of death; as manifestations of death. Blanchot's formulations of this enigmatic writerly persistence serve, whether by intention or not, as a critical frame for Beckett's fictive prose.

"Where is the end?" of writing, Blanchot asks. "Where is that death which is the hope of language? But language is *the life that endures death and maintains itself in it*" (GO, 54).[2] Death endures writing with its unique capability to temper and inscribe the limits of existential pretensions. But there is a dialectical interplay between writing and life. "The writer who writes a work eliminates himself as he writes that work and at the same time affirms himself in it. If he has written it to get rid of himself, it turns out that the work engages him and recalls him to himself, and if he writes it to reveal himself and live in it, he sees that what he has done is nothing, that the greatest work is not as valuable as the most insignificant act" (GO, 58). In Blanchot's dialectic, writing applies certain statutes of limitation to its existential base and frame of reference; but in return, a certain morbid life "rubs off on," becomes applied to writing. This is the unique persistence that Blanchot can characterize and Beckett recognize in his memorable fiction. Blanchot's formulations of writing's death are themselves memorable:

> We have questioned this meaning of the meaning of words at length, this meaning which is as much the movement of a word towards its truth as its return through the reality of language to the obscure depths of existence; we have questioned this absence by which the thing is annihilated, destroyed in order to become being and idea. It is *that life which supports death and maintains itself in it*—death, the amazing power of the negative, or freedom, through whose work existence is detached from itself and made significant. (GO, 61)

Writing, in Blanchot's formulation, not only furnishes life with certain limits: it detaches life from itself, "perpetuating an irreducible *double meaning*" (GO, 61). Blanchot inscribes the dramaturgy here of what we might call, following Artaud, "Life and its [Writerly] [Morbid] Double." Yet writing derives a certain sublime or uncanny power from its ability to "maintain itself" in the face of this death. This is the polymorphic persistence that both Blanchot and Beckett celebrate.

Blanchot describes an essential relationship between writing's inherently resolute but duplicitous persistence and a certain silence: "But this endless resifting of words without content, this continuousness of speech through an immense pillage of words, is precisely the profound nature of a silence that talks even in its dumbness, a silence that is speech empty of words, an echo speaking on and on in the midst of silence. And in the same way literature, a blind vigilance which in its attempt to escape from itself plunges deeper and deeper into its own obsession" (GO, 50). So Beckett too, in a way described compellingly by Carla Locatelli in her contribution to the present volume "Unwording beyond Negation, Erasures, and *Reticentia:* Beckett's Committed Silence," arrives, through a sometimes playful and sometimes nihilistic sifting of words, at a silence that is at once expressive, eloquent, morbid, and persistent.

Can a profoundly intense and deliberate silence, ask the following essays in different ways, claim a political significance? Or is silence forever consigned to the marginality of apoliticality and complicity? This is a variant on a question posed before: is it possible for the seemingly neutral discourse conditioned by a high level of linguistic attentiveness to be more compellingly political than the discourse of head-on political engagement? These questions find themselves situated at least in the backgrounds of the following essays, even where not directly engaged. Beckett's *The Unnamable* ends with the sense of poignant and overdetermined silence formulated with such elegance by Blanchot. I cull some of the "operative" lines from the conclusion to this novel as a means of emphasizing the centrality of these questions to the essays that follow. What is the political status of some of the most compelling phrases with which Beckett articulates his own unique silence, one that he reaches only on the far side of writing?

> I know that well, it will be the silence, full of murmurs, distant cries, the usual silence, spent listening, spent waiting, waiting for the voice, the cries abate, like all cries, that is to say they stop, the murmurs cease, they give up, the voice begins again, it begins trying again, quick now before there is none left, no voice left, nothing left but the core of murmurs, distant cries, quick now and try again, try what, I don't know, I've forgotten, it doesn't matter, I never knew, to have them carry me into my story, the words that remain, my old story, which I've forgotten, far from here, through the noise, through the door, into the silence, that must be it, it's too late, perhaps it's too late . . . they're going to abandon me, it will be the silence, for a moment, a good few moments, or it will be mine, the lasting one, that didn't last, that still lasts, it will be I, you must go on, I can't go on, you must go on, I'll go on, you must say words, as long as there are any, until they find me, until they say me . . . perhaps they have carried me to the threshold of my story, before the door that opens on my story, that would surprise me, if it opens, it will be I, it will be the silence, where I am, I don't know, I'll never know, in the silence you don't know, you must go on, I can't go on, I'll go on. (TN, 413–14)[3]

11. We say of Beckett that he was a "postmodern" writer and dramatist. There are as many meanings to this predication as there are commentators who have contributed to the debate. The discourse of postmodernism, whether understood as Beckett's own elaborate representation-games, critical articulations of his postmodernist strategies, or as interventions by writers who, in their "creative" work, deploy certain of these strategies, makes an ample impact upon the following essays. For one, among the first doctoral theses anywhere on Beckett's fiction was written in the early sixties by Raymond Federman, who went on to become one of the most generative authors of theoretically sensitive postmodern fiction, whose contributions include *The Voice in the Closet, Double or Nothing,* and *The Twofold Vibration.* Federman co-organized the Buffalo conference with me; his near omniscience regarding the Beckett world is reflected in the distinguished writers who assisted at the colloquium and contributed to this volume. Interestingly, Federman's seniority as an author of postmodern fiction enables him to become a *subject* as well as the contributor of a compressed essay on Beckett's

Company. This phenomenon is most evident in Marcel Cornis-Pope's essay, "'Going to BEthiCKETT on the Way to Heaven': The Politics of Self-Reflection in Postmodern Fiction," where Federman himself appears as a translator of a Beckettian sensibility into the ambiance of contemporary fiction. Federman's intense activity as a site of postmodern speculation and inscription can be discerned in the chapters by Brian McHale and Christian Prigent as well. McHale traces the migration and extension of a distinctively postmodern space explored with particular poignancy by Beckett to science fiction and contemporary fiction and cultural criticism. Interestingly, Cornis-Pope explores the transition between McHale's two major contributions to postmodern theory in his own pointed overview of the field. In "A Descent from Clowns," Christian Prigent articulates the parameters of a uniquely Beckettian environment in terms directly relevant to contemporary poetics. Of all the authors encompassed in the present volume, Prigent is the most skeptical of the applicability of political categories and modes of thought to Beckett's writing. At the same time, Prigent's writing sample is infused, page by page, by the incessant vitality that in Blanchot's meditation constitutes writing's complicit *answer* to death. Even while Prigent rejects the conference's and the volume's pretext, his essay is not at all out of its company.

12. This brings us to the issue of how a group of inventive writers and scholars was able to respond to an arbitrary and by no means universally acknowledged *topos,* one I must say that emerged from my own deliberations on postmodernism, my encounters with the late Kafka and Joyce, Heidegger, Adorno, Borges, Bernhardt, De Man, and Derrida. Many of my own attempts to compose meaningful illuminating accompaniments to significant artifacts have presupposed an ultimate, tragic, but unabridgeable abyss between the linguistic and the political. My instinctual reaction has always been that the order of politics culminates in choices and actions that are by their very nature selective, and reductive in this sense; whereas it is the very "nature" of language to embody and dramatize the expansion and inherent multiplicity of the possibilities embodied in thought and conceptual choices. Implicit in this attitude, which is not my own, but that has a long tradition in deliberations such as Kant's, of the "disinterest" that it is incumbent on Western idealism to inculcate into its many subfields, is the image of a certain "neutrality" surrounding the "purest," that is, most experimental "creative" or conceptual projects. The neutrality that I am conjuring up here is in the form of a literal "surround," an insulation, in the tradition of the frame around the Romantic image or fragment, separating "pure" or "genuine" works from the contingencies of sociopolitical and economic life.

A good and highly creative segment of the literary world in North America has currently turned its attention to conditions and phenomena whose acknowledgment and elucidation will not fare very well within the sublimated insularity legitimated by such neutrality. Particularly compelling is the interface between considerations of the impacts exerted by late capitalism and by the history of colonialism on current conditions of economic life, nationality, race, ethnicity, class, education, "free" thought, and writing. It is not clear to me that the received tradition of the "incompatibility" of conceptual work to tangible conditions is going to be terribly fruitful for such studies; just as I am not certain that clear-cut "heroes" and "villains" in a political sense are going to emerge from these investigations. My hunch is that, in keeping with the extreme sensitivity and sophistication that Western conceptual models have achieved, many of the true goats and villains in the histories of capitalism and colonialism are going to end up situated in a matrix of social forces and contingencies almost as complex and differentiated as the network of language itself. This is, of course, no reason to "foreclose" these investigations.

Beckett is an author whose writing elicits a powerful sense of the "detachment" and "neutrality" that often inhere to the "cutting edge" of conceptual and scientific work. The emergence of a political dimension in his writing will "rack up" a powerful point on the side of asserting literary theory's not-total detachment from the world. But as soon as we begin to discern the contours of something political in Beckett, it will have almost as many different definitions as there are thinkers who describe it.

In this respect, the current volume is a testimonial to the inventiveness and independence of the writers who composed it. Along with Locatelli, one of the contributors who most intensely explores the play between Beckettian discourse and problems in contemporary critical theory is Gabriele Schwab. Beckett's politics, according to Schwab, destabilizes the territorialization of subjects that inevitably results from the wider system of language. "Beckett erases the binary oppositions" in which "the territories of language and the discourses of Western philosophies" are rooted. Beckett has done the "groundwork for a postmodern politics that keeps its currency among intellectuals to this very day: the engagement of the writer is carried out on the boundary between living and being, I and Not-I, subject and object. More radically than any other writer, Beckett has turned these issues into a textual politics." Locatelli, in keeping with her seminal exploration of silence in Beckett and literature in general, distinguishes between the silent testimony to our century's cataclysmic events that became a metaphor for its particular moral bankruptcy and Beckett's "'engaged' silence, one that resists the ethical perfection of the ethical ambivalence of silence itself." Cornis-Pope takes the opportunity, in his essay, to clarify his own definition of the postmodern. While composing his own position paper, in which a systematic and antipragmatic self-reflexivity becomes the attribute of postmodern fiction to which all others are subservient, he furnishes a wonderfully condensed overview of the formulations in the postmodernism debate anticipating and contrasting with his own. In Cornis-Pope's view, the relentless self-reflexivity that one finds embedded in Beckett's prose, and rendered explicit in Federman's experiments and formulations, implies a politics that stands on its own merit. Such a narrative politics, in Federman, involves a "hesitation between articulation and silence, *said* and *unsaid*." Brian McHale, starting out with Beckett's *The Lost Ones,* is willing to "export" the unique spatiality elaborated in this text to fields and works that couldn't be further afield: contemporary malls and airports, Pynchon's *Gravity's Rainbow,* the science fiction of Robert Heinlein, J. G. Ballard and William Gibson, Federman's *The Twofold Vibration,* the criticism of Frederic Jameson, Mike Davis, and Dale Carter. In some respects, the extrapolation of a political dimension from Beckett's writing is less problematical in McHale's approach than in the others: the nature of the contemporary space that is McHale's *vehicle* is so distinctive that to a certain degree it implies its own politics of concerned claustrophobia. Yet on metaphoric and critical levels McHale's own "space trip" approaches an exuberance that may not always be apparent in the Beckett-inspired environments that he characterizes. Raymond Federman, in tracing Beckett's gravitation toward "the voice of language" in Beckett's *Company,* points at the implicit politics of sociability in that voice—and its antipathy to "the gestures and actions of Racism, Anti-Semitism, Chauvinism, Nationalism . . . and all the other isms." In her essay, "The Same Old Hag: Gender and (In)Difference in Samuel Beckett's *Trilogy,*" AnJanette Brush explores the curious indifference with which Beckett describes the human body, especially with regard to sexual difference. Invoking a varied range of critics including Butler, Ben Zvi, Foucault, Cixous, Clement, and Moorjani, Brush finds that Beckett does make a contribution to the discourse of gender precisely in denying the traditional differences. Erudition is a human endeavor that may or may not be conceived as being political. In the twentieth century a certain resolute erudition embodies its own intrinsic politics, one not unlike Walter Benjamin's persistence in his critical vocation even as his world was being dismembered around him. As suggested above, Christan Prigent is the volume's lone dissenter in refusing to posit some sort of *politics* that Beckett's distinctive complex fiction-games join. I, for one, remain convinced of the existence of some interstice at which the Beckettian *poetics* that Prigent so vibrantly dramatizes *overflows* into a political dimension. I am certain that this interstice plays a pivotal role in Prigent's contribution, however inexplicit it remains.

Christopher Devenney's essay, "What Remains?," continues along the line of articulating the extreme complexities and difficulties with which the endeavor of identifying a political "payoff" to Beckett's discourse is fraught. For Devenney, the resistance to politics, whether its articulation is aesthetic or nihilistic, is profoundly political, by virtue of the interpretative violence for which it calls. There is no unambiguous political message to a resolutely violent script; in Beckett's insistence upon the nonutilitarian deployment of language, however, we may discern the basis for a critique of cultural politics.

It is difficult to determine whether Raymond Federman's centrality to this volume takes the form of his overall status as a seminal interface between Beckett and the thinking public and within the community of those whom Beckett has inspired, or whether it is distilled into his commentary on *Company.* To these crucial contributions, he has added what is as close to a definitive statement as this volume encompasses, "Beckett [for] Nothing," an essay whose configuration as a colloquy of textual registers is a Beckettian performance in prose. The volume closes with this silent as well as resonant refrain: within its terms, there is, literally, nowhere else for it to go.

13. Introducing a collectively produced work varies from playing cards in that in the former activity, there is an advantage, even an imperative, in showing one's hand. That function completed, the best that the introduction-author can do is get out of the way and allow the contributions to the discourse to "write" for themselves. I do this gladly, and with sincere appreciation to the authors and conference participants for their patience with a particular, and not unarbitrary, question. I believe that readers of the following essays will find themselves rewarded with a certain coherence of inquiry and perspective, even where Beckett's discourse and age are defined by their skepticism toward totalization and their indifference to ready-made answers.

Notes

1. Jorge Luis Borges, *Ficciones* (New York: Grove, 1962), abbreviated "L."

2. Maurice Blanchot, "Literature and the Right to Death," in *The Gaze of Orpheus,* trans. Lydia Davis (Barrytown, N.Y.: Station Hill Press, 1982), here and henceforth abbreviated "GO."

3. Samuel Beckett, *Three Novels by Samuel Beckett: Molloy, Malone Dies, The Unnamable,* trans. Paul Bowles, in collaboration with the author (New York: Grove Press, 1958), abbreviated "TN."

1

COMPANY
The Voice of Language

Raymond Federman

In the meantime let us try and converse calmly, since we are incapable of keeping silent.

— *Waiting for Godot*

ENTERING THE TEXT

A voice comes to one in the dark. Imagine. Company begins with these words. And again, relentlessly, another of Beckett's fictions asks us to imagine a voice reaching someone in the dark. But let us not be fooled to believe that it is the voice of memory that speaks here, as it does in most works of conventional fiction. Beckett's fiction does not need memory (biography/autobiography) to sustain itself, even though some critics are insisting that *Company* is Beckett's most autobiographical work simply because images of a mother scolding a child, of a father wandering in a rainy landscape (Ireland?) to escape the horrors and pains of his wife giving birth to a child, simply because snapshots of a father and son having an argument, of a man wondering if his lover is pregnant, come and fracture the flow of words of this enigmatic text. No, certainly not, Beckett does not need the support of memory to sustain his fiction, nor does he need the pretense of the past tense on which conventional fiction relies to retrieve images from the past.

All that is needed to keep going, to keep the fiction going, are words. Or as Beckett put it more than forty years ago: "Words, words, this farrago of silence and words, of silence that is not silence and barely murmured words. Or to know it's life still, a form of life, ordained to end, as others ended and will end, till life ends, in all its forms. Words, mine was never more than that, than this pell-mell babel of silence and words." (*Text for Nothing*, 6—c. 1950). The voice of Beckett's fiction has been warning us for a long time now that it is all words, that life is but rhetoric:

11

"this pell-mell babel of silence and words." Moreover, Beckett has been warning us all along that language itself is a fiction. Referring to the paradox of his own fictional predicament, The Unnamable puts it this way: "About myself I need know nothing. Here all is clear. No, all is not clear. But the discourse must go on. So one invents obscurities. Rhetoric."

LISTENING TO THE TEXT

A voice comes to one in the dark. Imagine. And the text of *Company* pauses. Hesitates. Space.

Then the text is set in motion again. The voice speaks again: "To one on his back in the dark." A new proposition has been introduced: the one in the dark who is being reached by the voice is on his back. Consequently, the one whose back has been named must now react to the voice: "This he can tell by the pressure on his hind parts and by how the dark changes when he shuts his eyes and again when he opens them again." And so another logical semantic movement results from the combination of the words: *voice, dark, back, eyes.* The text is now committed to these words, and to the linguistic movement in which these words are caught. Once again fiction has been set in motion by the voice of language. However, we are warned, "Only a small part of what is said can be verified." Only what the voice says, and what is heard by the one on his back in the dark can be verified. It is as simple as that. And so, when the one on his back in the dark hears "you are on your back in the dark," only that much "he must acknowledge," only that much can be heard/accepted/recorded. And the text emphasizes: "That then is the proposition." Here, as in all of Beckett's later fiction: "Beyond what is said there is nothing."

Digression 1

Closed place. All needed to be known for say is known. There is nothing but what is said. Beyond what is said there is nothing. What goes on in the arena is not said. Did it need to be known it would be.

—*Fizzles* 5, c. 1976

LOCKED IN THE TEXT

Indeed, in Beckett's fiction there is nothing beyond the text. Nothing beyond language. That is the essence of Beckett's work. Its aesthetics. Its politics. Or as the unnamable tells us: "I'm not outside, I'm inside, I'm in something, I'm shut up, the silence is outside, outside, inside, there is nothing but here, and the silence outside, nothing but this voice and the silence all round."

We have progressed only a dozen lines into the text of *Company*, and what we have encountered so far are repetitions and permutations of words, brief verbal articulations, murmurs. What simplicity. And yet, what complexity already in this *Company*. In the space of a few sentences already three narrative voices within voices have been heard: (1) an impersonal voice (omniscience of language); (2) a body being spoken to and of (the being of fiction—the told); (3) a narrative voice (the teller) who addresses the one on his back in the dark (the body) in the second person (*you*—in the French text the familiar *tu*). This multiplicity of voices forces one to wonder: who is speaking here, to whom, and of whom? But again we have been warned, a long time ago, by the unnamable, to never try "to tell the teller from the told."

Fortunately for us *Company* explains itself on this question: "Use of the second person marks the voice. That of the third that cankerous other. Could he speak to and of whom the voice speaks there would be a first. But he cannot. He shall not. You cannot. You shall not." That is how the notion of *company* functions in the world of Beckett's fiction—voices within voices that can never tell if they are speaking or are being spoken. To put it differently: the other, in me, speaks my language which is my way of being in the other, of being the other. Or as Rimbaud discovered for himself, and for us as well: "Je est un autre/I is another."

Company: same old voice rattling. Same old Beckettian cracked voice mumbling, murmuring, ejaculating its fiction in the dark. But this time it is The Voice of Language that speaks here in this text: "Devised deviser devising it all for company."

PROGRESSING IN THE TEXT

"I am making progress. It was time" (*Text for Nothing*, 4). Things are getting extremely complicated in this apparently simple text. Not only has the narrative voice splintered into a plural voice, but the notion of the *other* has now been introduced: "If the voice is not speaking to him it must be speaking to another." But which other? *Company*. If the other (*he*—third person) could speak to and of whom speaks the voice, then there would be a third (person) in the text, and perhaps a first (person) too. There would be *Company*. But this cannot be ("He cannot. He shall not speak") because: "Apart from the voice and the faint sound of his breath there is no sound." Why? Because the weak sound of his breath (of language?) tells him so.

Digression 2

Suddenly one remembers *Breath* (*Souffle*—in French), Beckett's thirty-second dramaticule, or what he described to me as a dramatic comma—the first and last breath of humanity: two (*vagitus*—Beckett's own term) cries heard on a pile of rubbish as the light rises and falls. In Beckett's fiction or drama, the voice of language multiplies and demultiplies as it emerges from silence and vanishes back into silence: "Till finally you hear how words are coming to an end," in *Company.*

REFLECTING ON THE TEXT

Have we regressed? Are we again cornered into the unique sound of a single voice? No. Because even when raising such a question, the *He* can only ask if it is to him and of him that the voice speaks. And besides, "The voice comes to him now from one quarter and now from another. Now faint from afar and now a murmur in his ear. In the course of a single sentence it may change place and tone." What the hell is going on here?

What is going on—what we are seeing, hearing, witnessing, imagining (as we have been asked to do at the beginning of the text) is the essence, the pure essence of fictional discourse. But still, one wonders, who speaks here, whose voice is this? Recalling the unnamable (that other old Beckettian voice that could not go on and yet kept going on almost in spite of itself—"in the silence you don't know, you must go on, I can't go on, I'll go on" we hear again the same questions the unnamable asked at the beginning of his tale in order to establish his fictional being and his fictional space: "Where now? Who now? When now? Unquestioning. I, say I." However, in *Company,* it is no longer The Voice of Fiction that speaks, that demands where, when, and who it is, but The Voice of Language itself—a voice that speaks in the dark, beyond time, space, and being. In *Company,* even the pretense of fiction (of story that is) has been abandoned. The fragments of stories (the so-called autobiographical images and snapshots) that seem to come from an elsewhere, from the past, are here simply to create a semblance of narrative order to prevent the words from dwindling into unintelligibility. This is why *Company* gives the impression of progressing almost logically. But this is because the text is constructed word by word into a beautifully and tightly wrought structure that closes upon itself. Thus the images and snapshots surging from the past and dispersed throughout the narration become incompatible with the voice's obsessive stream of words directed toward the one on his back in the dark. As such these remnants of memories undermine their own validity and credibility as stories or as anecdotes.

Digression 3

"I don't know why I told this story. I could just as well have told another. Perhaps some other time I'll be able to tell another. Living souls, you will see how alike they are."

— *The Expelled*—c. 1946

Beckett's obsessions have been constant: "So given am I to thinking with my breath" (*Text for Nothing*, 7). At least since the trilogy of *Molloy, Malone Dies, The Unnamable,* he has been resolute in his refusal to allow the fable (the illusion of storytelling) to entrap his characters, and simply allow language to move toward meaning*Lessness.* Even if in *The Unnamable* the questions of fictional time, space, and being (what used to be called in conventional fiction: plot, setting, character) could only be resolved by attributing the sound of the narrative voice to an invisible, unreachable, and certainly unreliable, and at times malicious power that spoke through the unnamable ("it speaks through me"), here in *Company*, at last, as in most of Beckett's later texts such as *Imagination Dead Imagine, Ping, Lessness, Ill Seen Ill Said, The Lost Ones, Fizzles, Stirrings Still,* the distance between the teller and the told has been reduced to a "rumor transmissible ad infinitum in either direction" (*How It Is,* c. 1963)—certainly the greatest definition ever given of language.

Digression 4

. . . and so on, until all trace is lost, owing to the shortness of human memory . . . and so on, until all trace is lost, on account of the vanity of human wishes.

— *Watt,* c. 1942–45

THE PARADOX OF LANGUAGE

In *Company* as in all of Beckett's later texts, fictional pretenses (and pretensions) have been erased. Language finally becomes the means of getting where the voice wants to go and at the same time the obstacle that prevents that same voice from getting there. Beckett has taught us that language is both what gets us where we want to go and prevents us from getting there. But somehow, Beckett would say, we must do the best we can with this deficient language, and try to "converse calmly, since we are incapable of keeping silent."

Digression 5

"There is no communication because there are no vehicles of communication. Even on the rare occasions when actions and words happen to be valid expression of personality, they lose their significance on their passage through the cataract of the personality that is opposed to them. Either we act and write for ourselves—in which case action and writing are distorted and emptied of their meaning by an intelligence that is not ours, or else we act and write for others—in which case we act and write a lie." This Beckett wrote more than sixty years ago, in his little book entitled *Proust,* and having no other choice, he spent the rest of his life, before he changed tense (on December 22, 1989), verifying this statement in his work.

BECKETT AND FICTION TODAY

Here lies the dilemma that confronts fiction today: how to work with a language that is both a means of communication and an obstacle to communication. That certain writers, critics, theoreticians of fiction (including editors and publishers) still insist on writing, or on asking for a fiction which will relate, represent, describe, explain the world to us, and us in the world, and this from a *moral* and even a *commercial* standpoint, is to miss totally the crucial question of where fiction is today, what it must do, what it can do, what it has to do—and not what it is asked to do. The role of fiction today, its most important function, is to question not only itself, its own medium, its own possibilities (however irritating such self-reflexiveness may be), but to question especially its own language, and therefore, by extension, question "the language of the tribe."

Beckett may never have said it explicitly, but his work does suggest that one can always blame political, social, economic, even cultural evils for the injustices and immoralities of our time. However, when looking more closely, one realizes that these injustices and immoralities do not reside only in the gestures and actions of racism, anti-Semitism, chauvinism, nationalism, and so forth, but that they reside above all in the language of racism, anti-Semitism, chauvinism, nationalism, and all the other isms.

Beckett, of course, understood this many years ago, and has been telling us over and over again to listen to The Voice of Language, for it is there that we shall confront our moral crisis.

Recently two black South Africans played the roles of Gogo and Didi in *Waiting for Godot* as though the play had been written, had always been written for them, and in the process demonstrated that the language of this "tragicomedy" speaks directly to and of their social and political problems. Or as Didi says in *Waiting for Godot:* "At this place, at this moment of time, all mankind is us, whether we like it or not." Such a statement, however ironic it may be, reveals how close Beckett has always been to the truth of language, and the truth of human existence.

Unless we examine, reexamine the words of our language, we will never solve our social, political, cultural problems. The primary role of the writer today is to listen to The Voice of Language. That is what Beckett has been telling us for more than sixty years. He told us—and *Company* of course speaks directly to us and of us—not to trust the old words, "the old credentials," as they are called in *Watt,* not to make "a pillow of old words for a head" (*Watt* again). Yes, that is what Beckett has been telling us relentlessly, as he held siege in his room and battled with language. If we fail to listen to The Voice of Language, the voice that speaks to us inside our language, if we refuse to examine it, down to its most basic functions, we shall never achieve justice, liberty, equality, fraternity on this planet. This, I believe, is the implication of *company* in the work of Samuel Beckett.

Company, in its seemingly simple lexicon, and yet so complex narrative structure, is a work of fiction about being with *others,* about speaking to *others* and being spoken by *others,* but also about being unspoken by the absence of *others,* as the he/we/you of the text listens in the dark, eyes closed.

Company is a work of fiction about communication, but not communication in the sense that the impatient Gentleman or the elegant Lady requests of a fiction writer (especially an experimental fiction writer) who has ventured in front of an audience to discuss or read new fiction. "But Sir! What about communication?" the impatient Gentleman or the elegant Lady asks. To which the experimental writer (very much influenced by the work of Samuel Beckett) replies: "Yes, what about it?" Those who ask that fiction (novels or stories) communicate something merely want to be reassured in what they already know. That is what makes of fiction a lure. We think we are going to find in it the expression of our unity, whereas in fact fiction only manifests our desire of it. Beckett has certainly taught us that through all the detours that one takes or that one wishes, the subject who writes will never seize himself in fiction, he will only seize the fiction that, by definition, excludes him. And that, of course, is also true of the reader.

Communication, in that sense, would merely be a perpetuation of the same old confusion, the same old prejudices, the same old morality—ready-made language. Communication, Ladies and Gentlemen, is also, Beckett would say and has been saying all along, the transmission of the unknown, of the new, of the different, of the unexplainable, of the unnamable, and even the unspeakable. Yes: "There is no communication because there are no vehicles of communication." Or rather, the vehicles we once used are now obsolete, old-fashioned, useless, inefficient, and therefore the primary function of fiction today, of literature, is to invent new vehicles so that we can again speak to each other beyond all the prejudices, injustices, and immoralities of our present state of *company.*

At the end of *Company* one reads this sentence: "Numb with the woes of your kind you raise none the less your head from off your hands and open your eyes." A seemingly harmless sentence, perhaps a bit too lyrical, and even too dramatic, but that states for us the hope that someday, like the one on his back in the dark, we too will raise our heads above the evils of our time, "turn on the light above," and speak a new, purified language. However, if we insist on wanting to remain in the darkness of our present condition, "with face upturned for good labour in vain at y[our] fable," then we shall never emerge into the light, but only "hear how words are coming to an end," and with these dying words we will continue to perpetuate "the fable of one with you in the dark. The fable of one fabling of one with you in the dark."

That would certainly be bad *company.*

2

UNWORDING BEYOND NEGATION, ERASURES, AND *RETICENTIA*

Beckett's Committed Silence

Carla Locatelli

FRAMING THE PROBLEM

Most poststructuralist theories of reading seem to have engaged in the establishment of the "unreliability" of whatever pronouncement a text makes, but without then questioning the *limits* of the unreliability principle.[1] Thus, in the light of current tropological conceptions of the sign, the connection between engagement and silence acquires a particular relevance, but comparable perhaps only to the difficulty of defining it.

The hegemony of the nonphenomenal principle of figuration in language does not only attest to the self-deconstruction of (certain) texts; it has de facto also produced a pragmatic extension of the allegories of reading from theoretical texts to "descriptive" and "fictional" ones, often uncritically applying to them the principle of the impossibility of reference. De Man's idea of literature as the "figural potentiality of language" has probably encouraged the application of such analogy: "Rhetoric radically suspends logic and opens up vertiginous possibilities of referential aberration. And although it would perhaps be somewhat more remote from common usage, I would not hesitate to equate the rhetorical, figural potentiality of language with literature itself."[2]

However, not only does the hegemony of the figural displace the referentiality of discourse; it also represses the possibility of further discussion of the event-quality of any utterance, erasing the radical difference that actual uttering produces, regardless of what is (not) being said.[3] Furthermore, the radical alternatives of actual utterance versus nonuttering cannot be ignored in a discussion of silence, since they *make* a crucial difference (though they do not necessarily *say* it).

The expansion of rhetoric *at the expense of* phenomenology, seems a regrettable effect, since the choice of a rhetorical strategy waives the right to "talk phenomenologically," but by so doing it also relinquishes the task to prove that the phenomenal world does not exist. Still, we should remember that the impossibility of saying something about reality (granting the confusion of the figural with the referential) also establishes the impossibility of assessing its negation. In very simple, if somewhat reductive terms, we could say that not being able to say something is no proof that this something does not exist. In Nietzsche's words: "Once we have devaluated these three categories ['*aim,*' '*unity,*' and '*truth*'], the demonstration that they cannot be applied to the universe is no longer any reason for devaluating the universe."[4]

Even the famous, and variously misread Derridean statement that "there is nothing outside the text" does not necessarily imply that what is unsayable does not exist.[5] Furthermore, we should remember that this assertion has elicited different interpretations, either all inclusive or exclusive, in relation to ontology.[6] This seems possible precisely because the notion of "text" remains so problematic. However, the effects produced by poststructuralist conceptions and rhetorical options of reading have actually (and regrettably) limited the variety of current theoretical discourses, repressing the ones that do not subscribe to what has become an epistemological assumption; namely, pantextualism, and its corollary of textual unreliability.

Indeed, the hegemony of the rhetorical option of reading forecloses certain crucial problems, such as the statute and role of silence, both in communication and in relation to the linguistic system. This hegemony also marginalizes or represses the critical discussion of the event-quality of (non)writing and reading.[7]

In this respect, it is interesting to note that Beckett, too, described the unreliable condition of the writer, but he managed to point to the vigilance of "the eyes staring behind the lids, the ears straining for a voice not from without."[8] Before returning to the issue of representation in language, we must note that "not from without" does not quite mean "from within," but points to a space that resists representation. In other words, Beckett's vigilance takes into consideration both the unreliability of "representational" knowledge, and the actual effect of the unsayable: "I'm the clerk, I'm the scribe, at the hearings of what cause I know not. . . . Then what a relief, what a relief to know that I am mute forever, if only it didn't distress me."[9]

In the light of the plurality of discourses that could proliferate around a thematics or semiotics of silence, the absence of a systematic discussion in contemporary theory is striking. As a matter of fact, after the phenomenological meditations produced in the sixties, the post-Heideggerian "poetics of silence" developed around the seventies, and after some of the "hermeneutics of suspicion" that regarded silence as the only demystified status of preverbal authenticity, we seem to have accepted without further questioning the critical hegemony of a certain type of pantextualism, in the sense that we have abandoned investigation of what possibly lies "outside the text" but *can* be a component of communication.

However, in relation to hermeneutics, we must remember that Jürgen

Habermas's "universal pragmatics" has highlighted the fact that communication is more than language, even though language is the basic prerequisite for communicative action.[10] Furthermore, within the disciplinary domain of linguistics, the study of "pragmatics" has shown the importance of turn-taking in dialogue, whereby silence can be considered one instance or component of such turn taking, or one instance of communicative cooperation also in collective textualized procedures (such as ritual and protocol).

However, the "reduction" of silence to "pause(s)" reduces the scope of the problem, and we notice that neither traditional metaphysics nor speech-act theories alone, nor the latest tropological protocols, have provided complex and encompassing enough definitions of texts that could work for the interrogation of the statute, function, or "nature" of silence. In other words, in spite of the fact that silence is often still conceived as the "void" in a text, the question of what is a text remains so problematic that we actually cannot ask how that "void" really works.

Preliminary to the issue of silence and engagement, then, is the question of how silence has become de facto the interdict of current theoretical discourse. Does a questioning of silence still sound so "metaphysical" in its formulation that theoretical interrogation has to be bound solely to discourse?

But wouldn't this option "essentialize" and absolutize language, still implying the logocentric assertiveness of predicates, while apparently focusing only on the variety of verbal forms? I am obviously thinking all the way back to Plato's *Sophist,* but I am also wondering if the problem could not be reduced, for our present purpose, by clarifying a theoretical point regarding reference in literature. Marcello Pagnini has convincingly argued that in literature there is always an introjection of referents, because the communicative model itself is represented in it, even when there is apparent direct communication.[11]

In this light, it becomes clear that the representation of silence in literature can *constitute silence only as a represented object,* without alluding to it as a system comparable to language itself. And moreover, because of the fact that hearing, unlike seeing, does not involve spatial reference, we tend to associate silence with absence. Yet, as Adrienne Rich warns us: "Silence can be a plan/ rigorously executed// The blueprint to a life// It is a presence/ it has a history a form// *Do not confuse it/ with any kind of absence.*"[12]

How far can we go in believing that we are resisting logocentric concerns, when our rhetoric reproduces logocentered conceptions of the sign and implies a belief in pantextualism? Rhetorical "materialism" may turn out to be so logocentric and absolute, that it forecloses the visibility of silence, an issue that seems at once unavoidable in a theory of textuality, and avoided by current criticism.

It is important to note that most of the contemporary approaches to language have failed to develop "weaker" predicates of silence, and this is a fact that would help to explain why silence remains rather unexplored, but ipso facto still metaphysically conceived, even when it is conceived as a meaning (i.e., as nothing-ness, void, death, etc.), or pragmatically, as pause, suspension, or fragmentation. However, critical thinking about the representation of silence cannot leave intact our conception of language, in the sense that once the representative dimension of language has been scrutinized, the hegemony of pantextualism has to be seriously challenged. *Molloy* challenges it this way: "There could be no things but nameless things, no names but thingless names," and the *The Unnamable* infers: "I shall have to speak of things of which I cannot speak."[13]

The traditional representations of silence as an absolute (albeit mostly a negative one) reveals a strong logocentric implication, and shows that we are still susceptible to the ontotranscendental trap of representation. In order to relativize it, I suggest we make a heuristic distinction between silence as *communication* and silence as *meaning*, and silence as *context* and silence as *text*.

At one level, there is silence as "materiality" and "wholeness" in which silence is the resisting residuum that emerges unassimilated beyond thinking various forms and typologies of silence. This silence has traditionally been referred to as "mystical," but actually it is the silence we "feel," but cannot name or "see" anywhere in language. It is the unnamable that "unaccountably lingers on," and about which Beckett notes: "It is in outer space, not to be confused with the other."[14]

Here, as elsewhere, a spatial designation prevents Beckett's silence from being mystically connoted; the "very essence of the soul," described by Meister Eckhart as the *locus* of silence, becomes in Beckett the a-topic (u-topic) of an "outer space" denoted as neither wholly physical nor mental, but as a space "not to be confused with the other."[15]

At this point, Beckett would probably remind us of the silence that we experience beyond "the music of indifference [*that*] covers our voices," but also of the fact that "we no longer hear ourselves being silent."[16] The "sand of silence" ("*sable/ du silence*") to which one of his poems refers, is inaudible (notice the enjambement marking the end of the line, and signifying the suspension of a split meaning). The implicit reference to the countless grains, which we designate "uncountably" as "sand" alludes to the countless images ("music of indifference") in which silence is always disfigured. We *silence silence* through our countless logocentric representations; Beckett shows it by displacing silence in the paradig-matic sequence: "*coeur temps air feu sable/ du silence.*" Not unsurprisingly, the poem ends by asserting that "*je ne m'entende plus / me taire.*" The "music of indifference" is precisely the music where silence is not heard/understood and thus *makes* no difference, because it is conceived semantically or pragmatically (not as "materiality," "wholeness," or "system"), but only as the result of the interpreta-tion(s) produced by (acts of) language, which circumscribe it.

As a matter of fact, it is the presence of the linguistic system or of linguistic acts, which makes silence surreptitiously "needy" of interpretation. We should remember that the interpretation of silence (be it semantic or pragmatic) is not the "hearing/understanding" of the presence of silence. Emily Dickinson makes this distinction very clearly in one of her poems, whose scope moves far beyond the conventional romantic poetics of the unutterable: "The words the happy *say*/ Are paltry melody/ But those the silent *feel*/ Are beautiful."[17] To think "words" start from silence, rather than understanding silence starting from words, is a challenge that we have not yet taken up in our current interpretive endeavors.

Whenever silence becomes a figure of *evidentia* (even as discursive *reticientia*), it turns into a thematics of silence, or into a logocentered icon. Real silence is simultaneously heard/understood ("felt"), but cannot "be kept," because, strictly speaking, it cannot be designated *qua* silence by the linguistic system (which makes it understandable by always separating its being heard from its being understood). In this respect, we must also remember that when silence is made visible as the silence of listening, it fails to coincide with listening because it is still determined in relation to language and, specifically, in relation to the pragmatics of communication. In other words, silence cannot possibly be represented *qua* silence by the linguistic system, but can surface through it, procedurally, beyond discourse, and even beyond discursive silences, that is, beyond pauses, which signify it. As soon as silence is thought or named it invariably becomes the *idea* of silence, the concept of silence, the meaning of silence, or even the various meanings of specific situational instances of silence (the variable meanings of a pause). Significantly, *The Unnamable* poses the crucial question: "*what* can be said of the real silence, I don't know."[18]

When we represent silence, we usually conflate two heterogeneous levels of reference: the ontological and the semantico-pragmatic; furthermore, when we designate silence as body-less language, we repress its ontological level, and actually confound silence with the absence of language. Predictably then, silence is always found "lacking." Furthermore, we sometimes radicalize our projection of language onto silence, and "reify" our repression of the "singular" difference of silence by conceiving it as the foundation of language. When this unutterable "other" of what is said or written came to be connoted as the evidence of "the infinite continuity of language itself," such belief was then expanded into the unquestioned "evidence" of the pervasiveness of the semiotic, or produced the implied pantextualism of rhetorical reading, which does not seem aware of "the great, invisible labyrinth of repetition, of language that divides itself and becomes its own mirror."[19] We should note the fact that when "language becomes its own mirror" mimetic dissolution does not mean the impossibility of reference, nor ontological dissolution, but simply the realization of self-referentiality in discourse.

Years ago, in his *Archéologie du savoir* (1969) Michel Foucault had warned us against the temptation of believing in some intrinsic silence of writing, a theme he discussed again in other important works, such as "Theatrum Philosophicum" and "Language to Infinity,"[20] where he developed his well-known arguments on the "genitality of thought" and its "singularity." We cannot turn the absence of language into the paradoxical guarantee of the continuity of the linguistic production; as Foucault pointed out, discourse cannot be taken as a symptom of the eternal absence from itself on which language builds itself.

At this point, it is appropriate to wonder if the obsession to deconstruct texts has produced a less obvious but more tenacious form of rhetorical logocentrism, one that ignores language at work, the "singularity" of such work, and "the signs that might appear from this /and which/ must be read as ontological *indications.*"[21] In spite of their rearticulation of complex notions, such as repetition, reiteration, erasure, supplement, and so on, rhetorical readings seem to endorse "the fundamental role of protecting thought from its 'genital' singularity."[22] In other words, we still need to ask more unsettling questions on the *limina* (boundaries) of language, and certainly we need to do so before we tackle the issue of silence.

Beckett was not totally immune to these suggestive hypotheses typical of the "hermeneutics of suspicion." In fact, he expressed a belief in language "like a veil that must be torn apart in order to get at the things (or the Nothingness) behind it."[23] However, we must notice that it is precisely an onto-referential imperative that drove Beckett's linguistic deconstruction, so that he came to conceive not so much the "absence of language" as, eventually, the nonlinguistic condition of the real, and hence of the visibility of "things" or "Nothingness." In the "German letter" quoted above, Beckett also proves to be fully aware of the difficulty of moving beyond logocentered articulations: "I know there are people, sensitive and intelligent people, for whom there is no lack of silence. I cannot but assume that they are hard of hearing."[24] In other words, only if we move through, and beyond linguistic (dis)figurations, can we feel the "lack of silence" produced by logocentered representations; we are no longer hard of hearing, and no longer does "the music of in-difference cover our voices." When silence makes a difference, we no longer silence it.

Therefore, a "correct" representation of silence, something like a performative allusion, should always and necessarily be "plural," that is, articulated simultaneously by different systems of signification; it should be divided and procedural in order to keep a trace of the difference inherent to silence-(in)-representation. For example, it should be related to both the sound system and the linguistic system, combining sound and words, laughter and words, or words and music. Representation of silence could also be expressed through other semiotic systems (for example through the alternation of light and dark), lest logocentrism pervade it, and repress the fact that silence is not translatable into language, nor is to be assimilated to it. If we borrow May's words in *Footfalls* we can remember that: "the motion alone is not enough, I must hear the feet, however faint they fall."[25] The mind alone is not enough: silence has to be heard-understood, and so should always be "doubly" represented.

REPRESENTATION AND SILENCE REPRESENTATION

In taking up Beckett's challenge, we must remember that it is precisely because of its noniconic structure that silence relieves language from the compact solidity of its representational power. As a matter of fact, silence can play an important role in the mobilization and deconstruction of representation since it is neither pure negativity, nor the absence of language, but a system of signification other than language.

If silence appears as a negative, it is because, as Maria Carmela Coco Davani has clearly indicated: "silence acquires its negative characterization through empathy" with the linguistic system, or with other rhythmic and sound systems, such as music, or noise.[26]

Beckett himself has foreseen the possibility of semantic projection from segments of the verbal chain onto silence, and has exploited the semantic possibilities of this projection every time he has prescribed a pause in his dramatic texts. Pauses play an extremely significant role in all of his plays, and may be interpreted in a great variety of ways. They amply show how the meanings of a silence located within a representational system are bound to change, and that they are related to the semantic components of that system.

Furthermore, together with his *dramatic use* of silence, Beckett has also *described* silence, as "holes" and as "enormous pauses,"[27] thus showing both the necessary relation of "semantic silence" to the linguistic system, and a material, "nonsemantic silence" that cannot be properly designated by the linguistic system. Seen in this light, pauses are the correlatives of visual synecdoches, a great many of which are central to the structuring of Beckett's late plays. Fragmentation through silences and pauses works there as more than a suspension of the linguistic or representational continuum: it works as a recontextualizing semiotic device that creates the horizon for systemic signification of both language and silence. In other words, fragmentation in discourse, that is, within the verbal chain, constitutes a way of expressing the limits of language as context, and can allude to silence as another possible context, comparable to language in this respect.

In the "German letter" previously quoted, Beckett has also warned his readers about the interpretive fallacy that makes silence visible, but always as already interpreted: "I know there are people/ . . . / for whom there is no lack of silence. I cannot but assume that they are hard of hearing. For in the forest of symbols, which aren't any, *the little birds of interpretation,* which isn't any, *are never silent."*[28] It seems to me that, together with his usual criticism of symbolic over-tones, Beckett is also pointing to a current interpretive obsession whereby silence can only be defined as interpretation. Because we move "in the forest of symbols," but, much like Dante, we get lost as soon as we move beyond babbling, beyond a basic articulation, silence confronts us with the elemental materiality of a nonsym-bolic meaning; silence disregards that "internal difference, / Where the meanings are."[29] Silence is extraneous to linguistic discretion: *qua* silence it is an undivisible "indifference" which, however, makes a whole difference.

Critics have been too ready to call this nonverbal ontology the domain of the absurd when it is in fact just another "side" of the semiotic domain. On the other hand, we can understand this conception of the absurd as the result of a defensive mechanism: in fact, as long as the preverbal is still defined in relation to language, the interpretive domain is predictably "compelled" to exorcise the radi-cally insensate.[30] We protect ourselves from "folly" with "the word." We talk to make sense, and yet, the dramatic *enjeu* of Beckett's work has shown us the ambivalence of such a defense from the insensate: the "word" is itself a "folly for to need to seem to glimpse / . . . /what—/what is the word—// what is the word."[31] In other words, the "word" threatens to ensnare us into the infinity of its own self-reflection.

However, once room is made to conceive silence without linguistic discre-tion and interpretive projections, once we no longer are "hard of hearing," because we have somewhat delogocentered silence, then the human "intentionality of thought" can be reframed, and bound to the symbolic frame.

The Nietzschean parable opening *On Truth and Lying* (1873) exemplifies well the thematics of the inanity and absurdity of "sense": "In some remote corner of the universe that is poured out in countless flickering solar systems, there once was a star on which *clever animals invented knowledge.* That was the most arrogant and the most untruthful moment in 'world history'—yet indeed only a moment. After nature had taken a few breaths, the star froze over and the clever animals had to die. / Someone could invent such a fable and still not have illustrated adequately how pitiful, how shadowy and fleeting, how purposeless and arbitrary the human intellect appears within nature. . . . For *that intellect has no further mission leading beyond human life."*[32]

In modern times, the liberating exploration of flat surfaces can indeed replace the vertigo of sublime heights, but only so long as we do not then imply that these surfaces are "beyond human life." Instead of a mystical elation, we are called to feel the antisublime detachment of perceiving that the desire to make sense outside the human domain is as senseless as the desire to make language absolute. Modern elation needs to wait for the liberating effects of a "nomadic" relativization, ensuing from a vision of the "word" as an ambivalent "*pharmakon*."[33]

In the Beckettian "letter" which I have repeatedly quoted, silence is also connoted as a sort of *metalinguistic device* because of its systemic compatibility with language, and its assigned function is that of eroding language so as to "contribute to its falling into disrepute."[34] The task of the writer is thus defined by Beckett within a frame conjugating cognition and ethics, whose purpose is demystification.

Writing is located by Beckett at the level of enunciation, that is, at the junction of two systems: silence and language. "Is there any reason why that terrible materiality of the *word surface* should not be capable of being dissolved, like for example the *sound surface,* torn by enormous *pauses,* of Beethoven's Seventh Symphony, so that through whole *pages* we can perceive nothing but *paths of sounds* suspended in giddy heights, linking unfathomable *abysses of silence?*"[35] "Materiality" is articulated: "word surface" and "sound surface" are to be "torn by enormous pauses," and it is also conceptualized: "sound surface" becomes "word surface," and are then turned into "pages" and "paths of sound," showing "abysses of silence."

However, we should not confuse the metalinguistic function of silence with some sort of authenticity inherent to it, even if the systemic indivisibility of silence may have lead interpreters to connote it as the very *locus* of authenticity, much as the unexplored culture of "primitives," which seemed homogeneously monolithic to extraneous onlookers, made them appear quintessentially authentic. However, this way of posing the issue of authenticity here remains within a logocentered and metaphysical thought, one that predictably conceives silence as the opposite of language.

Within the logic of "the same" silence can only be conceived metaphysically, and eventually, as we have seen, as an antidote to linguistic mystification. We should instead try, following Beckett's example, to delogocenter our conceptions of silence, and valorize its "singularity" in order to readdress, eventually, the issue of linguistic authenticity.

SILENCE AND ENGAGEMENT

The connection between silence and engagement is to some extent foreclosed precisely by the tropological beliefs pervading postmodernist theories of literature and of the political, where the issue of witnessing is doubly jeopardized: not only because of the problem of establishing evidence (in relation to reference), but also by the impossibility of "defending" the evidence that may be given. However, we must remember that: "To bear witness means, on the one hand, a calling in, but at the same time it means, for the one who calls in, to stand for it. Man is who he *is* precisely in the witnessing of his own *Dasein.* Witnessing means here not an additional expression of humanity coming to the fact, but rather, it adds to the construction of the human existence (*Dasein*)."[36]

The example of Primo Levi, and of many Holocaust survivors, dramatically bears witness to the impossibility of witnessing, and yet most of them refused to fall into silence. Witnessing has been fulfilled precisely by actually repeating the coexisting obligation and impossibility of answering for the evidence provided, so that visibility could be conferred to this radical contradiction.[37] Linguistic and aesthetic self-reflexivity have never become for Levi a reasonable alibi for a morally acceptable silence.

Other intellectuals, on the contrary, have managed to make the connection between silence and engagement seem fortuitous, or untenable, either by decreeing the absolute semiotic domain of the tropological, or by fanatically prompting the absoluteness, that is, the ahistoricity of moral principles, and the specific assertiveness of moral predicates. The latter invariably become impatient or resentful with apparently "issueless" struggles, presumably leading to moral "nihilism."[38]

In this respect, it is easy for Beckett scholars to remember that in the fifties and sixties many critics displayed negative reactions toward Beckett's work, precisely on the ground of its ethical ambiguity.[39] This is less the case today, but the contemporary absence of questions around the connection between silence and engagement may itself be a sign of the repression of the conflict of interests that such a connection involves, both outside a text and inside it. I am thinking, for example, of the ambivalence of de Man's emblematic assertion: "The passage to an ethical tonality does not result from a transcendental imperative but is the referential (and therefore unreliable) version of a linguistic confusion."[40]

In this context, it is easy to see how textual indecidability may actually foreclose the possibility of analyzing, or even raising, the silence-engagement issue. From an ethical point of view, the dogma of indecidability presupposes a forgetting of the fact that witnessing is "not an *additional* expression of humanity coming to the fact," as Heidegger has suggested, but that witnessing is a component of the very construction of human existence. Critical interrogations today should then focus on the extent to which current conceptions of language erase silence's differences in relation to language, and silence's own difference.

Beckett has already developed this double investigation by displaying a concern with both an ontology and a "linguistics" of silence, powerfully synthesized in another one of his poems: "que ferais-je sans *ce silence* gouffre *des murmures*/ . . . /sans voix parmi les voix/enfermées avec moi."[41] Here, the image of both the silence of whispers ("silence . . . des murmures") and of the silence of "voiceless voices . . . that throng my hiddenness" (as Beckett himself rendered the English version of the poem), points to the imperfect silence through which Beckett has responded to the double-bind imperative of having to speak *through* the absence of language. It is precisely the full assumption of this imperfection that makes Beckett's silence an "engaged" silence, one that resists the absolute perfection of the ethical ambivalence of silence itself: "No truly, no matter what, *I say no matter what,* hoping *to wear out a voice,* to wear out a head, or without hope, without reason, no matter what, without reason. But it will end, a desinence will come, or the breath fail better still, I'll be silence, I'll know I'm silence, no in the silence you can't know."[42]

DELOGOCENTERING SILENCE: REPETITION AS LINGUISTIC CONTEXTUALIZATION

In the elucidation of the *enjeux* of Beckett's silence, I want to show that his project "to fail as no other dare fail" is not only an aesthetic procedure characterizing his deconstructive poetics, but is also an ethical imperative, born out of his refusal to repress human impotence. As a matter of fact, with no simplification of the expressive double bind, his poetics aimed at no less than deconstructing the "esthetic axiom that expression is an achievement."[43]

Yet, in Beckett, the very acceptance of speaking, and of speaking voicelessly (itself a way of voicing silence), prompts the recognition of the dignity of the voice, still coming even when it is clear that no epistemology can back it up. There is no epistemology of the voice, but its dignity can rely on its exercise, an exercise recognizing the unity of *phoné* and sense.[44] Beckett's version of the dignity of the voice, in spite of the lucidly assessed failure of the ability to express, is summarized in a short passage of *From an Abandoned Work:* "No, there's no accounting for it, there is no accounting for anything, with a mind like the one I always had, always on the alert against itself, I'll come back on this perhaps when I feel less weak."[45]

A mind "on the alert against itself" is a mind that coherently makes the hermenutical choice of *différance;* it is a mind capable of noematic reflection, and yet not content with the "parenthesizing" of supposed objectivities (that ultimately, however, produce "no accounting for anything"). Thus, the Beckettian promise to "come back" ("I'll come back on this") highlights the fact that repetition is not only a necessary move in order to show the impossibility of an abstract meaning (of the content of the "accounting"), but it is also the only way in which the accounting impossibility does not become a mere abstraction, negative and closed.

Rather than a strategy of "parenthesizing," repetition constitutes the silent voic*ing* of the impossibility of accounting. Through repetition, a silent voicing keeps its relationship with the present of the enunciation; therefore, the Beckettian promise of return alludes to "a voice that keeps silence,"[46] and implies the ethical resistence to the barter of the silence-of-impossibility with a silence-of-choice.

Having acknowledged in themselves "a mind . . . always on the alert against itself," some intellectuals have dissolved the responsibility of responding, either by decreeing the untenability of whatever pronouncement can be made, or by making transcendental the negativity of knowing. Beckett, on the contrary, made the ethical choice of always "coming back." He responded to his restless "counterthinking" with a dialogical antidogmatic practice, a dialogism that allowed him to show that the unspeakable does not dissolve that of which it cannot speak. We could describe Beckett's achievement using a quotation from Celan's poems: "The no longer nameable, hot, audible in the mouth."[47]

The failure imperative, of having to return in order to move beyond any image, but *through* that image, can show both the inherent conflict of said and saying (the war within the trope described by Nietzsche), and can also "return" to silence its unexchangeable integrity. By refusing to fall into mere silence, that is, by "daring to fail," Beckett offers witness to the unspeakable and inexplicable authenticity of relations, including the indescribable relation to the real world. This relation, however, must not be denied, not even by way of absolute epistemic negations. The world can only be referred to through failing representations, but silence is an improper object of barter if exchanged with expressive impossibility. In this respect, Beckett humorously comments: "Then what a relief, what a relief to know that I am mute forever, if only it didn't distress me."[48]

The world has to be alluded to, invariably missaid but said, because: "There is nothing but what is said. Beyond what is said there is nothing. . . . This is known because it needs to be said."[49] One can see that the impossibility inherently acknowledged by allegorical readings is subsumed by Beckett as the very form of a "going on," as the (bad) figure of a procedural temporality that in the late Beckett is reduced to the minimal "on," itself a crucial indication of a silence in discourse.

The duration of discourse, rather than diegesis; and discursive enactment, rather than rhetoric, confer visibility to a reference to silence, and to the silence of reference:

> No, no souls, or bodies, or birth, or life, or death, *you've got to go on without any of that junk,* that's *all dead with words,* with excess of words, they can say nothing else, they say there is nothing else, that here it's that and nothing else, *but they won't say it eternally,* they'll find some other nonsense, no matter what, and I'll be able to go on, no, I'll be able to stop, or start, another guzzle of lies but piping hot, it will last my time, it will be my time and place, my voice and silence, a voice of silence, the voice of my silence.[50]

The Beckettian mobilization of tropes in the light of temporality ("it will last my time") produces a radical change in the semantics of world models, certainly not because it condemns us to the effect of atemporal allegory, but because it inscribes duration (a silent component) in the "singular" figures that articulate such models ("it will be my time and place, my voice and silence").

We should also notice that Beckett manages to name here three "modes" of silence in a precious critical distinction hardly to be found elsewhere in contemporary literature or criticism: (1) my voice and silence; (2) a voice of silence; and (3) the voice of my silence. He confers visibility to an unspeakable procedural ontology, beyond the diegesis of narration. By deconstructing even discursive negations, he exposes a logocentric abductive fallacy: "they can say nothing else, /*therefore*/ they say there is nothing else." However, the translation of an expressive impossibility into a dogmatic epistemological negation, or the transformation of a power issue into an ontological one, will prove untenable with the passing of time, and not simply because reference is unassessable and unreliable. Beckett is suggesting that the conceptualized (or allegorical) impossibility of expression will wear out: "they won't say it eternally."

The silence of representation and the indecidability of reference in Beckett (signified by the obviously ahistorical and nonrealistic content of his icons), leads him to acknowledge the impossibility of representing otherwise than representing ill, but not to admit that the failure of representation is equal to referential absence. Rather than sealing the conflict of rhetoric and grammar with a decree of impossibility, Beckett suspends the very negativity of the unsayable by enacting it over and over: "But there is not silence. No, there is utterance, somewhere someone is uttering. Insanities, agreed, but is that enough, is that enough, to make sense? I see what it is, the head has fallen behind, all the rest has gone on, the head and its anus the mouth. . . . But the heart's not in it any more."[51]

Insanities are enough to make sense, and to prove that "there is not silence," since what is said can be contradicted, but not erased into not having been said. "There is not silence" as something is always uttered: silence cannot be kept, but the insanity of "insanities" can be amended, by the practice of an ethics of the heart. Maurice Blanchot suggested something similar when he wrote: "Silence cannot be kept; it is indifferent with respect to the work of art which would claim to respect it—it demands a wait which has nothing to await, a language which, presupposing itself as the totality of discourse, would spend itself all at once, disjoin and fragment endlessly."[52]

Beckett's concern for the place of "the heart," expressed right in the middle of a declaration of expressive failure, implies the possibility of establishing the dignity of the voice. At the same time, the indication of the possibility that "all the rest has gone on" even if "the head has fallen behind," eventually amounts to saying that the impossibility of talking about facts (because there are only interpretations) should not produce a negation of the world, but eventually only reaffirm the commitment of the enunciative engagement: "make sense who may."

In this respect, we can say that for Beckett any allegory of reading needs to be renewed by constant reassessment: the practice of reading is needed to testify to the impossibility of reading, lest the saturation of the unknowable and unsayable on the part of the known and said forecloses the very question of speaking. Again, we should remember Blanchot's words in order to understand Beckett's silent language: "It is upon losing what we have to say that we speak . . . by a sort of prolepsis, not so as finally to say nothing, but so that speaking might not stop at the word—the word which is, or is to be, spoken or taken back. We speak suggesting that something not being said is speaking."[53]

A passage from *For to End Again* can highlight the Beckettian deconstruction of reference, together with his resistence to the allegories of reading, and his speaking through the failure of language: "And dream of *a way* in a space *with neither here nor there* where all the footsteps ever fell can never fare nearer to anywhere nor from anywhere further away? No for in the end for to end yet again by degrees or as though switched on dark falls there again *that certain* dark that *alone certain* ashes can."[54] "Dark" invariably falls, "again" and "again," but not without progressively qualifying itself "in the end for to end yet again," as "that certain dark," "that alone certain ashes can" display.

Beckett's imperfect silence challenges the very assertiveness of predicates, even of negative ones, by actually sometimes repeating them: "Leave it so *all quite still* or try listening to *the sounds all quite still* head in hand listening for *a sound*."[55] It is important to notice the transformation of reference going from the first "all quite still" referred only to space, to the second "all quite still" referring to sound, an apparently identical reference that has however subsumed movement, into an iconic rendering of auditory stimuli. This translation from space to sound is quite important, particularly because of the fact that silence is not visual, and while perceiving its iconic representation we may fail to remember the metaphorical quality of the linguistic vehicle that represents it.

Furthermore, here, the passage from "sounds" endowed with meaning, to silence, the silence of stillness, produces the visibility of "a sound," whose materiality is finally released from the implications of a semantic network determined by discourse. The difficulty of listening to "fundamental sounds," that is, "for a sound" beyond "the sounds all quite still" derives from the pervasiveness of the symbolic, and implies here a listening produced by the fatigue of a delogocentering struggle.

Beckett challenges our imagination to conceive of silence not merely as absence of speaking, but beyond it, and also beyond the semantic articulations of listening. This cognitive exercise works against our habits of listening, which is always a listening for, so that silence comes to be understood in our contemporary culture only as part of a predetermined informational universe. In fact, silence is usually described according to linguistic morphology, rhetoric, and semantics, thus remaining unheard *qua* silence. "The indifference of postmodernity" described by Henry Sussman comes to mind in relation to this cultural habit, which saturates silence instead of "expressing" it: "The indifference of postmodernity is anxious-depressive, fusing an endless annexation of qualifications with a fatal resignation to the predetermination of an entropic universe."[56] The "endless annexation of qualifications" makes silence visible only as a paradigmatic component within the domain of the linguistic system, which, indeed, functions as "the predetermination of an entropic universe." Informational entropy may be the modern expression of traditional logocentrism, and it may lead to ignoring the radical difference of silence, a difference that is ontosystemic, and resists translation and discretion into semantic, syntactic, and pragmatic units.

FIGURES OF SILENCE AND POSITIONS OF ENGAGEMENT

It is only through the contextualization of language, achieved by putting discourse on discourse, that Beckett found a powerful way of representing silence without transcendental overtones and even without the usual logocentered hyperdeterminations. Language has to somehow double itself in order to speak through the absence of language, so as to reproduce the ontosemiotic movement that makes silence "audible." The contextualization of language allows silence to become "intelligible," beyond a system of linguistic representations.

Beckett has "voiced" silence through the dramatic mixing of semiotic codes (spatial, visual, rhythmic, etc.), which he combined with a number of subractions within the linguistic system. He has then assembled this dynamic polymorphism through a discursive syntax that contradicts expected combinatory patterns. As Angela Moorjani suggested: "rhythmic patterns detached from linguistic/symbolic meaning go back to the time preceding the synchronicity of language and body rhythm that comes with the acquisition of language."[57] In other words, Beckett reached all the way back to the silence of symbolic "origins," to a point anterior to the establishment of conventionally regulated space-time relations, before a discursive syntax presides over the formation of world models.

Cascando, Footfalls, and *Ohio Impromptu* are strikingly emblematic in this respect; repetition combined with a systematic de-automatization of gestures confers visibility on silence, by blocking or suspending the representational efficacy of linguistic images. It is by failing that language beckons toward silence, and makes it visible beyond itself, and as the ineliminable (and yet unspeakable) residuum of linguistic allusion: "and there all *at once* or *by degrees* this *whiteness to decipher.*"[58] In this sense we can say that repetition does not saturate the space of silence in

Carla Locatelli

these plays, nor does it connote it as transcendental, but makes it visible as a semiotic system, rather than the "Grund" of the linguistic system, or one of its paradigmatic alternatives.

In order to make silence visible *qua* silence (and not as absence of language), Beckett had to create texts in which the culturally assumed mobilization of contexts into texts was reversed: the text became the context of a nonrepresentable text: that is, of the text silence, thus made visible as silence. These texts contextualizing silence were the stunning performative narrations, and narrative performances of the late Beckett: scripts-contexts that "act/ualize" silence through a sort of contextualizing semiosis.

When the reduplication of context is represented in a text (for instance, when a scene of reading a text is included in a play), the transformation of the greater text into a context, signifies a movement that may then allude to a silent "outside." This new context has acquired visibility through isomorphic textualization within a previous text, and through the dialectical contextualization that has occurred therein. Silence, the unrepresentable by definition, is thus made visible by a text made context from within a text, susceptible then of being contextualized by a greater context (i.e., the text can be contextualized by silence).

Given the fact that there is no such thing as the silence of silence, the representational procedure could not possibly be different: the text has finally to textualize itself, as a misplaced context of the unrepresentable. Thus, the text becomes the context of a non-metaphysical, but dynamically textualized, and yet unrepresentable silence. In Beckett's words, the text breaks its context by duplicating it within itself, so that another possible context (silence) can acquire visibility as a prescripted absence: "it will be the silence, *the one that doesn't last,* spent listening, spent waiting, for it to be broken, for the voice to break it, perhaps there is no other."[59]

As it is often the case with major theoretical questions, the Beckettian work has enriched the spectrum of the conceptual definitions of silence, also in relation to its different *enjeux*. Thus, different statutes and figures of silence have emerged in time, enriching the contemporary notions of it in original ways.

One of the ethical outcomes of this proliferation of figures of silence is the Beckettian establishment and elucidation of the difference between what *cannot* be said and what one *has to* say, even when the latter includes the former. The formula "I can't go on. I'll go on" is proverbial in this respect. We must remember that Beckett's acknowledgment of the expressive impossibility never resulted in his acceptance of silence as the last word, and even less, in his subscription to the indifference of a "nothing to say" or dogmatism of "nothing to be said." As a matter of fact, his "nothing to say" is made dialogical by the very impossibility of saying, because the enunciation is inscribed in it, and unsettles any conclusive statement, including the ones actually said. In other words, the "nothing to say" has to be said in order to let silence be silence, that is, in order to leave silence untranslatable, unexchangeable, and unassimilated to some (im)possibility of saying.[60]

In this respect, we can understand why even the tale of "the failed witness" always needs to be told, over and over, in spite of its referential failure, and precisely in order to resist the ineliminable impossibility of saying. As Primo Levi suggested: "I must repeat," even with no prospect of success; "I must repeat" because only through failing the "ideological coercion . . . surreptitiously built into language" will not remain absolutely silent.[61]

The "failure imperative" acquires particular significance even when there is neither referential accuracy nor verifiability in the tale told. Furthermore, even if in understanding there are no facts but only interpretations, the diachrony of tropes does make a difference; actually, it makes the difference that could unveil, at some specific point, the war of concept and figure in every trope and the cultural valorization of that cognitive war. The Beckettian invitation to "fail as no other dare fail" valorizes tropological diachrony and the dignity of the voice; it is an ethical imperative, as well as a cognitive one, in the sense that it underscores the fact that silence cannot be equated with the unsaid.

Not a dogma or an irrefutable evidence, but just a risk, brought into a communicative relation, can erode the pervasiveness of dominant cognitive paradigms, in the light of historical understanding and of tropological diachrony. In Beckett, the actual practice of discourse (of a discourse that has qualified itself as expressively impotent) is the only antidote to a silence always susceptible of being exchanged for meaning, albeit a nihilistic one (absence, indifference, impotence, etc.). Significantly, Maddy in *All That Falls* (1957) declares: "Do not imagine, because I am silent, that I am not present, and alive, to all that is going on."[62]

The Beckettian silence is the nonexchangeable content of an alternative to language, as well as a semantic component of the linguistic system; in that case: "the voice listens, as when it speaks, listens to *its* silence."[63] The fear of semantic totalization does not prevent Beckett from *using* words in order to make silence speak, even when he is fully aware of the undecidability of meaning and of the proliferating aporias of his discourse. The opening of *The Unnamable* sets the epistemic coordinates in which the Beckettian meditation on silence will then develop: "What am I to do, what shall I do, what should I do, in my situation, how proceed? By aporia pure and simple? Or by affirmations and negations invalidated as uttered, or sooner or later?"[64]

As we all know, Beckett chose to practice the second alternative; his entire work can be seen as a resistence to the "pure and simple aporia" that dichotomizes silence and language. "He condemns himself to writing because he knows that silence would be a sacrifice (thus a substitution) of silence itself, which is the true, desperate desire of each one of his sentences."[65]

Rather than predicate silence, Beckett "situates" it. Therefore, it should not be mistaken for a thematics in his work, a thematics established once and for all and recurrently revisited, nor should it be conceived as a mere rhetorical *locus* of persuasion (as in *theologia negativa*). It should not even be thought of as an onto-linguistic "necessity." In fact, throughout his career, Beckett has shown us that silence always needs to be alluded to, but not to be "qualified," within a linguistic perspective. If anything, it has to be disqualified (as a semantic component of language), and delogocentered, so as to remain, precisely and powerfully, silence.

Beckett has shown us that the amoral silence is always subject to penetration by any empowering defacement; in fact, it thrives on interpretive hyperqualification; the ethical silence, on the contrary, resists the indifference of nihilistic totalizing. The amoral silence substitutes the event with informational entropy; the engaged silence asseverates the unspeakability of the event alluded to by the repeated missaying.

Therefore, the oscillation between silence and language cannot come to the halt of an aporia: silence cannot be dissolved by logorrhea, and logorrhea cannot be dissolved by silence. The "obligation to express" is neither positive nor negative; it is the need to asseverate our existence, through the word that makes us disappear.

The paradox of necessity and impossibility that silence puts before us shows the ultimate untenability of the boundary between presence and absence, positive and negative, through the systemic heterogeneity but coexisting ontology of our human "silent language" and "linguistic silence." This existential aporia may be described, quoting Celan, again: "'We are strangers.'/ As when in silence, 'two silences fill our mouth'."[66]

Notes

1. Although a tropological critique of the sign has been largely developed and inspired by the works of Paul de Man, most poststructuralist writers still seem to subscribe to it in full. For a valuable introduction to the problem, see Paul de Man, *Allegories of Reading* (New Haven and London: Yale University Press, 1979), and Jonathan Culler, *On Deconstruction* (Ithaca, N.Y.: Cornell University Press, 1982).

2. De Man, *Allegories of Reading*, p. 10.

3. In spite of the fact that the following statement comes at the end of "Reading (Proust)," I hardly believe it should be taken as conclusive: "what we call time is precisely truth's inability to coincide with itself." De Man, *Allegories of Reading*, p. 78.

4. Friedrich Nietzsche, *The Will to Power*, ed. W. Kaufman (New York: Vintage Books, 1963), p. 194.

5. "[W]hen it is said about the deconstructive perspective that there is nothing outside the text, then I say to myself: if deconstruction *really* consisted in saying that everything happens in books, it wouldn't deserve *five* minutes of anybody's attention." Jacques Derrida, "Deconstruction in America: An Interview with Jacques Derrida," *Critical Exchange* 17 (Winter 1985): 1–33, quotation p. 15.

6. For example, see Geoffrey Galt Harpham's comment: "the notorious statement that there is nothing outside the text really means there is nothing outside context. Any 'text' implies all the structures called 'real,' 'economic,' 'historical,' socio-institutional, in short all possible referents." In "Derrida and the Ethics of Criticism," *Textual Practice* 5. 3 (Winter 1991): 389–98.

7. In this respect, some current feminist theory provides an interesting movement of "resistence to theory," worthy of attention particularly because of its erosion of the circular (but closed) effect of allegory. I should also like to mention here the works of Rodolphe Gasché and Marcello Pagnini, because of their critique of the extension of the allegorical interpretive option. See Rodolphe Gasché, "In-Difference to Philosophy: De Man on Kant, Hegel, and Nietzsche," in *Reading de Man Reading,* ed. L. Waters and W. Godzich (Minneapolis: University of Minnesota Press, 1989), pp. 259–94; and *The Tain of the Mirror: Derrida and the Philosophy of Reflection* (Cambridge, Mass.: Harvard University Press, 1986). Also see Marcello Pagnini, *The Pragmatics of Literature,* trans. Nancy Jones-Henry (Bloomington: Indiana University Press, 1987).

8. Samuel Beckett, "Texts for Nothing, V," in *Collected Shorter Prose 1945–1980* (London: John Calder, 1984), p. 85.

9. Ibid.

10. Jürgen Habermas, *The Theory of Communicative Action,* trans. T. McCarthy (Boston: Beacon Press, 1984); and *Texte und Kontexte* (Frankfurt: Suhrkamp, 1991).

11. For a discussion of the introjection of the communicative model in literature, see Pagnini, *The Pragmatics of Literature.* See also A. Whiteside and I. Issacharoff, eds., *On Referring in Literature* (Bloomington: Indiana University Press, 1987).

12. Adrienne Rich, "Cartographies of Silence," in *The Dream of a Common Language* (New York: W. W. Norton, 1978), p. 17. Italics mine.

13. Samuel Beckett, *Molloy* (New York: Grove Press, 1955), p. 41; and *The Unnamable* in *Three Novels by Samuel Beckett* (New York: Grove Press, 1958), p. 291.

14. Samuel Beckett, "Horn Came Always," in *Collected Shorter Prose 1945–1980* (London: John Calder, 1984), p. 194.

15. For a philosophical discussion of silence, see Bernard P. Dauenhauer, *Silence: The Phenomenon and Its Ontological Significance* (Bloomington: Indiana University Press, 1980); for a theological discussion, see Massimo Baldini and Silvano Zucal, eds., *Le Forme del silenzio e della parola* (Brescia: Morcelliana, 1990). For a semiotic discussion, see Gian Paolo Caprettini, "Per una tipologia del silenzio," in M. Baldini and S. Zucal, *Le Forme del silenzio,* pp. 423–30. See also Ugo Volli, *Apologia del silenzio imperfetto* (Milan: Feltrinelli, 1991); and Pier Aldo Rovatti, *L'Esercizio del silenzio* (Milan: Cortina, 1992). In relation to

Beckett, see Hélène Baldwin, *Samuel Beckett's Real Silence* (University Park and London: The Pennsylvania State University Press, 1981); John Fletcher, "Bailing Out the Silence," in *Samuel Beckett's Waiting for Godot,* edited with an Introduction by H. Bloom (New York: Chelsea House, 1987), pp. 11–22; Georges Bataille, "Le Silence de Molloy," *Critique* 58 (May 1951). Now translated as: "Molloy's Silence" in *Modern Critical Interpretations: Molloy, Malone Dies. The Unnamable,* edited with an introduction by H. Bloom (New York: Chelsea House, 1988); Tom Bishop, "The Temptation of Silence," in *As No Other Dare Fail* (London: John Calder, 1986), pp. 24–29.

16. The actual Beckett poem reads as follows: "musique de l'indifférence/ coeur temps air feu sable/ du silence éboulement d'amours/ couvre leur voix et que/ je ne m'entende plus/ me taire." Samuel Beckett, *Collected Poems in English and French* (New York: Grove Press, 1977), p. 44.

17. Emily Dickinson, poem 1750, in *The Complete Poems of Emily Dickinson,* ed. Thomas J. Johnson (Boston: Little, Brown & Company, 1960), p. 709.

18. Samuel Beckett, *The Unnamable,* in *Three Novels by Samuel Beckett* (New York: Grove Press, 1958), p. 171. Italics mine.

19. Michel Foucault, "Language to Infinity," in *Language, Counter-memory, Practice,* edited with an introduction by D. F. Bouchard (Ithaca, N.Y.: Cornell University Press, 1977), p. 56.

20. Michel Foucault, *Archéologie du savoir* (Paris: Gallimard, 1969), English translation: *The Archaeology of Knowledge,* trans. A. M. Sheridan Smith (London: Tavistock, 1972); "Theatrum Philosophicum," and "Language to Infinity," in *Language, Counter-memory, Practice,* pp. 165–96 and 56–60.

21. Ibid., p. 57.

22. "The morality of goodwill, which assists commonsense thought, had the fundamental role of protecting thought from its 'genital' singularity." Michel Foucault's "Theatrum Philosophicum," in *Language, Counter-memory, Practice,* p. 182.

23. Samuel Beckett, "German Letter of 1937," in *Disjecta: Miscellaneous Writings and a Dramatic Fragment,* edited with a foreword by Ruby Cohn (London: John Calder, 1983), pp. 51–54, translation pp. 170–73, quotation p. 171.

24. Ibid., p. 152.

25. Samuel Beckett, *Footfalls* (1976), in *Collected Shorter Plays* (London: Faber and Faber, 1984), p. 241.

26. "In ogni caso si può dire che il silenzio acquisti la sua caratterizzazione negativa per simpatia." Maria Carmela Coco Davani, *Godot il crack del codice* (Palermo: Flaccovio, 1977), p. 105.

27. Samuel Beckett, "German Letter of 1937," in *Disjecta,* p. 172.

28. Ibid. Italics mine.

29. Emily Dickinson, poem 258, in *The Complete Poems of Emily Dickinson,* p. 118.

30. The pioneering studies of Julia Kristeva, and especially *La Révolution du langage poétique* (Paris: Seuil, 1974), introduced the distinction between the "semiotic" and the

"symbolic." Among other feminist critics who analyze the extent of the patriarchal symbolic, and focus their attention on the "preverbal" state, I will mention: Dorothy Dinnerstein, *The Mermaid and the Minotaur: Sexual Arrangements and Human Malaise* (New York: Harper & Row, 1976); Nancy Chodorow, *The Reproduction of Mothering: Psychoanalysis and the Sociology of Gender* (Berkeley: University of California Press, 1978); and, with specific reference to Beckett, Angela Moorjani, *The Aesthetics of Loss and Lessness* (New York: St. Martin's Press, 1992).

31. Although only the semantic movement of the entire poem can do justice to the expression of the radical and irreducible ambiguity ("folly") of language, I have taken the liberty of quoting only the ending of Beckett's "what is the word" in *As the Story Was Told* (London: John Calder, 1990), p. 134.

32. *Friedrich Nietzsche on Rhetoric and Language,* ed. and trans. S. L. Gilman, C. Blair, and D. J. Parent (New York: Oxford University Press, 1989), p. 246. Italics mine.

33. I am obviously referring here to Jacques Derrida's *Plato's Pharmacy,* translated with an introduction by Barbara Johnson (Chicago: University of Chicago Press, 1981).

34. Beckett, *Disjecta,* p. 172.

35. Ibid.

36. I refer to Martin Heidegger's essay on "Hölderlin and the Essence of Poetry" (1934–35), quoted in my own translation. For the original, see "Holderlin und das Wesen der Dichtung," in *Erläuterungen zu Hölderlins Dichtung,* 4th ed. (Frankfurt: Klostermann, 1971), p. 36: "Zeugen bedeutet einmal ein Bekunden; aber zugleich meint es: für das Bekundete in der Bekundung einstehen. Der Mensch ist der, der er ist, eben in der Bezeugung des eigenen Daseins. Diese Bezeugung meint hier nicht einen nachträglichen und beiherlaufenden Ausdruck des Menschseins, sondern sie macht das Dasein des Menschen mit aus."

37. See, in particular, Primo Levi, *I Sommersi e i salvati* (Turin: Einaudi, 1986). English translation: *The Drowned and the Saved,* trans. R. Rosenthal (New York: Simon & Schuster, 1988).

38. We should keep in mind that, historically, most "liberation struggles" (of slaves, bourgeois, blacks, women, gays, etc.) originate from oppressions that have no cultural visibility, hence they may seem "issueless," but we should also remember that once visibility is achieved, the definition of specific issues often functions as a way of controlling further changes and securing real shifts in power.

39. Beckett's reception at that time displays interesting oscillations of appreciation, mostly linked to how "nihilism" was understood by critics. Georg Lukàcs had a powerful influence on the development of Beckett criticism, and ironically so, when he was modifying and attenuating his criticism against Beckett (see "The Ideology of Modernism," in *The Meaning of Contemporary Realism,* trans. J. Mander and N. Mander (London: Merlin, 1963), pp. 17–46. Quite surprising, because not really attuned to the main theses of his *Negative Dialectics,* trans. E. B. Ashton (New York: Continuum, 1983) and *Minima Moralia,* trans. E. F. N. Jephcott (London: Verso, 1984), is Theodor Adorno's viewpoint on

Endgame (see "Versuch, das Endspiel zu versthelen," in *Noten Zur Literatur II* [Frankfurt: Suhrkamp Verlag, 1961]; in English, see "Trying to Understand *Endgame*," in *Samuel Beckett's Endgame*, Modern Critical Interpretations Series, ed. H. Bloom [New York: Chelsea House, 1988], pp. 9–40). In more recent times the works of both A. Alvarez, *Beckett* (Glasgow: Fontana/Collins, 1973) and Luciano Codignola, *Il teatro della guerra fredda* (Urbino: Argalia, 1969) could be read as echoes of the disapproval of those "masters."

40. De Man, *Allegories of Reading*, p. 206. Important resistence to this view has been developed recently, and should be remembered. See, for example, *Reading De Man Reading*. I should also like to remember, as a contrasting example to de Man's rhetorical deconstructive practice, Barbara Johnson's work, which has consistently been engaged in investigating the possibility of translating the indecidability of textual deconstruction into political awareness. Significantly, the title of her earlier book *The Critical Difference* (Baltimore: Johns Hopkins University Press, 1980) is echoed in the following: *A World of Difference* (Baltimore: Johns Hopkins University Press, 1987). While not rejecting de Manian "rhetoric," the *telos* of Johnson's work seems altogether different.

41. Beckett, *Collected Poems in English and French*, p. 59. First published in *Transition Forty Eight* 2 (June 1948): 96. Beckett's English version, significantly different, reads: "What would I do without this silence where the murmurs die/ . . . /among the voices voiceless/that throng my hiddenness."

42. Samuel Beckett, "Texts for Nothing VIII," in *Collected Shorter Prose 1945–1980* (London: John Calder, 1984), p. 97.

43. "The kind of work I do is one in which I'm not master of my material. . . . There seems to be a kind of esthetic axiom that expression is an achievement—must be an achievement. My little exploration is that whole zone of being that has always been set aside by artists as something unquestionable—as something by definition incompatible with art." Samuel Beckett, "Interview with Israel Shenker," in *The New York Times*, May 5, 1956; reprinted in L. Graver and R. Federman, eds., *Samuel Beckett: The Critical Heritage* (London: Routledge and Kegan Paul, 1979), pp. 146–49, quotation p. 148.

44. For a discussion of the unity of *phoné* and sense, and of the unity of thought and voice in *logos*, see Jacques Derrida, *Speech and Phenomena*, edited, translated, and with an introduction by David B. Allison (Evanston, Ill.: Northwestern University Press, 1973).

45. Samuel Beckett, "From an Abandoned Work," in *Collected Shorter Prose 1945–1980*, p. 131.

46. Derrida, *Speech and Phenomena*, p. 84.

47. "Das nicht mehr zu Nennende, heiss,/ hörbar im Mund," Paul Celan, "Ein Auge, Offen" in *Sprachgitter* (1959), *Gesammelte Werke*, vol. 1, Poetry I (Frankfurt: Suhrkamp, 1986), p. 187. English translation: *Speech-Grille and Selected Poems*, trans. Joachim Neugroschel (New York: E. P. Dutton, 1971). The poem: "One Eye Open," p. 139.

48. Samuel Beckett, "Texts for Nothing, V," in *Collected Shorter Prose 1945–1980*, p. 85.

49. Samuel Beckett, "Closed Space," in *Collected Shorter Prose 1945–1980*, p. 199. The ethical *enjeu* of the statement: "there is nothing but what is said" surfaces again and again in Beckett's late works, and particularly in *Worstward Ho*. For a discussion of this "theme," see Carla Locatelli, *Unwording the World: Beckett's Prose Work after the Nobel Prize* (Philadelphia: University of Pennsylvania Press, 1990).

50. Samuel Beckett, "Texts for Nothing, X," in *Collected Shorter Prose 1945–1980*, p. 105. Emphasis mine.

51. Samuel Beckett, "Texts for Nothing, X," in *Collected Shorter Prose 1945–1980*, p. 104.

52. Maurice Blanchot, *The Writing of the Disaster*, trans. Ann Smock (Lincoln: University of Nebraska Press, 1986), p. 29.

53. Ibid., p. 21.

54. Samuel Beckett, "For to End Yet Again," in *Collected Shorter Prose 1945–1980*, p. 181. Emphasis mine.

55. Samuel Beckett, "Still," in *Collected Shorter Prose 1945–1980*, p. 185. Emphasis mine.

56. Henry Sussman, *Afterimages of Modernity* (Baltimore: Johns Hopkins University Press, 1990), p. 176.

57. Moorjani, *The Aesthetics of Loss and Lessness*, p. 207.

58. Beckett, "For to End Yet Again," in *Collected Shorter Prose 1945–1980*, p. 180. Emphasis mine.

59. Beckett, *The Unnamable*, in *Three Novels by Samuel Beckett*, p. 414. Emphasis mine.

60. Shoshana Felman, "After the Apocalypse: Paul de Man and the Fall to Silence," in S. Felman and Dori Laub, M.D., *Testimony: Crises of Witnessing in Literature, Psychoanalysis, and History* (New York and London: Routledge, 1992).

61. Primo Levi, *I Sommersi e i salvati*, p. 37.

62. Samuel Beckett, "All That Falls," in *Collected Shorter Plays* (London: Faber and Faber, 1984), p. 27.

63. Samuel Beckett, *The Unnamable*, in *Three Novels by Samuel Beckett*, p. 408. Italics mine.

64. Ibid., p. 291.

65. "Egli si condanna a scrivere perche' sa che il silenzio sarebbe il sacrificio (e quindi una sostituzione) del silenzio che e' il vero desiderio disperato di ogni frase." Carla Locatelli, *La Disdetta della parola: L'Ermemeutica del silenzio nella prosa inglese di Samuel Beckett* (Como: Artegrafica Guarisco, 1978; reprinted: Bologna: Patron, 1984), p. 6.

66. ". . . Wir sind Fremde.)/ . . . / zwei/ Mundvoll Schweigen." Celan, "*Sprachgitter*," p. 167. English translation in *Speech-Grille and Selected Poems;* for the poem "Speech-Grille," see p. 109.

3

THE POLITICS OF SMALL DIFFERENCES
Beckett's The Unnamable

Gabriele Schwab

PRELIMINARIES

If I were a literalist about the term "politics" my argument today would be that Beckett's engagement lies with the new class of intellectual bums, the lumpenproletariat of lay philosophers and old humanists who have been layed off, burned out by or dropped out of postmodern academia. But then again, this perspective might be too much of a projection of the bankrupt and run-down schools of humanities at the universities of California where—to use Beckett's famous juxtaposition in his Proust essay—the "suffering of being" is slowly but inevitably replaced by the "boredom of living." Since I am less of a literalist, I will talk about Beckett's struggle with and against the system of language that, for him, is a territory of politics in the sense that language as a system works toward the territorialization of subjects. While mapping out and traversing the territories of language and the discourses of Western philosophies, Beckett erases the binary oppositions in which they are grounded. If we were to find a formula for his territorial politics we might say that he swallows up the spaces of difference, differentiation, and discrimination in language in order to unsettle the basic premises of language as a system.

"The thing to avoid is the spirit of system" says the unnamable, quite in tune with the Proust essay's juxtaposition between the "boredom of living" and the "suffering of being" (*Proust,* p. 8). The latter is achieved through a specific mode of attention to the world, a form of "un-systematic" thought or "free play of every faculty" (p. 9) in which objects are perceived "as particular and unique and not merely the member of a family" (p. 11). Written in 1931, these assertions lay a groundwork for a postmodern politics that keeps its currency among intellectuals to this very day: the engagement of the writer is carried out on the boundary between living and being, I and Not-I, subject and object. More radically than any other writer, Beckett has turned these issues into a textual politics in which

42

language ceases to be the object of the writer and becomes instead his form of thought and mode of being (instead of living).

The engagement here is thus not a commitment to political issues, but to the very issue of writing and form as politics. Such writing needs to practice a certain "indifference" toward the possible referential worlds of language in order to draw attention to itself as politics. If this "gravitation toward a certain indifference" is, as Henry Sussman has argued, "as much a style and a conceptual position as an affective state," then it also entails a certain politics of desire. Writing becomes self-effacement rather than self-constitution, displaying a willful indifference toward the unequivocal constitution of a writing subject. Beckett even radicalizes this process: ultimately his writing renders the very distinction between subject and object or I and Not-I indifferent—not because it is no longer a concern, but, on the contrary, because it becomes impossible to maintain the difference in the particular form of thought practiced as writing.

The form my paper takes is less a continuous line of argument than a series of reflections that explore Beckett's relationship to postmodern categories and their political implications. More specifically, my talk plays out a sequence of three "lines of flight" or "spiralling loops" in *The Unnamable* in order to draw out the epistemological implications of Beckett's politics of small differences. One might also call this a politics of difference at its vanishing point, a politics that takes a radical stance in relation to issues of authorship, otherness, and the interpellation of the subject (Althusser). In particular, I want to trace those movements through language that attempt to collapse or reconfigure the system of binary oppositions that underlies our linguistic and philosophical traditions. Theorists from Benveniste and de Saussure to Lacan and Bateson have defined linguistic information in terms of difference. Beckett's discursive strategy of collapsing differences through linguistic procedures reveals a commitment to rethinking some of our most cherished epistemological and cultural premises about difference and otherness as well as about being in language and relating to objects or others. I have chosen to focus on *The Unnamable* because this text invokes Beckett's concerns in their most abstract and pure, but also in their most relentless form. It resonates with pervasive concerns of postmodern politics such as authorship and authority, subject and otherness, the myth of origin, authenticity, or self-presence, and the limits of textuality and subjectivity.

POSTMODERN PARANOIA AND PARADOX

He speaks of me, as if I were he, as if I were not he. (p. 163)

Without a distinction between I and Not-I, it would seem impossible to establish a relationship to any form of otherness. And yet, the unnamable tenaciously clings to a notion of anonymous others as instances of interpellation who force him to speak of himself, who determine the rules of his language games, who impute a self and a voice on him, and who want to define him as a living being. At times, he fantasizes that he is indebted to them, expiating a crime unknown to him. There are also concrete others, characters from the earlier books of the trilogy. At the beginning, he describes how Malone passes by him, though not without immediately qualifying that it could also be Molloy with Malone's hat. Since he mistrusts his sensory organs as instruments of reality testing, he also doubts if these characters even exist outside of his imagination. He remains equally undecided about whether a cry he hears comes from himself or from another "definitely not human" creature.

At that stage he still perceives others as figures who are at least temporarily differentiated from him. But as soon as the pure form of an other manifests itself, he compulsively effaces it. His constant oscillation between differentiation and dedifferentiation erodes the boundaries between different characters. He even inverts the logical possibility of understanding the whole textual world as his own projection, by claiming that he has been invented by the other characters. For him, the boundaries between inventing and being invented no longer obtain.

The most tangible modes of relating to self and other are also the most extreme poles: paranoid rejection, on the one hand, and de-differentiating fusion on the other. The first marks the pole of a politics of postmodern paranoia, the latter one of a postmodern nostalgia for the primordial and the undifferentiated. In language, the first manifests itself as a paranoia of textual self-reflexivity, the latter as a *delire* that resists the constraints of sense and verges on the boundaries toward nonsense and schizophrenia. The dynamic interaction between the two poles of paranoia and nostalgia is enacted as a playful merging of primary and secondary processes in language. This interaction generates a singular form of the "political unconscious" in which the unconscious appears not in the form of repressed psychological or ideological material but as a "form of thought" (in the sense in which Beckett uses this term in his Proust essay). To put it differently: in its spiraling loops Beckett's discourse brings forth the unconscious implications and ideological underpinnings of the forms of thought that mark the tradition of Western philosophies.

The unnamable enacts both postmodern paranoia and postmodern nostalgia for the primordial—with one important qualification: even his nostalgia is marked by paranoia and, most importantly, both positions are mockingly exposed by the narrator's sarcastic and comical voice as futile relics of traditional "human" concerns. However, due to their persistence in the unnamable's forms of thought or, if one likes, in his political unconscious, the latter must be endlessly reiterated—albeit in a mode of simulation.

If the death of the subject is one of the most tenacious epistemological configurations of postmodernism, Beckett explores its most relentless consequences. His commitment is to avoid any trace of self-manifestation and the paranoid structure of his discourse is an effect of this politics of continual self-erasure. The most prominent strategies of this self-erasure are negation and "othering." Both strategies result in the blurring of any conceivable boundaries that could demarcate a speaking subject. The most simple strategy of "othering" follows the logic "I am Not-I" into and through all its possible ramifications. The unnamable likes to think of himself as invented by others from whom he eventually becomes indistinguishable, but his imagined fusions with others are never symbiotic unions that create a primordial oneness. Rather they are involuntary fusions induced by the logic of his own discourse or calculated acts of mimicry intended to deceive the others: "I'll put myself in him, I'll say he is I" (p. 159).

At the most simple level of textual self-reflexivity, the diffusion of boundaries between I and Not-I appears in the form of a question of who invents whom.[1] Hyperconscious of his own fictionality, the unnamable long ago left behind any historical convention of distinguishing between the real and the imaginary. And yet, the question of the real seems to reappear through inversion when the unnamable begins to question the fictionality of fiction. While contemporary theories challenge any strict distinction between the real and the imaginary, Beckett's diffusion of boundaries is ultimately more radical. Instead of simply assuming a dissolution of the boundaries and a respective revaluation of the real as an "absent cause" (Althusser/Jameson), as an "effect of structure" (Lacan), or as a "simulacrum" (Baudrillard), Beckett's texts suggest a complete reorganization of the relationship between reality, fiction, and subjectivity on a different level of complexity and abstraction. The virtuosity with which the unnamable ultimately avoids the demarcation of boundaries between the real and the imaginary or between I and Not-I indicates that instead of passively enduring he actively practices a diffusion of boundaries.

The poststructuralist figures of the *mise-en-abîme* is here not the endpoint but the starting point of a discourse that, instead of discarding questions of reality or the subject, tries to explore them under new premises. The *esse est percipi* serves as a ground for the production of endless fictions of subjectivity, showing, then, the process of exploration as one of invention. Basil, for example, under whose gaze the unnamable seems to assume the form that Basil has invented for him, embodies the persecuting and petrifying gaze of the Other. Basil mobilizes the unnamable's existentialist heritage. In trying to escape Basil's gaze, he traces the self-referential spirals of a Kierkegaard, a Sartre, or a Laing—including the postexistentialist spirals of a Lacan—to a point where they disperse under the illusion of infinity.

The determination of the subject by the gaze of the other/Other is, however, only the beginning. Translating this problem into its textual equivalent—the determination of the subject by the voice of the Other—the unnamable envisions speaking in alien voices. Yet it remains unclear whether others have disowned his voice or, vice versa, he has disowned the voices of others. He keeps inventing literary characters who seem to speak from within him, or whose voices he speaks—and whose invention he might be. The inversion of the creative act, in which characters invent their author—a core problem of literary self-reflexivity explored by Pirandello and Borges—is brought to its extreme in *The Unnamable.* A simple inversion would still maintain the boundaries between I and Not-I. This is why the unnamable must problematize the inversions as such. The problem of inventing or being invented no longer obeys a logic of "either . . . or" but a paradoxical logic of "both . . . and." The unnamable stylizes himself as the creator of literary characters who invent him, thus casting the question of authorship in terms of the more general problem of the subject in relation to voice and language.

This telescoping of inverted acts of invention ultimately feigns the disowning of another voice: that of the author, Samuel Beckett, who by inventing the unnamable, is in turn invented by him. One must only prolong this endless perspective of inversions far enough back into the past to arrive at an ironical invocation of the God of the Old Testament as the original creator. The unnamable, of course, immediately rejects the idea of such a creator God and its related myth of origin as another perspective imposed by others: "They also gave me the low-down on God. They told me I depended on him, in the last analysis" (p. 13).

The God of the Old Testament, who, like the unnamable, refuses to be named, possesses the very self-identity of an "I am who I am" from which the unnamable removes himself further and further in his discursive spirals. Absolute self-identity with one's own speech, without *différance,* is, however, the Other of the unnamable's discourse, its tacit obsession.[2] Due to the paradox of feigning absolute self-identity as the Other, the unnamable transforms the "I am who I am" of the Old Testament into his endless chain of paradoxical counterformulas such as "I am he" or "Where I am there is no one but me who am not."

Self-identity or fictionality of the subject, differentiation between the real and the imaginary, speech as a medium of realization or fictionalization of the subject—these are the obsessive questions that over and over force the discourse of the unnamable back to reiterating the old metaphysical questions and their reformulations in contemporary theories of language and subjectivity. The unnamable shows how, driven toward their extreme implications, they can only be reformulated as a paradox. While he probes the paradoxes of both absolute self-identity and self-presence of the subject in discourse, he at the same time indirectly questions the possibility that a literary subject can ever *not* be identical with its discourse. Deliberate shifts between the positions of a philosophical versus an empirical versus a literary subject inevitably create epistemological ambiguities and paradoxes.

Beckett creates a literary subject as textuality that posits itself as transtextual, a subject who organizes his whole discourse under the premise of his absence from his own speech. For the unnamable, the paradox of representing the unrepresentable is the ultimate paradox of subjectivity—for empirical, philosophical, and fictional subjects alike. To complicate matters, he playfully maintains the notion that absolute self-identity in language is at least conceivable. In fact, he demonstrates that such a notion is intrinsic to the notion of unrepresentability, since only the dream of an absolute identity of the subject with its self-representations can engender the notion of unrepresentability.

Being aware that self-presence in discourse is impossible, the subject is faced with the choice of either continually producing new self-projections or renouncing every attempt at self-presentation. The choice of endless self-productions leads to a hermeneutic of the subject; the choice of renunciation, to a mystic philosophy of the subject. The unnamable moves between these two poles—between the extremes of an endless hermeneutic circle of self-production and an unattainable self-presence through mystic silence, between absolute and irreducible individuality and an existence beyond individual forms. His discourse settles for neither the one nor the other, even though he extends it toward both extremes.

The two poles of discourse, endless self-exegesis and mystic silence, both maintain the notion that there is something beyond language. If one understands self-presence as what is unrepresentable and cannot be translated into language or conceived in terms of any referential meaning, the movement of hermeneutic self-interpretation would strive toward a form of representation beyond meaning. But this would also mean a movement against the philosophical conception that argues we cannot meaningfully speak about what resists meaning; the unnamable rather demonstrates that we cannot meaningfully silence what resists meaning and that we therefore must voice it in paradoxical speech acts. The spiraling discourse of the unnamable thus constitutes less a Sartrean hermeneutic of silence than a hermeneutic of paradox within which categories such as absolute individuality and irrevocable mediatedness, I and Not-I, and subject and object collapse into each other.

SPEAKING TOWARD SILENCE

My mind at peace, that is to say empty. (p. 31)

Even though the unnamable can never embrace the notion of mystical silence, his spirals of representational negativity seem to imply a secret teleology of ultimate silence, if not a politics of meditative self-detachment from words and worlds. Silence forms an imaginary endpoint, if not the last myth, of this tortured discourse. In mystical philosophies silence evokes the self-presence of a *unio mystica* between the subject and the world. But the unnamable does not share the optimism of mysticism and knows that it would not suffice simply to stop talking in order to breach the gap between language and the subject. He intimates that a mere renunciation of speech would not grant the peace of an empty consciousness; rather it would provoke a metaphysical *horror vacui*. Nevertheless, the notion of silence as the only possible space of an impossible self-presence persists throughout the text. While speaking, the difference between the subject and its speech cannot be transcended. Only silence could possibly erase this difference. Since a first person narrator is by definition condemned to speak, he can at best use his discourse to project himself toward silence.

With this project, the unnamable follows the traces of Kierkegaard's sickness unto death. Speaking toward silence, this character seems to be afflicted by all three variations of the Kierkegardian sickness at once: he is "in despair at not being conscious of having a self" (Kierkegaard's *uneigentliche Verzweiflung*), "in despair at not willing to be oneself," and "in despair at willing to be oneself."[3] For Kierkegaard the sickness unto death is rooted in an endless self-reflexivity that causes an imaginary "despair of infinitude."[4] The unnamable, who cannot define himself between the boundaries of life and death, reveals obvious traits of a self-reflexivity that creates infinity. Endlessly dealing with ending and not being able to end, his "speaking toward silence" moves toward an "evaporation in the infinite."[5] The infinite discourse of the unnamable is stylized as the speech of a nonliving being who fantasizes mystic silence as an unattainable teleology: "Strange task, which consists in speaking of oneself. Strange hope, turned toward silence and peace" (p. 31).

The infinite spirals of discourse reveal the structure of a secularized, profane negative theology. Just as negative theologies attempt to clear consciousness of every trace of a representation of God in order to approach God as pure nothingness, the unnamable tries to clear his consciousness of every trace of a representation of his self in order to experience himself in silence as pure nothingness— hence his dream of ultimate silence and an empty mind at peace. The dilemma of this antirepresentational politics of language, however, results from the unnamable's compulsion to put this attempted progression toward silence into language. To speak of himself while at the same time obliterating every trace of the self becomes a paradoxical task that resembles solving a koan in Zen Buddhism. In fact, the unnamable deliberately plays with such affinities to mysticism and Eastern philosophies. His desire for a complete emptiness of mind and his fantasies of death and rebirth have adapted some of their assumptions to his own cultural situation and heritage.[6] Yet to adopt positively a mystic philosophy would entail what the unnamable tries to avoid: a concrete definition. He thus evokes notions of mysticism only to assert that they remain as alien to him as all the other philosophies that have imposed their traces on his mind.

Silence and infinite discourse are the two poles of a contemporary obsession with transcending the conditions of representation and the symbolic order. They also mark a politics of profound suspicion—against representation, manifestation, confinement. Negatively or positively, all these attempts rely on the figure of self-presence and struggle with irreducible difference and imaginary self-formation. The dream of a pure speech that would allow for self-presence while retaining absolute individuality has a long tradition within mysticism. We find it, for example, in the notion of an Adamic language in both Christian and Jewish traditions. Contemporary philosophies revitalize this notion as a problem of self-realization versus mediation or self-alienation by the symbolic order. The unnamable shifts the focus from the phenomenon of self-presence within discourse to the paradox within the notion of self-presence as such. If the experience of self-presence is ineffable, its philosophical representation is haunted by paradox. The unnamable, however, shows that such a paradox is necessary and relevant for any self-reflective presentation of subjectivity.[7] The dream of mystic silence is therefore not an endpoint, but an unattainable counterpoint of his discourse.

Since the unnamable takes it for granted that he can neither be silent nor attain self-presence in speech, he performs a paradoxical act of speaking against language. This seems to be the only way of speaking while avoiding any manifestation of the subject within speech. In order to speak against language, he tries to empty language of its semantic content. The changes in the forms of his discourse might be read as a progressive fulfillment of this program. Since the unnamable negates all self-determination in speech, we are reduced to focusing on the ways in which he materializes himself in the forms of his discourse. What happens to this speech, once the unnamable withdraws more and more semantic crutches? At times, it seems as if he has won a new freedom from those symbolic mediations he has rejected as impositions from anonymous others. But then again, the singularity of his speech threatens to catch up with him and make him assume an unwanted identity. Hence his task also to distance himself from the *forms* of his speech.

FORM IN MOTION

*it drags on by itself, from word to word, a labouring whirl, you
are in it somewhere, everywhere (p. 161)*

The unnamable's compulsive use of discursive strategies of negation and othering
increasingly reduces what can still be said, and, at the same time, requires ever
more complex forms of negation. Initially, this discourse still obeys the basic rules
of secondary process speech. Moreover, the richness and eccentricity of the unnamable's vocabulary, as well as his abundant philosophical allusions and the
complexity of his reasoning, testify to an unusually high linguistic competence, a
solid and broad education, and a hyperreflective mind. However, the very rules of
discourse and the philosophical erudition he displays so eloquently belong to a
symbolic order and a cultural tradition that he tries to escape.

As the compulsive negation of every utterance keeps his discourse spiraling
around the same problems, its rhythm accelerates centripetally—with the effect
that the spirals become narrower and narrower. Despite its general tendencies
toward dissolution, the discourse possesses a precise inner structure, which at first
follows the dynamic of a hyperactive mind, but then assumes more and more an
internal dynamic of accelerated speech. The traditional function of negation—
namely, to provide a criterion for judgment and differentiation—is discredited.
Instead, negation is used to subvert the very foundations of language and subject.
"With the yesses and noes it is different, they will come back to me as I go along
and how, like a bird, to shit on them all without exception" (p. 4). The subversion
has a double edge: by negating the very strategy of negation, the unnamable
performs a double negation that usually transforms into an affirmation. His
negations, however, operate at different levels of abstraction, and therefore fail to
be affirmative. Instead they create an entropic self-reflexivity, a process of unending doubt during which the unnamable uses the most basic operations of speech in
order to put himself as the subject of his own speech in question. This has the
paradoxical effect that, on a merely formal level, the unnamable indeed circum-
vents complete absorption by his speech. In other words, despite all assertions to
the contrary, he escapes what postmodern theories describe as a disowning of the
subject by its speech.

At the same time, as we recall, he formally maintains the norm of self-
presence in speech. His insistence on these two incompatible attitudes toward
language makes it nearly impossible to define his relationship to his discourse
without becoming oneself entangled in contradiction or paradox. One possible
resolution is to read the formal qualities of discourse as symptomatic of the status
of the subject. The high degree of reflection alone can be taken as a signal that the
unnamable does not simply succumb to a regressive dissolution of speech—not

even when, toward the very end, he increasingly abandons the discursive mode in favor of sounds and babbles, which remind one of the primary process speech of early childhood.

But instead of resulting from a regression to linguistic undifferentiation, these dissolutions turn out to be a product of the most extreme differentiation. With the ever more complex refinement of his thoughts, the unnamable has reached a point where further differentiation can no longer be translated into greater precision.[8] The loss of precision creates the impression of secondary undifferentiation. Instead of founding an I, which would require a reduction of complexity, the unnamable performs an implosion of complexity that results in a diffusion of the I. But instead of passively succumbing to primary process, he radicalizes this mode of speech by generating it from within the secondary processes. The goal, as Floyd Merrell writes, is not an archaic pleasure in using primary process, but a secondary pleasure in controlling it: "Beckett goes a step further; he desires to bring the primary process under his domain, to make words, creativity, laughter, and *aporia* possible when two or more ordinarily incompatible domains are intersected."[9]

Speech in this process remains irreducibly ambivalent: on the one hand, the unnamable denounces it as an instrument of reducing complexity; on the other hand, he uses language against the conventions of speech in order to increase complexity. If language can ground the subject, this function can also be inverted. The unnamable produces paradoxes of subjectivity from within the dynamic of speech to subvert both language and the subject. After all, we need language even to think the paradox of "I am Not-I." For the purpose of probing this paradox, the unnamable performs the most complex operations of language and exaggerates this performance to a point where language itself becomes paradox. This enables him to develop a subtle critique of language within his speech. But, at the same time, nearly inadvertently, the difference between subject and language begins to vanish more and more. The unnamable pushes the assumption of a subjectivity beyond language *ad absurdum,* since he produces his paradoxical subjectivity from within language. It would be simply inconceivable without the very language he deems so inadequate. Instead of announcing the end of the subject, *The Unnamable* reveals the insistence of the subject in language—albeit against its own will.

For the unnamable, the unavoidable subject effect of language appears as a coercion—an imposition of a symbolic order that is Other. But, as J. E. Dearlove has shown, such a rejection of the power of language can only be motivated if we concede that there is a nonverbal core of the subject: "On the one hand, he [the unnamable] is the formless, fluid speaker who rejects all that is alien to the nonverbal core of himself. On the other hand, he resides in the fixed shapes and external orders of his spoken words."[10] It is precisely this tension between a subjectivity in language and its nonverbal core that drives the unnamable to invent himself as a paradox in language. Far from effacing the words and silencing the voices in order to reveal a subjectivity freed from language—the nonverbal core of his empty mind—the unnamable develops a hermeneutic of paradox in order to document his inseparability from language at the precise moment when he attempts to locate himself outside the symbolic order. Instead of dissolving his subjectivity into nothingness, he infinitely expands it through operations based solely on language. In light of the unnamable's paradoxical discourse the notion of a subject freed from language appears as reductive as the notion of a language freed from the subject.

EMOTIONS IN LANGUAGE

nothing but emotion, bing bang (p. 170)

Since the unnamable can become neither identical with nor different from his discourse, he oscillates between the complementary fictions of a nonverbal core subjectivity and a discourse without subject. This oscillation regulates the shifting distance to his own utterances as well as the rhythm and affective dynamic of his discourse. As all fictions about ourselves, the fictions of the unnamable, too, reveal an intense affective cathexis. It is difficult to decide how much affective distance the unnamable really possesses to his own discourse. It might indeed even seem impossible to decide when the unnamable is controlling his discourse and when he is losing himself in it. This distinction, however, becomes crucial for interpreting the figuration of his subjectivity. The unnamable reiterates the complex dynamic between master and slave as a dynamic between language and subject. As we have seen, he uses negation to prevent himself from being subsumed by language, but the further he drives this process and the more complex it becomes, the more he is in danger of becoming identical with his discourse. Negation turns into negative fixation.

This dynamic can be traced within the rhythms of speech. Initially, his discourse remains segmented by passages with short sentences that obey conventional rules of grammar and punctuation. Even the spirals of argumentation can be followed without too much difficulty. Increasingly, however, passages of speech and sentences dissolve into rhythmical fragments. Ever longer, uninterrupted sentences finally merge into a flood of mere parataxes. The affective cathexis of speech seems to increase proportionally to the decrease in its designative or semantic definition. This much, at least, we could conclude if we read the formal and rhythmical elements as affective expressions. We would notice the accelerated rhythm, the repetition of highly affective core words such as "silence" or "I," and the emancipation of formal qualities from semantic connotations, often exaggerated to the point of linguistic nonsense: "I'll laugh, that's how it will end, in a chuckle, chuck, chuck, ow, ha, pa, I'll practise, nyum, hoo, plop, pss, nothing but emotion, bing bang, that's blows, ugh, pooh, what else, oooh, aaah, that's love, enough, it's tiring, hee, hee" (p. 170).

Insertions of asemantic conglomerations of sounds recall the spontaneous production of so-called glossolalia—a form of linguistic nonsense that is supposed to indicate a breakthrough of the pleasure principle in language.[11] The more the discourse begins to resemble primary processes, the more its energies seem to increase—which would confirm Freud's hypothesis of a decrease of energy in secondary processes.[12] But the unnamable only mimics this original discharge of affect. In announcing his glossolalia as "inarticulate murmurs, to be invented" (p. 170), he reveals a fully conscious and intentional utterance. If he has to "invent" archaic forms of language, their function does not unfold spontaneously. Instead, they are used in a calculated way to void the semantic content of discourse. The assertion "I'll practise" makes it clear that the unnamable does not produce linguistic nonsense in a spontaneous game with words and sounds. Rather he uses nonsense as one of the possibilities to subvert his discourse even further and to enhance his paradoxical pleasure of controlling the pleasure principle.

He practices yet another form of regression when he uses foul language to spice up the fantasies of his body. The sarcastic pleasure he takes in obscene and scatological fantasies also enhances their ability to undermine the potential philosophical gravity of his reflections. Significantly, these interspersed vulgarities emerge whenever his discourse threatens to assume conceptual density or reach a level that smacks of philosophy. He particularly likes to fall back on them when his hyperconscious reflections collapse under their overcomplexity. As in the case of the glossolalia, the affective cathexis of these obscene images of the body is broken. They are not, as one might expect, used as a spontaneous assertion of the pleasure principle against the dominance of the reality principle and the cultural exclusion of the organic drama of the body from language. Rather the unnamable uses artificial phantasms and obscene images of the body in a calculated way as an aggressive rhetorical strategy against the civilizing forces in language. Once again, his subversion is not a spontaneous regression, but a reflected and controlled act of speech.

On one level, the recourse to nonsense or to the obscene is just a further step in the unnamable's resistance to philosophical conceptualization. The dynamic of form in his discourse is governed by shifts in rhetorical strategies. Such shifts are necessary because the unnamable wears each strategy out by overusing it. We can thus conclude that, paradoxically enough, the unnamable deliberately uses rhetorical strategies like nonsense or obscene language, which commonly counteract reflection, not only in order to mock reflection and self-consciousness, but also to defer the failure of his self-reflexive spirals. He has it both ways: he undermines conceptual self-definition, but at the same time he neutralizes any traceable affective cathexis of his discourse. What appears at first glance to be linguistic traces of affect turns out to be only a willfully deceptive mimicking. His disguised "indifference" or affective abstinence then becomes just another strategy of speaking without manifesting himself.

This, of course, counteracts the initial impression of an increasing affective cathexis of language. Since, at the semantic level, affects are only mimicked, the last resource for measuring the unnamable's indifference or distance toward his speech is its changing rhythms. There are no signals in the text to indicate that the unnamable deliberately controls these rhythms. One could therefore assume that the more he tries to distance himself from all semantic manifestations, the more he inadvertently inscribes himself into the rhythms of his speech. This perspective would account for the increasing formal dissolution of language. Due to longer and longer paratactical sentences, speech becomes more and more leveled. Repetition of core sentences, words, and syllables make the whole discourse more rhythmical but also more monotonous. The rhythm of speech begins to dominate over the semantic content, especially since its increasing uniformity and redundancy undermines the sparse reminders of narrative tension. The text eventually gains a stronger equilibrium toward the end, but it appears to result from textual entropy rather than from the narrator's mental balance. The unnamable seems to have eventually succeeded in emptying language of semantic content, but this does not help him in finding the peace of an empty mind.

With his repetition of sounds and rhythms toward the end of his discourse, the unnamable activates an ancient technique of separating language from meaning, which has been used for centuries in the most diverse cultural contexts. Children love to keep repeating a word until its meaning disappears behind the sound. Eastern meditative practices use the repetition of internally spoken mantras in order to transcend consciousness. In all these practices sound and rhythm detach language from meaning, yet only to endow it with magic or spiritual power. Evidently, however, the unnamable does not use language like a mantra or a playful nonsense game. Despite his dream of the meditative peace of an empty mind, his frenzy to avoid semantic manifestation ties him negatively to semantics. His hypersuspicious awareness of the semantic traps of language is maintained until the very end. Instead of moving toward silence, his discourse moves away from it. After a deceptive transitory period of rhythmic stabilization, his rhythms become increasingly hectic and ruptured. As Bruce Kavin writes, "The literature of the ineffable, in contrast to the language game of OM, accepts the conditions of time and fragmentation."[13]

We can conclude that even the ultimate recourse to rhythm and sound is marked by the unnamable's fundamental ambivalence toward language and subjectivity. The rhythms of speech form a countermovement to silence and reveal, behind all suspicion, a deeply rooted negative fixation to language. If the unnamable's speech were indeed a speech toward silence, its emptiness would have to be both semantic and affective. The forms of discourse, however, reveal how silence is at best a superficial teleology, an impossible dream performed by the unnamable in full knowledge that it can never be attained. Silence as the declared goal of speech is counteracted by the practice of speech.

The unnamable, who never wanted to occupy a space within language, seems to dissolve into the forms of his discourse. He, who wanted to renounce the use of the pronoun "I" in order to destroy the illusion of an identity with his speech, ends up producing a discourse more prolific in "I's" than any other conceivable text of the same length. *The Unnamable* ends as it began: with a paradox, one that swallows up the "politics of indifference." There is no conceivable counterpart to Beckett's "indifference": engagement as well as difference depend upon a form of thought that pursues the "politics of small differences" to a point where they vanish and yet matter more than ever, infinitely and infinitely: *Less*. The dream of silence, dream silence, generates an encompassing spiral of utterances that leads the speaker back to the impossible origin of his unending speech: "before the door that opens on my story, that would surprise me, if it opens, it will be I, it will be the silence, where I am, I don't know, I'll never know, in the silence, you don't know, you must go on, I can't go on, I'll go on" (p. 179).

POLITICAL EFFECTS

If Beckett's discursive loops compel us to reconsider the premises of our philosophical tradition, they equally compel us to reconsider our notions of the political. In the same way in which Beckett resists the pedagogical lure of concrete messages or political manifestos, he also resists the allegorization of the political. His most pertinent concern is what we might call, following Jameson, the "ideology of form." There is no referential ideology to Beckett's politics, despite the fact that his characters move through all conceivable ideological figurations of our time. Even when he engages the most controversial issues of postmodern politics—such as the death of the subject, the end of representation, and the vicissitudes of the gaze of the other (to name the most obvious ones)—he refuses to let these issues become the foundation for a political program or a theoretical orthodoxy. Rather, he stages a grotesque language game that carnivalizes our whole philosophical tradition as well as our postmodern politics and exposes with hilarious humor and biting sarcasm the commonplaces of a paranoid or nostalgic relation to our cultural and philosophical baggages. Beckett not only leads us willfully and with malicious pleasure into the epistemological traps and dead-ends of the philosophical traditions that we postmodernists like to trash, he also challenges the ideology of form inherent in postmodernism and postmodern figures of thought. Driving them toward their most impossible consequences, he exposes a long tradition in which our relationship to otherness and difference is marked by cultural paranoia and nostalgia. In this microperspective, politics appears not only as the well-known monolith of ideology, but as a most fragile fabric of discursive figurations replete with emotion, desire, and unconscious effects.

Last but by no means least, Beckett practices a politics of difference in the very form of his discourse. If it is true that the boundaries of our language are the boundaries of our world, then Beckett expands these boundaries simultaneously in two opposite directions: toward the most rigorous self-reflexivity and formal abstraction as well as toward the most playful use of the unconscious energies of the primary process. This expansion is a political act that affects language, subjects, bodies, voices, and emotions alike. A voice that is neither I nor Not-I, subject nor object performs speech acts on the tightrope toward the impossible. Yes, politics then becomes an issue of territory, interpellation, and otherness, but only from the perspective of a subject who says: "Where I am there is no one but me who am not."

Notes

1. Regarding Beckett's metalanguage and textual self-reflexivity, cf. also Manfred Smuda, *Beckett's Prosa als Metasprache* (Munich: Fink Verlag, 1970).

2. Regarding a critical reading of Derrida from the perspective of Beckett's texts, cf. Floyd Merrell, *Deconstruction Reframed* (West Lafayette, Ind.: Purdue University Press, 1985), chap. 7: "Beckett's Dilemma: or, Pecking Away at the Ineffable," pp. 165–95.

3. Cf. Søren Kierkegaard, *Fear and Trembling* and *The Sickness unto Death,* trans. Walter Lowrie (Garden City, N.Y.: Doubleday Anchor Books, 1954), p. 146.

4. Ibid., pp. 163–64.

5. Ibid., p. 166.

6. Regarding Beckett's affiliations with mysticism, cf. also Waltraud Goelter, *Entfremdung als Konstituens buergerlicher Literatur, dargestellt am Beispiel Samuel Becketts: Versuch einer Vermittlung von Soziologie und Psychoanalyse als Interpretationsmodell* (Heidelberg: Carl Winter Verlag, 1976), pp. 209–26.

7. Cf. also Bruce Kawin, "On Not Having the Last Word: Beckett, Wittgenstein, and the Limits of Language," in *Ineffability: Naming the Unnamable from Dante to Beckett,* ed. Peter S. Hawkins and Anne H. Schotter (New York: AMS Press, 1984), p. 195.

8. Manfred Smuda has pointed out that with increasing complexity in Beckett's texts, the possibilities of writing have proportionally decreased. In this development, *The Unnamable* marks a turning point in Beckett's development toward the later, minimalistic

texts. Cf. Manfred Smuda, "Kunst im Kopf—Becketts spaetere Prosa und das Imaginaere," in *Samuel Beckett,* ed. Hartmut Engelhardt (Frankfurt: Suhrkamp, 1984), p. 212.

9. Merrell, *Deconstruction Reframed,* p. 191.

10. J. E. Dearlove, *Accommodating the Chaos: Samuel Beckett's Nonrelational Art* (Durham, N.C.: Duke University Press, 1982), p. 61.

11. Cf. Sigmund Freud, "Jokes and Their Relation to the Unconscious," in *Standard Edition,* vol. 8. Cf. also "Der Witz und seine Beziehung zum Unbewussten," in *Gesammelte Werke,* vol. 6, pp. 139–43.

12. Cf. Sigmund Freud, "Formulations on the Two Principles of Mental Functioning," in *Standard Edition,* vol. 12. Cf. also "Formulierungen ueber die zwei Prinzipien des psychischen Geschehens," in *Gesammelte Werke,* vol. 8, p. 233.

13. Kavin, "On Not Having the Last Word," p. 201.

4

A Descent from Clowns

Christian Prigent

for Jacques Demarcq

I came to Beckett late in life and read him incompletely. He barely counted in my professional education as a writer. Not that Beckett has been either indifferent or foreign to me. On the contrary, when I open any one of his books I have the sensation of coming home. I could, it seems, speak with the mouth that had formed these words, breathe in its rhythm. And while this is certainly an illusion, it is not vain. I simply note the sensation of familiarity, a sensation normally parsed out in guarded portions. Few authors work such an effect, a power . . . of *truth*. What is the order, the nature of this truth? This is the question.

DISCHARGING MOM

It is 1951. *Molloy* has appeared and I reread the beginning. "I am in my mother's room. It's I who live there now. I don't know how I got there" (p. 7). The narrator continues: "In any case I have her room. I sleep in her bed. I piss and shit in her pot. I have taken her place. I must resemble her more and more" (p. 8).

Living in the maternal language, sleeping cuddled within it, pissing in its chamber pot, identifying with it, subsidized by its law, all in a sort of happy imbecility. Here, in a nutshell, is the dream of any speaking being, that which most certainly pledges him to the community, subjects him to the social contract. This is his consent to the world and the means by which he sometimes even manages to draw pleasure from it.

The author of *Molloy* has, on the contrary, just left his mother's room. He has decided to abandon the maternal language. Molloy writes ("so many pages, so much money" [p. 7]), as does Beckett. But the first "stammer[s] out his lesson, the remnants of a pensum one day got by heart and long forgotten" (p. 41). The second prepares himself "to fix it up for them, their nonsensical jargon." The first pledges himself to the mother while the second sends her away.

This was not easy: "Ah, the old bitch, a nice dose she gave me, she and her lousy unconquerable genes" (p. 109). Still, Beckett chose to write in a foreign

58

language. Against the pseudofamiliarity of an amniotic speech, he chose the worrisome strangeness of another language. From that point on, he wrote as an alien. Each word that fell from his pen broached the inadequacy of both the language and the world. He wrote in and out of separation: "all language," he wrote, "is a departure [*écart*] from language."

I do not know if Beckett intended all this. It is of little consequence to me. I only note that in order to "find his language" he left his own maternal, native language. In order to speak he had to depart. And I will retain this allegory, for it suggests that all speech is a departure. A speaking being is a being on the move. Because he speaks, he is expelled. Speaking is parting, being parted from and imparted to one's self. As soon as he speaks the speaking being loses his complicity with the world, the approval of that which is. Here, as at many other points, Beckett joins Artaud.[1]

I continue reading. The mother is dead. The search for her cadaver is the subject of the gesture. The mother's dead body is the undiscoverable Grail toward which our infirm hero limps. It is a journey of despair. Not that the cadaver is nowhere to be found. Rather it is everywhere, both within and without the seeker. It is the language, the maternal space granted to being. "They're in there, perhaps, in what they've just said," remarks the unnamable. The cadaver is the "clattering gabble, which can only have stopped during her/its brief instants of unconsciousness" (p. 22).

Beckett knows this. But Molloy doesn't, for he is within that which he seeks without. "I don't know how I got there" (p. 7), he declares. He circles, marking out the As and Bs. He marches himself inside. He speaks with the cadaver in its/his own mouth. He runs to "mommy." He tries, in any case, to believe that this is possible ("And from time to time I said Mother, to encourage me I suppose" [p. 122]). But everything goes wrong: the hat is lost, the shoelace breaks, the spirit moves "in slow motion," the bewildered pilgrim turns ineluctably around and around.

"You do what you can," he says. And he can do little. This is not surprising. The maternal language is of a suffocating familiarity. It kills. "On its charity," one doesn't live, one dies. And if the mother tongue is implacably mortifying, this is because it has died a pitiful death. "One might say that you sometimes do battle with a dead language," Beckett will soon write in *All That Fall*. And Molloy asks himself: "For example my mother's death. Was she already dead when I came? Or did she only die later? I mean enough to bury her. I don't know. Perhaps they haven't buried her yet" (p. 8). The maternal language is always already dead: nothing easier than to resemble it; nothing more natural than to submit to this maternal affection; nothing more tempting than to die in it while reproducing it at the same time. "All I need now is a son," Molloy muses, uncertain whether or not he has performed the requisite act. "But I think not. . . . It wasn't true love" (p. 8).

The true love is, without a doubt, the mother, and this love might properly be called a death wish. To love one's mother is to make a pact with something inert, with "nature." Like Molloy, one turns over in his mouth the small ritual stones, the deathly accumulation of exhausted words. "This collection of imbecilic remarks, it's certainly from them that I got it," grumbles the unnamable. "And this murmur that strangles me, it's they who have stuffed me with it." At the same time and in a similar spirit, Bataille expressed the anguish of feeling his grandmothers alive in his throat, and Ponge set himself the task of "speaking against words . . . the already given and foul habits that have contracted so many mouths."[2]

This is, indeed, a program for writing. This program is, mutatis mutandis, Beckett's. To speak against words, this is an attempt to clear a space in which one might "begin differently." Otherwise, one's mouth tainted by its adhesion to the dead body of the mother, one persists only in "beginning at the beginning like an old ballocks" (p. 8), *made over,* fashioned ever and again identically to the morbidity of the same, to the eternal decrepitude of an idiot who bows to an impure world.[3]

The program has a technique. To begin differently, suggests *Molloy,* implies the forgetting of "names," of "proper spellings," and "half the words" we ever knew. And the possibility of this survival (of freedom?) tainted by failure, resides in a resistance to the familiar, in a disabled language, in language obscured and impoverished. (In 1968 Beckett would say, "At the Liberation [of France], I set myself again to write—in French—with the desire to impoverish myself still further.") The chance for rebirth, renaissance, rests within what Ponge has called the "divine necessity of imperfection"[4] and within the "careful carelessness," the "incorrigible illiteracy," that Artaud would adopt. And it rests in Rimbaud's taste for "erotic books without any orthography," "idiot refrains and naive rhythms." This survival assumes the embrace of stupidity: "I knew Molloy and all the rest the day that I became conscious of my own idiocy."[5] In other words, we must succeed at failing, endow ourselves with a lack of competence, in order to quit being "comprehended" by the maternal (language). "Pardon me, my very dear mother," thus wrote Hölderlin, "if I do not make myself completely comprehensible to you."

This is the first lesson. On this point, as on many others, Beckett is a radical. And herein lies the power of truth of which I spoke. Unlike Molloy, Beckett leaves his mother's room. He mocks the maternal idyll. He refuses a determination that is atavistic. He writes in another language. This means that Beckett does not number himself among those who believe in inhabiting language like a family home. For Beckett, there is no family language, no *natural* language. (In *Waiting for Godot* we will reach a crinching: "We must turn resolutely toward nature.")

In short, Beckett admits nowhere a belief in the transparency of language able to carry the weight of any "existential" message. For Beckett there is no content of knowledge or experience to be transmitted in and at the discretion of language. No illusion of communication. What communicates, he says, are the vases. And, in his *Proust,* he wrote: "There is no communication because it has no vehicle." This is why, before all else (before, for example, being the bearer of a philosophical vision of the "human condition"), Beckett's literature is a protest both violent and droll against the reduction of the powers of language to those of communication. Beckett knew very well that speaking is not only communicating. And his subject is the estrangement of the foreign, the infirm and infamous matter of language, the moments where "even words betray you," the ineluctable obscurity, the hinge and the wound borne by this truth that language is not only, not first, a "vehicle of communication," but the blade of separation.

Beckett would say of his vocation as a writer that it intends the "indestructible association that persists to the last breath of the tempest and of the night into the light of understanding." He proposes language as a encumbered space, an opaque matter, a problematic datum. "Night" is a permanent resident in this space that chaotic obscurity constructs. This place of *obscure clarity* is the only space in which literature can invest itself because it is the space wherein the speaking being engenders itself and dies to the extent that there also arises and dissolves the meaning with which he pretends to endow his life. "And if I'm ever reduced to looking for a meaning to my life, you can never tell, it's in that old mess I'll stick my nose to begin with, the mess of that poor old uniparous whore and myself the last of my foul brood, neither man nor beast" (p. 23).

All of this must be taken into evidence. But we know quite well that the recognition of these truths as such is little to be found in the literary world of the present. And we ought likewise to recall the context in which (and against which, perhaps) Beckett wrote. For in those years, the years of *Molloy,* there was an eminent philosopher (Sartre) and his doxa of the day. When this doxa embroiled itself (as it often did) with literature, if affirmed that "style must pass unseen," that words are "transparent," that "the eye traverses them," that "it would be absurd to slip between them windows of frosted glass." Beckett thought, evidently, just the opposite. He knew that we must "consider words by themselves," even if this entails their "loss of meaning."[6] For the loss of meaning and the meaning of this loss (the knowledge that meaning is all at once lost and ultimately loses itself again and always) is the very question of literature.

POETRY, YES OR NO?

Vladimir: You should have been a poet.
Estragon: I was. (Gestures to his rags.) Isn't it obvious?

— *Waiting for Godot*

Beckett's work could be placed, thereby, in a logic of modern "poetic" language.

We recall the first poem of *Spleen et idéal,* in *Les Fleurs du mal:* "When, by a decree of the sovereign power / The Poet in this weary world appears, / His mother, terrified, aghast, blasphemes, / Clenches her fist at God." At the far edge of modernity Baudelaire defines literary language as an exception to the maternal language. The poet accomplishes this language that tears men from their natural inertia (from the morbidity of the maternal). He mocks the world and terrifies Mother, Nature, and Earth. Bataille likewise adopted this train of thought. "A poet does not justify—he does not accept—Nature altogether."

Writing draws on the maternal language,[7] draws it out to betray it.[8] (Rimbaud speaks in much the same way in his *Poètes de sept ans*). Beckett, who had carefully read Proust and Joyce, knew that poetic language is not necessarily proper to "poetry." He certainly knew that it is "poetic" language that is both the maximum extension of language and the accomplishment of its vocation. But he also knew, for the *rupturing* experience of writing demonstrates it, that this vocation was not simply to reproduce things, that, on the contrary, it is the task of poetic language to perforate the opacity of things. He knew that the artifice violently displayed in poetic language, the inhumanity of its rhetorical excess, its asocial obscurity, are not the approbation of the world, the celebration of the existent, the hymn to the natural, but rather an assumed strangeness, a heightening of the spasmatic paralysis induced by the rupturing function of language. Beckett the writer, the reader, the critic, knew, therefore, that playing the game, both serious and vain, of poetry, intensifies even more cruelly the separation already intrinsic to language. ("Must I write verse to separate me from other men?" asked Ducasse.)

After so many mysteries Beckett might have declared that we belong to the world neither body nor soul and that, speaking beings that we are, beings, that is, not swallowed up within the muteness of the world, we do not accept entirely to be part of its physicalness. But the inverse is just as true. Like several other of the great "poets," he might have declared that our bodies of flesh expulsed into the world, and with no other place but this place, nor do we belong simply and without lack to language.

Writing, thus, is not the illumination of things, but rather the accomplishment of this lack, this separation, this . . . metaphysical (or, in Jarry's terms, "pataphysical") remainder. It is the amplification of the unspeakable rumor, the confused buzz of voice that circulates between named things. It does not name the world, but rather casts rhythms against the verbal decor that one calls "reality," and, "born of an impossible voice," says "an unfeasible being." Writing attempts an approach on the in-significant foundation of the unnamable across the unsignifying plain of the namable. "At the end of my oeuvre, there is this dust: the namable."

Our "poetic" word thus misses the mother who instills the world in us by instilling us in it. We both are and are not echoes in her chamber. We are not entirely in her bed and something of us pisses elsewhere than in her nocturnal grail. Our poetic word is this leap beyond the world and beyond the mother, beyond the mundanity of discourse. It is another beginning. "Here's my beginning," says Molloy, closed within the chamber (p. 8). We need another chamber, not a chamber that will replace the first ("It must mean something or they wouldn't keep it"), but that will launch the written as a shrinking of the deathly ascendancy of the world and its common language.

Perhaps one could have expected Beckett to write poetry. One might easily imagine a poetics of separation, of this "we are not in the world." One might have expected sarcastically arid poems in the style of Bataille, or poems hammered and torn like those of Artaud, despairing doggerel like Queneau's, or comically uncouth like Michaux's.

The first of Beckett's texts in French are, in effect, brief poems. We see him tempted by a sort of lyric expressionism ("musique de l'indifférence / coeur temps air feu sable / du silence éboulement d'amours / couvre leurs voix et que / je ne m'entende plus / me taire"). He tries on the rhythmic and sonorous language of a modernity intent to "remunerate the defect of languages." ("Bois seul / bouffe brûle fornique crève seul comme devant / les absents sont morts les présents puent.") But these forays are relatively minor and are quickly abandoned (even if we still might very well call poetry the upsetting polyptotons and the exploded derivations of his *Worstward Ho* or the taunt jazz syncopations of *Mal vu mal dit*).

I remark, as have others, no doubt, that Beckett decidedly left the chamber of the maternal language at the moment when he decided upon the form that would homogeneously embody his novel trilogy: the first person monologue, the "species of imagination so tainted by reason," the ratiocinative ruminations of *Molloy, Malone,* and *The Unnamable*.

This choice was first of all a decision to relieve from its uninterrupted dominion the distant and disaffected third person narration of the realist novel. But it was also, without any doubt, a decision to hold at bay, to bring down (to oust, I might say) the subjective "I" of the poetic tradition (that which continued to speak in the Beckettian poems of the thirties). The I named (Molloy, Malone) or unnamed (the unnamable) is in all respects the trivialized ectoplasm of the lyric

I (this expressive subjectivity, filled to the brim with "true" feelings). This I descends from the other I, it is its descent (as from a bed) and its cadaverous double. The other (the poetic I) experiences the agony of death in this I, an agony even more voluble for the gag it must wear.

The hysterical logorrhea of Molloy's "I" has nothing to do either with the I of lyric confidence or that of a hysterical unfolding of expressionism. This is to say, in terms that drive the nail home, Molloy and Malone (etc.) would be Beckett, *if Beckett weren't a writer.* This detail makes all the difference. For it says that writing is not communicating (either knowledge, opinions, emotions, complaints, passions . . .) in the unrestrained authenticity of and simple belief in the affective transparency of any language. It says that writing is an artificial excess, an ambivalent distance (wherein humor and horror mingle), an inauthentic monstrosity that coldly saves and saves itself from the idea of salvation, from the belief in the expression and attractive adhesion of meaning.

It was perhaps to give form to these affirmations that Beckett *reduced* poetry, exhausted its subjective expressivity, humorously differed (in the comic catastrophe) the expressive proximity of sorrow and tragic confusion. And perhaps the incorporation, the disincarnation of the Beckettian creature is itself to be read as the allegory of this gaunt posture of emaciation in the face of poetic language.

This will come more clearly into focus if we stop to review the state in which poetry found itself in 1948.

I have said that poetic language accomplishes the vocation of language, the separation, the de-parture of speech. Still, its most cherished dream is rather, as we all know, that of adhesion, incorporation, adequation to the body, and uterine fusion with the things of the world.[9] This dream is reactive. It is the dream of separating oneself from separation. It imagines some happy reunion with the world. It wants to redeem the sin of separation and suture the wound of the inadequacy of words and things.

When it seeks to objectify itself in the symbolic order, this dream undertakes, for example, the remotivation of signs, the struggle against arbitrariness, the ambition to "remunerate the fault of language" that was, for Mallarmé, Jarry, or Khlebnikov, one of the determining axes of the rhetorical endeavor of poetry. But in its most mundane and idealistic guise, this dream generally contents itself merely to sing reconciliation, idyllic celebration, a hymn to fusion. "I am Creation's Inspector," wrote Claudel, "the one who verifies the present, the solidity of the world is the stuff of my beatitudes."[10]

The poetry dominant in the day of *Molloy* was occupied by this dream and pledged itself, with ritual seriousness, to its rhetoric. The "Great Poets" of the day modulated the dream and embroidered on its humanist prophesies. What was true for a true believer like Claudel was equally true for those of weaker faith, or even those who claimed not to believe at all. Thus Saint-John Perse wrote in 1946:

"The poet is also with us travelling the common way of our time. . . . His occupation among us: to clarify messages. . . . By virtue of his total adhesion to that which is, he binds us to the permanence of being. And his lesson is that of optimism. For the poet, a single law governs the entire world of things."[11] René Char defined poetry as "the life of the future residing within a newly qualified, newly defined, man," and he saw this man "planted in the harmonious soil of the future."[12] And Tzara, the former Dadaist, declared that "the profound sentiment of the poet tends toward the transformation of the present world into a world in which man can once again be entirely in accord with himself."[13]

These oracles of the ideal and their convivial pathos (*harmony, accord, same, permanence* are their master words) may have produced some beautiful verse, something to warm the morose hearts of humanity. But we see very well that Beckett could not do otherwise than to challenge these sugarcoated truths, these exultations. This is why, whenever he could, Beckett reduced to the order of the ridiculous the principle rhetorical vector of poetry's allure, the metaphor, the figure that would mend the dislocation and fragmentation of the world.[14] All that poetry bears secularly with it of an hysterical assent to the existent, of the dream of fusion, of the devotion to a worldly idyll, could only seem false and derisory, a garrulous babble, to this man who had adopted the gesture of the unnamable and the passion of negativity. All of Beckett's writing traverses and is traversed by an opposition to this agreeable phantasmagoria and its singing horizons, an opposition to tragedy sanitized and humanized.

Beckett could thus approach poetry, but, as Bataille would say, only "to miss it," only to designate its denial of its own generative vacuity and only to demonstrate how it converts its own acute consciousness of separation into the pathos of reconciliation.

LOVE, POETRY

It is in a celebration of romantic love, a love that thus symbolizes the redemption of separation, that poetry most often incarnates its dream of fusion and a perfected humanity.

Eluard's 1929 collection of poems entitled *L'Amour et la poésie* occupies the intersection of these two forces. In 1948 Eluard counted himself a member of a neoclassical "fraternity," writing lyrical love poems under the banner of the *uninterrupted*. On his flank, Aragon was celebrating, in pompous alexandrines, a redemption by love (this is between *Les Yeux d'Elsa*, of 1942, and *Le Roman inachevé*, of 1956). And no small number of tender masters were composing a mélange of earthy ecstasy, sentimental botany, and sensitive elegy (Fombeure, Cadou, the school of Rochefort . . .).

Molloy says: "I would have made love with a goat, to know what love was" (p. 77). But this knowledge never happens. Molloy has forgotten the name of his "true love" (Ruth, Edith?). No meeting, no complicity, no being-together, no adequation. And the world? "A path just wide enough for one where two never meet."[15]

Molloy, no more than Moran, has met *Obidil,* alias Libido. He is no more sure than Moran that she even exists. The body of the other? It is ectoplasmic, insipid, or repugnant. And the body of the self? It is only a problematic knot of loss, confusion, infirmity that only knows to make itself taunt and thin. The sex? Only a "torn bag," "nothing more to get from it." No problem. Nothing more is expected from it. For Molloy, sexual intercourse simply does not work, it is "an idiot's game" leading only to a derisory, null, and atonal miscarriage. Ergo, "If they had removed a few testicles into the bargain I wouldn't have objected" (p. 47).

Of the body we see above all the trivial and the sordid. The "rectum" or "asshole" is everywhere, its activity intense. "What do you want, I pass gas in response to everything and nothing." This is not the anal obsession of a jovial gallic humor. Nor is it even the Freudian emblem of "everything that is forbidden." It is rather a descent of and from the heights of a phantasmagorical love. Thus, in that atrociously atonal and disaffecting story of comic cruelty that is *First Love,* the Narrator traces the name of the Beloved (Lulu, alias Anne) in "a heifer's dried out dung," "immemorial bovine excrement," and then exclaims: "Would I have traced her name in old cow dung if my love for her were pure and disinterested? And with my finger to boot, that I then put to my mouth?"

The more etherial the fusional idealism, the more functionally base the real corporeal solitude. Beckett's tales reverse the "poetic."

> I apologize for having to revert to this lewd orifice, 'tis my muse will have it so. Perhaps it is less to be thought of as the eyesore here called by its name than as the symbol of those passed over in silence, a distinction due perhaps to its centrality and its air of being a link between me and the other excrement. (p. 107)

The theme of the anus and its low language become thus the emblems of the negative, the pataphysical and unnamable traces, the parodic, obsessional manifestations of the irreducible Other, the disappropriator and destabilizer of the communicating propieties of the maternal language.

We are thus once again to read allegorically. Molloy, the bewildered observer, simultaneously ploddingly obscene and meticulously clinical, combats the indigence of sex and notes the hurried nullity of copulation. Beckett, facetious and grim, combats language, challenges an ecstatic coupling with the naturalness of the maternal speech, sabotages the belief in a verbal rapport, makes of writing an . . . error of nature.

The "body," the "other," is a world, even in the guise of its alluring idealization, inimical to all familiarity. The apathetic miscarriage, the trivial catastrophe of the sexual union represents thus more generally in this fable the always missed union with the world that the speaking being always misses. It symbolizes the divorce of words and things, the misunderstanding inherent to communication. "What we call love is really exile." And art, the "apotheosis of solitude," etches the impossible and insupportable character of the nevertheless ineluctable community of speakers.

THE INSIGNIFICANT

Beckett's heroes are "people . . . hard to distinguish from yourself" (p. 9). Synthetic images, heraldic figures of speech, they wander in a space without distinction, the asylum of *Mal vu mal dit*, "the nonexistent center of a space without form." At first named (Molloy, Malone), they become progressively unnamable. At first wanderers and seekers, they become expectantly stagnant. The decor in which they either limp about or vegetate is always poor and informal, but very much the contrary of the naturalist or the sordid luxury (of detail) of the Sartrean novel. "It was on a road remarkably bare, I mean without hedges or ditches or any kind of edge" (p. 9), says Molloy.

For me what comes into focus is, in a sense, the staging of the insignificant, or rather of the in-significance of the present, of presence. This poverty is not of the order of an existential miserabilism (it does not even seem to me interested to stage a sort of bedraggled lumpen proletariat symbolic of "human misery"). Its stakes seem to me more formal, more concerned with the fact of the symbolic in itself and with the strange status that the speaking being has in the world. It forces a hesitation of plots, a fuzziness of figures, a rarefication of glances, an indetermination of meaning. It is poised in opposition to those strategies—the articulation of time, the formulation of spaces, the determination of names—by which the traditional, realist novel structures the world, sutures its vertigo and reabsorbs its nonsense into the coherence, the stability, the affective assurance of a fictional construct slipped into the place of the unnamable real.

This Beckettian drama is far from the order of realism even while it is not less than realistic (no more lacking in reality effect than the traditional novel). On the contrary, it is closer to being a more-than-realism. For it is a gesture born of the knowledge that, as Lacan has put it, "the real begins where meaning ends." This gesture knows the real to be that which resists the symbolic. It intuits a world full of unnamable things and bodies, resistant to the constitution and organization of meaning. It faces and faces up to the real as an object that can only be missed (the dead mother and her elusive corpse, or perhaps the Godot who never comes, or the anti-Christ who keeps us cooling our heels).

With its somnambulistic words, it surveys a chaos without either form or formula. Its outside, the space wherein we experience things and bodies, is only a suspense without voice, a gaping vacancy within language. Writing maintains a tension toward this unnamable object. It is this erring, this catastrophic expectation, that desires the real even as it knows that this desire desires its own lack, its own failure, its own dilapidation and degradation into the insensate. Writing experiences the *cruelty*, in Artaud's sense of the term, of meaning.[16]

Fiction most certainly describes this experience. What we read in Beckett is the story of this interminable errancy (of Molloy toward his mother, of Moran toward Molloy . . .)[17] which stages an indefinite expectation in which the object remains suspended as an emblem of the general suspense of meaning. Fiction is thus the fable of the strictly *unqualifiable* character of the real that literature seeks to invest, for its cause, its engendering force, resides only there, in this impossible qualification.

But the description of experience can also just as well be the ruin of fiction, undoing its descriptive order and infinitely impoverishing its "realist" guise (this is the trajectory from *Molloy* to *The Unnamable*, for example), reducing it to ridiculous ruminations and insignificant rituals (Molloy and his pebbles), condemning it to be nothing but the idle filling of an improbable expectation, leaving it to be ravished by the unnamable and turning like a confused dervish on the verge of speaking in tongues: "Unaugmentable unmitigatable inviolable sempiternal almost void."

But this is neither despair, haggard melancholia, nor an exhausted assent to the calamity of being. It is more a kind of health and truth, a mode of resisting the mortifying fixation of settings, figures, interpretations, meanings. Molloy laments that "the icy words hail down upon [him], the icy meanings, and the world dies too, foully named" (p. 40). If the world is (only) this "long confused emotion" (p. 32) of which Molloy speaks, writing is an attempt to elude all that would cloak, in the stability and sweet clarity of lexical mastery, the violence and obscure aridity of this emotion. "The danger resides in the neatness of identification."[18]

It is only in the fact that there exists the unnamable that there resides the chance to escape subjugation. And this is another of Beckett's lessons. Writing differs the moment in which the system of the language invades and re-covers the living chaos, names, and in naming it, flattens its depth, in an instant exhausts its vitality. Although this certainly soothes its agony, it also extinguishes, in the historical reconstruction of the past or the prophetic ordering of the future, the desire and free in-significance that make the present. ("Here I am cornered by the future," says a tired voice in *Nouvelles et textes pour rien*).

The goal of fiction is thus less to say than to badly say or to unsay, less to advance than to retard, less to clarify than to obscure. "Discourse is unavoidable. So we invent obscurities. This is rhetoric," says the unnamable. The tone is cynical. But it tells the truth. Rhetoric is that which endures *différance*, suspends determination, retards the gel of nomination. It is less a question of saying (something) than of speaking.[19] "I can't talk about nothing and still I talk." As long as one speaks (and, paradoxically, speaks in order to defer the maturity of the word), consent to the named, and mortifying, a priori remains deferred. This is the meaning of the fable. Molloy looks for a corpse, Moran looks for Molloy who looks for a corpse. Neither finds what he seeks. Space remains open, no perspective is closed off. Writing happens. It takes place in its no place, a place without judgment or verdict, only hesitation, indecision, suspense, enigma, the maintained opening of significations and the vertiginous stagger of *Worstward Ho*. Since "saying is poorly said, . . . better still to poorly say" is the only homeopathic exit.

BECKETT THE TRAGIC

Beckett's heroes are clownlike clones of the solitary Jansenist. They know what Lucien Goldmann called the "absolute and radical solitude of tragic man, the impossibility of the least dialogue between this man and the world." They await the improbable appearance of a sporting God who stood them up, dressed in a carnival outfit, but not without some similarity to the *Deus absconditus* of Port-Royal. As for the world, it is for them nothing but "this little residue of venomous trifles that one calls, because one is lazy, the non-I, or even the world."[20]

For the small human being inquisitioned by language, the torture is double, for both the heavens and the face of the mother along with the world that it would create simultaneously withdraw. Against the backdrop of this originary scene (this founding myth?) painted by *Compagnie*,[21] among others, Beckett's oeuvre affirms the separation to which language pledges the speaker. It submits that "we are not in or of the world." But it knows just as well that there is no other place to be than the present world. Flawlessly "tragic," it affirms that there can be neither viable compromise with the world nor redemptive transcendence of it.[22] The "lie" of religion is not part of his work. But nor does it posit a secular exit from this tragic impasse, the extenuating flight toward the horizon of the happy future of political utopia, for example.

Beckett wrote *Molloy* in the wake of the traumatic dehumanization of the war, a time when one tried to bring everywhere into relief the idea of man as the survivor of a barbaric disaster, one endeavored to revive humanism, tried to think and to write "after Auschwitz." It was the time of existentialism and its engaged humanism (*Existentialism and Humanism* appeared in 1946). It was also the time in which Camus, still far from his *Étranger,* sought, in the moral ideal of Revolt, to recover the possibility of human solidarity and the traces of a "human nature" bronzed in the fire of a solar vitalism (*L'Homme révolté* appears in 1951.) And it was, at least for a little while, a time for the euphoric procrastinations of communism (which we know likewise to have been a pretender to humanism: is not man the "capital most precious"?).[23]

Tzara, thus, who wished to redefine the objectives of poetry, wrote in 1948,[24] "the poet heralds the advent of a harmonious world in which man will never again be in contradiction with himself." As for the poetry of which I earlier spoke, it redoubled its fraternal effusions, sang the praises of the future and prophesied an Arcady purged of the anguish of evil. "To each foundering of proof, the poet responds with a salute to the future," ecstatically intoned René Char. Even Francis Ponge, usually more of a realist and less bedecked, let himself dream of a secular and modern redemption. Imbued with a sort of healthful and hopeful faith in the future, he proposed (in *Proèmes,* 1948) that man enter a "repair shop," and announced that "the new man," the man of the "future," would be equilibrated, and happy, relieved of tragic man's "enervation" and Heideggerian "worry" about "ontological or metaphysical problems."[25]

Despite their (profound) differences, these forms of humanism have all one thing in common: the idea of a possible eradication of ontological evil (by means of a redemptive praxis, for example)[26] and the projection of this cure into a secularized future (a society cured of malaise, the classless society of the Marxists, for example). They all speculate on the future of illusion. They all attempt to deny the tragic, to sublate the contradiction whose impasse it draws, to preserve an exit toward a world of heavenly beauty. At the time of *Molloy,* this perspective was nearly hegemonic. And it is against this backdrop, I believe, that we must appreciate Beckett's philosophical and political obduracy to sustain the tragic truth.

THE SOUL LAUGHS

In 1950 Beckett was a radical atheist, one who did not even believe in the new religion, the religion of man.[27] The space that he opened was absolutely without faith or law.[28] He gaped tragically at the unmitigatable anguish of being. Beckett brought humanism's divine man down from his utopic sky and released him, mad, muttering, and ill, by the wayside in a world without redemptive issue. He exposed his clownish truth, exposed the truth of his invariable descent as a clown from a clown, decked out in a language grotesque and stirring, a language of artifice stubbornly unready to be naturalized, repaired, rectified, purified, or re-educated by optimistic doctors or blood-stained reformers.

For there is still more heterodoxy than merely that of the "tragic." Beckett (the poet Beckett) could very well have continued in the guise of a victim confessing his injuries, could very well have persisted in a bleary-eyed lyricism or in the dull pathos of elegy. He could have steeped himself in the metaphysical moralism of a Cioran, in misanthropic and ill-tempered rumination, delectable nihilism, or a masochistic submission to philosophy's self-articulation (the "intelligent" lucidity of its supposed knowledge). In other words, he could have gnawed dully on the corpse of the mother.

But there is nothing of this in Beckett, no clinical display of the evil of being. There is rather a jeering dignity, the distance of a comic dissonance.[29] While it is certain that the space described, the time beaten, the being staged, are those of tragedy, the characters are unhappy fools, buffoons who know nothing. Beckett himself makes a clown of himself, dusts the incontrovertible tragedy with the power of farce, with the stuff of sentences perforated by a deadpan humor. Beckett's laughter thus breaks with the ultimate belief, that is, with the belief that the Tragic is philosophy's final word. For if one laughs at the final word then the word is final no more and an opening is made for the uttering all of those words that have not made obeissance to the maternal mummy. This fortifying truth buoys us when we read Beckett.

For the central thing with Beckett is that this sordid gesture, this gray epic of human unhappiness, this failure replayed again and again in tragic impasse, makes us laugh. We cannot say this often enough.[30] There is, in Beckett, a formidable gaiety. It is a gaiety wrenched from the darkness, an energy that resides in the movement of sentences emerging and stringing themselves together that lightens, softens, the unhappy weight of what they speak. For the repetitive form of the sentences (the simultaneously mortifying and outrageously funny inventiveness of their syntax) elides in a limited way what they describe, transcends the opacity of the tragic prison that our debt to language constructs around us. It is as if it were absolutely necessary that Molloy or Malone be radically manacled, destroyed, undone, so that, a contrario, in a sort of cold and grotesque altercation, the liberty of he who has cast them onto the scene of the novel might detach itself.

This would be a good occasion to recuperate a fine word (to free it from its zealous usage). Perhaps we should name *soul* (in the sense that Baudelaire gives the term) this sacrificial ebriety, this distance of despair and auto-irony that animates us, that disentangles us from our cadaverous language and relieves, by flashes, the existential depression that narrative insists upon us. This *soul* detaches us from the morose (hypochondriac) contemplation of the stupidity of things, of the over-whelming in-significance of the world, of the dismaying confusion of being. It secures a respite, the place to catch a breath, a space in which to *breathe* a little. With Beckett we see that the spirit who denies is the spirit who laughs, that what laughs is the soul, that the *soul laughs,* even that it is a soul only to laugh. Beckett's laughter is a spiritual spirit, a dissolving spirituality that resolves, by displacing and surpassing it, the contrariety (that nevertheless less linked the two) of stupidity (a dumbfounded submission) and an intelligence sure of its wily superiority but that errs ruminating its supposed knowledge. Beckett, and herein lies another facet of his power to truth, shows us this.

Thus, at the very moment when the whole of his work describes the speaking being as a being in de-parture from the amiability of the world and on the way to no place else, the one who writes laughs at this revelation. He opens thereby within and for himself a symbolic issue. But this issue has no other place than the experience of deracination itself, the short-circuited time peculiar to an attempt at writing that represents nothing but itself, nothing but the invention of sentences and perforating comedy.

The heart of the matter is that there is effectively nothing but the margin opened by this maneuver, for if it is the function of language to sever, then nothing (even silence, which separates the separate) can reunite the speaking being to the world. The only chance of triumph (punctual and fleeting) over the implacable datum that is "writing," the simultaneous defection and restoration beyond the pale of the sentence, the disarticulation of words and their rearticulation *in an even worse state than before,* is "to try better a worse gaping, different according as with words or not. According as so much the better the worse or no way."[31]

If Beckett seems so familiar to those of us prey to the passion of literature, if his work produces such a power of truth within the essence itself of the literary gesture, it is without a doubt that he gives us an inkling of what it is that *there is literature,* an inkling as to the cause of this startled look, this spasm that mimes a symbolic exit and exit of the symbolic (a tentative bound beyond-the-mother), the source of this paradoxical word that speaks and speaks only in order to relieve the conditions of a silence always claimed and always reported. "The search for a means to make things cease, to silence their voice, is what allows discourse to go on."

Beckett shows us that writing is this de-parture, this god-speed without any god, this ex-traction from a here without any elsewhere. He teaches us that to write, to craft a style (artificial or rhetorical), is to "succeed at failing," to abuse its bitter aftertaste, to set it back on separation, on strangeness.[32] Beckett practices comedy like a cathartic catastrophe, as a means to push to an extreme, "one time worse for all," the logic of this politics of the worst. "To say this best abomination. With words that abridge, to say the least best worst."[33] Writing, for Beckett, is something like the worst converted to laughter, a bantering homeopathic turn of the separated being on that which separates him.

THE RHYTHM OF LAUGHTER

If writing *in the worst possible way* draws its dynamism from the disengaged spirituality of laughter, it is that laughter, for Beckett, beats the time of writing and of reading. Laughter is rhythm.

There have been others (Ludovic Janvier above all) who have studied the details of the comic procedures of Beckett's prose. But what I would like to retain for our discussion is that the comic effect derives less from the content (situations, gags . . .) or the forms (puns, calembours . . .) than from a certain type of occurrence, the rule-governed rhythm of the comedic gaps. In the discursive movement peculiar to Beckett's characters there is a sort of spasmodic cycle of ruptured utterance, a ritournello composed of the defections of meaning petrified by ratiocination, a punctual repetition of burlesque skits, of absurd dislocations, of clownlike swaggers that perforate the soliloquy.[34]

Often, what makes us laugh is a disparity of tones or levels of language that emerges at relatively regular intervals in incidental clauses often explicitly set off between commas. Here we find whiffs of triviality, purely phatic hackneyed plots ("everything in its own time," "don't count your chickens before they're hatched," "it's good to know," etc.), idle asides, automatic idiolects (thus, in *Molloy:* "I thought I could see, vaguely on the horizon, the towers and steeples of a city that naturally nothing led me to believe was my own, *until further notice*" [my emphasis]), or self-evident truths, founding axioms launched from the wings into the abyss, idle political aphorisms ("Constipation in pomeranians is a sign of good health," declares Molloy).

At base, we find a number of paradoxical *points* that work their effects only to be radically blunted. In these literally in-significant, disaffected, neutralizing concepts, the sententious rumination, the maniac amnesia, the fastidious confession skids away, bogs itself down, collapses in a vague somnambulistic protocol. But after this "plop," the wave of the sentence reanimates itself, obstinately and stupidly. And this system—composed alternately of comic deceleration, of pausing on the abyssal images, the comicocadaverous stasis of meaning, and the stubborn receleration of logorrhea—constitutes the rhythm, the scansion, of the written.

Beckett's incidental clauses play the same *negative* role as Céline's ellipses. They are an unnamed sublation of the unnamable, an unremarked marking of the negative, a fissure in the homogeneity of the symbolic body, the thwarting of the alluring idyll between language and reality. The commas that propel them into the sentence divide the strength, grind the elocution, cause discourse and narration to miserably fail. Meaning is drolly suspended, rumination broken, monologue deflected. Rhythm manages these ruptures. Laughter shakes the logic of these failures[35] cast in the hardened material of the sclerosis of language (crusts of a ready-made meaning).

POLITICAL BECKETT?

We do not presume to change the manners of men, but we hope to demonstrate to them the fragility of their thought, and on what variable bases, on what caverns, they have fixed their trembling abodes.

—Antonin Artaud

A political discourse can perhaps be understood as a discourse that believes (and that reproduces this belief) in the adequation of word and thing (the exigency of "true speech") and that adopts a therapeutic perspective ("anguish must leave this earth," Gorbachev has recently said). The heterodox laughter of a literature like that of Beckett is first of all the unplaying of this game. It brings to audition something like the mute triviality of the negative, introjecting within the calm and assured positivity of the conference room jeering interruptions, voices from the wings, perforating jokes, and the carnival-like slogans of a despair without acerbity.

I cannot see any other way of situating the question of the political in Beckett. His writings are always on the side of the sterilization of the story, the erosion of imagination, the exhaustion of meaning.[36] They resist the stabilized constitution of figures and discourses. They set into motion a mechanized erosion of names and dissipation of decors. They systematically stage a frustration of the anticipation of any saving grace. Everything is fashioned to escape the declarative mode. Nothing solidifies into a positive platform, a political position (either protest against what is, or an exemplary narrative vision of what will be) that offers a possible civic transformation.

But, as I have noted, *Molloy*'s time was a time dominated by a humanist vision, by a belief in the positive role to be played by literature in the transformation of civic society, by the ideal of declarative engagement, and by a devotion to gurus of whom Sartre is always the model. Although with considerable variants, these modes of seeing held sway into the eighties, that is, to what has been called the death of the avant-garde (the alliance of political messianism and the "great irregularities of language").

It is from this event that we emerge. And we cannot help but find the declarations of our century's politically engaged authors a bit naive, a bit self-important, a bit ridiculous. I am not speaking exclusively of specialists, like Sartre, or of partisan trumpets like Aragon. I am speaking also of intellectuals and artists of greater subtlety and profundity (Breton, Bataille, even Ponge and, nearer to us, Guyotat). I recall their spontaneous belief in the interventionist powers of literature, the weight with which they seemed almost spontaneously to endow their own declarations on the issue (as if it were obvious, natural, that they be heard, responded to, followed by transformational repercussions).

These people still believed in the effects of the dynamism launched at the end of the nineteenth century. Art and literature had come into their own in relation to the powers that be. Intellectual and artistic prestige became the guarantor of an efficacious word exerting its power on the terrain of ideological influence and political action (emblem: the Dreyfus affair and the role of Zola).

Today this has come to an end. And everything seems to unfold as if the omnipresent media had paradoxically deprived intellectuals of their substance and impact, their power to affect the political. The agitated and cursory "debate of ideas" has replaced (and contradicted) the subtlety of thought. Philosophy, mediatized (mediatizable?), has contracted to a minimalist humanism (the Rights of Man becoming the horizon of thought). Art's destabilizing function has cleared the place for a massive positivity.[37] The loss of competence has been dramatic (and authorizes artists to speak with greatest authority about that in which they are not specialists).

Anyone who persists in "doing literature" without acceding to the fact that doing literature can only be an intraworldly diversion, a career path, a subjective confession, anyone who does not assent to the idea that literature can have no possible *social* impact, is today urgently confronted with the lacerating question. What end does it serve? What good is it? What meaning, in the world and for the world, in a society acutely suffering its lack of meaning and loss of Utopia, in a universe hungry for determination, positivity, clarity, for a heavenly plenitude, can the pursuit of this activity have, an activity that the world seems definitively to have marginalized, to have reduced to a sort of deliciously and pleasantly outmoded survival existing only beyond the bounds of society's serious self-reflection.

Beckett's texts do not, as is plain to see, furnish us with any easy answers to such questions. But what I would like to put into evidence is that their various rapports with the question of language, with humanist thought, with tragic vision, and with "homeopathic" laughter can help us in our own time to better pose the above questions. For Beckett's oeuvre is one of those (not so very numerous) that force us to ask ourselves why there is literature rather than nothing (rather than a linguistic usage exclusively contractual and social) and to try to understand what this enigmatic phenomenon makes manifest within the city, to understand its civic meaning, what it signifies for the community.

It seems to me that to read Beckett (caught up in the mélange of perplexity, jubilation, and hygienic despair that his reading forces) is to carry out an *experi-*

ment in which we find all that we read and decipher in this literature to be finally only a ring, a swollen excrescence around that which, impossible to articulate, is nevertheless its meaning, the articulation of its origin, of what interdicts silence.[38] This is the saying that says the impossible response to the question "Why write?" "Why is there literature at all?"

This question (and here, it seems to me, resides the source of the violent "power of truth" that Beckett produces) is the acute, symbolic form of an even more fundamental question: "Why do we speak?" "How is it that we speak?" "How is it that we are, are alone speakers?" And, finally, "what price do we pay for this gift?"

From at least the time of the Greeks we have understood politics to be a linguistic affair, the management in and by means of verbal exchanges of conflicts which otherwise would explode violently into actions. This forces the conclusion that the knowledge of what language is in effect, the knowledge of the uneasy rapport with the real to which it consecrates us, is a *politically necessary* knowledge because, for example, the fundamental political illusion (the illusion of secular utopias) is the illusion of a resolution of this specifically human malaise (the malaise specific to the speaking being).

The loss of meaning, the absence, the failed quest, the frustrated expectation, that Beckett's oeuvre indefinitely modulates, is perhaps that which, in his own epoch, one sought to recover and to reconstitute in the practice of ecstatic illusion inherent to all the visions of political utopias, the reveries of a perfectible humanity, and the various myths of a finally successful community. We sought to embody the meaning in a redemptive praxis in which it invests its desire to extroject existential malaise and to endow with meaning the life of the other in works, romantic or poetic, which are all, from the Sartrean novel to the oracular poetry "à hauteur d'homme" of a René Char or an Eluard, more or less the defense/illustration of these preoccupations. Beckett's literature, like that of several others but his more than most others, is, on the contrary, a sarcastic resistance to this positive determination. In more general terms, Beckett's literature, with its contradictions held up as pseudocorrectives, challenges the rational plenitude that each body of knowledge imposes on the world to make its chaos supportable. It engulfs, in a mortifying region, the articulation that narratives like to give time in order to symbolically suspend its menace. Its austere monstrosity and deadpan humor annihilates whatever dream we may have had to see in the art of literature the return of the prodigal speaker into his earthly home.

Like that of any "tragic" author, the oeuvre of Beckett situates first of all the rock of unalterable and unmitigatable malaise at the heart of "civilization." I have tried to recall that Beckett sets himself up on the threshold of the conscience of separation (symbolized by leaving the maternal language). It breaks with the maternal. It identifies being (insofar as speaking) with this rending. It refuses the natural-atavistic bound. It makes of this consciousness of separation the place, the object, the tool of literature, of a literature that treats the negative, withdraws itself from the thetic, interdicts positive declaration, unhinges the rules of communication. It likewise renders eminently problematic and implicitly raises the question of the relation of persons to those things that bind them together: language conceived as access to the social, as being hailed by the expropriating power of the community and its always potentially fascist strictures.

Beckett's literature tells us that there is something that cannot be named, qualified, determined, that there is something suspended and empty at the heart of the relation that persons, speakers, hold with the world, with things and their bodies, with others. A hole in the community that makes it simultaneously impossible and possible.[39] A void that makes community intolerable and that nevertheless gives it the elasticity, the porosity, without which the community becomes irrevocably panoptic, carceral, and totalitarian.

This something is in language and is language, is the fact of language.[40] To attempt to erase its trace, its blind spot, its remnant of obscurity (from the perspective of science, morality, politics, discourse, well-managed narrative)[41] is the objective of positive discourses (without which the community would sink into barbarity without laws). To bring all of this obstately in and through language is the objective of art and literature, without which the community would sink into the totalitarian barbarity of the Law.

In other words, the condition of being cut from the world nourishes in us a dolorous nostalgia. To be tied body and soul to the community of speakers could weigh us down to the point of throwing us into a schizophrenic state. We cannot not dream of a happy and redemptive homecoming, of a community at once supple and solid, and of the quieting of our neurotic sufferings. We must dream of abolishing the rupture, of escaping the prison. But if it is language that isolates and incarcerates us then escaping this prison implies escaping language. In the end this . . . acting-out amounts to madness. This is why madness is our peculiar temptation (along with violence, bestial abjection, mystical exaltation . . .).

But one does not escape language without likewise leaving behind one's being human. One does not withdraw oneself from language without withdrawing oneself from the human (and barbarism is the horizon of this unspeakable exit). This, then, forms the dilemma, in its customary sense but also in the silhouetted cursive of fiction, in which the Beckettian creatures operate. Does one remain in prison (cancel oneself out as free subject by submitting to the norms of the community, become, as the unnamable says, "reduced to reason," live stupidity, dress oneself in neurosis, speak only with the cadaver of the mother in one's mouth) or does one escape, without any voice, in the direction of barbarism, criminality, Winnie's potted autism or Lucky's mournful and delirious logorrhea? It's not surprising that we look for more clement skies, even if we secularize them under the heading of a gratifying Utopia.

Beckett is one of those who reduce, desiccate, these reveries. For him, the only solution is not only more modest, but it is not a *solution* at all. One can only exit language from within, by intervening in it (as Michaux likewise believed), by opening within it a provisional space of freedom, by rattling it with style and laughter, by working within it this symbolic bound that stays in one place (but is nevertheless a leap, "out of the rank of murderers," as Kafka said), this perilous and clownlike leap that is named literature, "excess of language," or "scripted gibberish." Without a doubt, there is no other civic meaning to this activity wherein solitude, says Beckett, finds its "apotheosis."[42]

Beckett was one . . . "resistant" to the catastrophic and exultant euphoria of an engaged and utopian humanism. This resistance had a footing in writing, art, in *this kind of form* of the experience and the work of language turned entirely toward negativity and a hopelessly sovereign laughter. And we can be certain that such resistance, while in modes certainly different but deriving from the same ethical and philosophical bases, remains very much and more than ever, the order of the day.

(translated from the French by Michele Sharp)

Notes

We have opted to follow the format of M. Prigent's original French text, in which citations of Beckett's text were used sparingly. When noted, all references are from Beckett's English translation of the trilogy, published as *Three Novels of Samuel Beckett* (New York: Grove Press, 1958).

1. "The mind's trinket / was that / the parting that is / always there / cannot / very well support itself there" (Ci-gît).

2. Or rather: "For the crowning horror, within ourselves, the same sordid order speaks, for we do not have any other words, nor any other great words (or sentences, that is to say, any other ideas) at our disposition than those of everyday use in this gross world prostituted for eternity" (Ponge, *Proèmes,* 1948).

3. Artaud likewise evokes (in his way) "this abyss of impure matter and moreover so nicely impure where the cadaver of Madame Death, of madame faecal uterine, madame anus, gehenna of excrement by gehenna, in the opium of its excrement, foment fama, the faecal destiny of its soul, in the uterus of its own foyer" (*Oeuvres complètes,* vol. 9, p. 174).

4. "Let the impropriety of terms permit a new induction of the human among signs already too detached from him and too dehydrated, too pretentious, too boastful. Let all abstractions be punctured from within and made as if to be founded by this secret passion of vice" (*Proèmes*).

5. The mother, as Rimbaud puts it in exemplary fashion in *Les Poètes de sept ans*, demands "intelligence."

6. These formulas are lifted from Sartre. ("Qu'est-ce que la littérature?" in *Situations* II, 1948).

7. I will not here open a discussion of . . . biography. But across many of Beckett's texts one can follow the traces of a difficulty with the mother, the one whom questions *exasperate* and who language *wounds* the child avid to know the world and anxious of all that separates him from it. Thus, in *Compagnie*, we read: "Raising your eyes to the azur sky and then to your mother face you break the silence, asking her if it isn't really much more distant than it seems. . . . For some reason that you never could explain this question must have exasperated her. For she sent your little hand flying and gave you an answer woundingly unforgettable."

8. "The lie, the lie, to lying thought" (*Molloy*, p. 36). See my essay, "Cette obscure clarté" in *Quai Voltaire* 7 (January 1993).

9. Bataille: "When accepting poetry changes it into is opposite (it becomes the matrix of an acceptation)! I hold to the leap by which I would exceed the universe, I justify the given world, I content myself with this. . . . Poetic delirium has its place in nature; it justifies nature, agrees to embellish it" (*L'impossible*).

10. From *Connaissance de l'est* (1900).

11. *Vents* (1946).

12. *Furreur et mystère* (1948).

13. *Le surréalisme et l'après-guerre* (1948).

14. It is thus that Molloy flies quaintly to his mother "on the clipped wings of necessity"! (p. 35).

15. *Pour et finir* . . .

16. "One could well imagine cruelty, without any rending of the flesh. And philosophically speaking, moreover, what is cruelty? From the point of view of mind, cruelty signifies rigor, implacable application and decision, irreversible determination, consciousness, in a kind of applied consciousness" (*Lettres sur la cruauté*, 1933).

17. "The important thing is that I never arrive anywhere," says *the unnamable*.

18. *Dante . . . Bruno . Vico . . Joyce.* Dubuffet says the same thing: "The more determinate the figure, the more diminished its signification," or, "I no longer want anything that bears a name," "Your sight will be fixed only when it is no longer determined by the names given to things." And, as Gilles Deleuze suggests in *L'Epaisé*, it is this resistance to determination, this bantering escape from all identification, this softening down of names that verges on aphasia, that produces within the minimalist ritual of Beckett's short

plays written for the television screen (precisely there where the luridly illuminated chromatic clarity of its representations—images, words, and scenarios—asphyxiates the real and gives us over to the *fabulous* grasp of represented, named, stabilized things that edit and articulate for us our sense of time and space) an "ennemi du dedans."

19. Here, again, the opposition to Sartre is radical.

20. *First Love.*

21. Cf. note 7, above.

22. We might recall those figures of *Le Dépeaplear* trapped in their cylinder and precisely unable to find any opening toward the sky.

23. Aragon's *Les Communistes* appeared in the same year as *Molloy.*

24. *Le Surréalisme et l'après-guerre.*

25. It does good to remark one more time that it is always the remainder of a devotion to *positivity* (the small, "too human," too communitary, too declarative residue left in a brain devoted to the paradoxically superhuman humanity of the adventure of language) that subjects these writers (Ponge, Tzara, Céline also, differently but all the same on the positivistic base of his therapeutic and prophalactic passion) into the trap, into the ridiculous and sometimes the odious.

26. "We no longer count ourselves among those who wish to possess the world, but among those who wish to change it. . . . *Praxis,* as both action in and on history, that is, as the synthesis of historical relativism and the ethical and metaphysical absolute . . . , this is our subject" (Sartre, *Situation de l'écrivain en 1947,* in *Qu'est-ce que la littérature?*).

27. Beckett's (almost) sole accomplice at the time was always Artaud, who wrote in *Sappôts et suppliciations* (1948): "I, myself, Artaud, feel like a horse, a non man." And in *Pour en finir avec le jugement de Dieu:* "If no one believes in God anymore, everyone believes more and more in man."

28. The fact, reported by Roger Blin, that *Waiting for Godot* was initially, in 1951, everywhere condemned for containing "neither woman, communist, nor priest," testifies to the strong inner relation between religion, the religion of man, and the devotion to the natural/maternal (the three powers against which Beckett wrote).

29. Beckett chalks this up to his "stupidity," his intellectual reticence, his lack of aptitude for "ideas."

30. Although it remains astonishing that this definitive aspect remains so little commented on.

31. *Worstward Ho.*

32. Or, to take the words of Ponge, "There is only one possibility: to speak against words. To carry them with us into the shame to which they lead us in such a way that they disfigure themselves. There is no other reason to write" (*Proèmes*).

33. *Worstward Ho.*

34. Laughter can be born as the inverse of the sort of abusive homogenization (and not at all "natural") of rhythm that appears in Beckett. It is this that happens with the

obsessional ritual repetitions that Molloy performs with the pebbles carefully transferred from pocket to pocket (and the syntax that describes the ritual itself becomes a kind of repetitive music). The question of rhythm, the devaluation, fundamentally mythological or biblical, grotesque and discretely droll that sweetly weaves a story like that of *Molloy,* is also, without doubt (of contrapuntal doubling), lodged in our brains like an imperceptible filigree, a figure hidden but ready to emerge from the trivial disguise it wears.

35. It is evidently not by coincidence that Beckett, in *Film,* animates Buster Keaton, the emblem of the clownlike (and of the hyperembattled) by means of a combat with things and his general inaptitude for the world. This is the cinematic archetype of the worst converted into laughter and the height of comicocatastrophic failure.

36. This continues, we well know, even to the rhythmed atomization and repetitive ritornellos of texts like *Worstward Ho. . . .* Molloy anticipates this in radical terms: "You would do better, at least no worse, to obliterate texts than to blacken their margins, to fill in the holes of words till all is blank and flat and the ghastly business looks like what it is, senseless, speechless, issueless misery."

37. Exactly the inverse of the effect sought by Beckett in his television screenplays (in *Quad*).

38. Cf. the passage already cited above, "The search for a means to make things cease, to silence their voice, is what allows discourse to go on" (*The Unnamable*).

39. In my opinion, this is the reason why Beckett deliberately chose to give to his highly anticivic work an explicitly civic role (by choosing theater, television . . .).

40. This is indeed exactly that to which, in 1950, a writer like Beckett and a philosopher like Camus (one of those philosophers of which Lacan remarked: "I call them *philosophers* because they are not psychoanalysts; they believe that words have no power") set themselves in radical opposition. On the one side, an ethics nourished on the cruelty of an experiment with language, on the other, the idealism of a voluntarist morality (revolution as the community's refoundational chance). This consideration is not only of retrospective import, for it is the heritage of Camus that makes an appeal to this largely mediatized thought that circumscribes the horizon of the "Rights of Man."

41. "Athletes, mechanics, philosophers, doctors have tried, one after the other, the most diverse methods. They did not understand that the evil which man had wrought could no longer be undone" (Lautrémont).

42. In a recent article (*Libération,* January 22, 1993) I have proposed that if we are absolutely intent on inscribing all of this within a sociopolitical register, we must at the very least risk the following. This vacillation of meaning, this assumed imperfection, this accepted malaise, this indetermination of principle so much a part of Beckett's work, in the language of politics must be named *democracy,* a democracy that sets itself against the attractive devotion to therapeutic futurologies, totalitarian assurance, the atavism of racial determinations, the luminous clarity of utopia. In their darkness, their difficulty, their strangeness (in their resistance to the a priori determination of Meaning and in the cruelty

of their emplotting of Evil), works like those of Beckett lay claim to a democracy under-stood as an accounting for the knowledge of the logos, as a disillusioned understanding and acquiescence to malaise, as a negation of the therapeutic political illusion, and as the least of all evils because it is the cruel knowledge of evil. All of this, in any case, rather than the bloody illusion of the great and dazzling projects that prepare to spring into being on every side.

5

"GOING TO BETHiCKETT ON THE WAY TO HEAVEN"

The Politics of Self-Reflection in Postmodern Fiction

Marcel Cornis-Pope

One does not translate Beckett, one provokes him to translate himself. . . . Our work was less one of translation than one of incitation and resonance.

—Ludovic Janvier, Beckett's translator

INCITATIONS TO REREADING

This essay is an incitation to rereading:[1] the first section will attempt a reconceptualization of the postmodern notion of narrative reflexivity along stronger political and sociocultural lines, and will seek to revalorize narrative innovation, integrating it more coherently with a theory of narrative and cultural articulation. The second section is concerned with revisionistic intertexts: reinterpreting Beckett through his postmodern resonances, and using these new Beckettian incitations to rethink the tasks of contemporary fiction. Beckett mediates in this perspective his own revision, as well that of postmodern innovation.

SELF-REFLEXIVITY AND THE IDEOLOGICAL RESTRUCTURING OF THE NOVEL

. . . I'm convinced that we must now move beyond mere fables, beyond the neatly packaged stories which provide a chain of terminal satisfactions from predictable beginnings to foreshadowed endings. We have come so far in the long journey

*of literature that all the stories whisper the same old thing to us
in the same cracked voice. And so we must dig in to see where
the raw words and fundamental sounds are buried so that the
great silence within can finally be decoded.*

—Raymond Federman, To Whom It May Concern *(1990)*

*I want the chance to shape my own future; to be able to make
decisions in reference to what I will or will not do. I want to
have some say in the programming of my own day-to-day
existence.*

—Clarence Major, *No* (1973)

In his 1988 reappraisal of "Self-Reflexive Fiction," Raymond Federman ascribed
to narrative reflexivity a strong ideological function as a facilitator of a critical
dialogue between author, text, reader, and culture. While "self-consciousness"
draws the reader into the workings of the text and its culture, "self-referentiality"
pits the author's consciousness against the rhetoric of his text.[2] In both versions,
reflexivity is more than a formal gimmick: its function is to extricate the novel
"from the postures and impostures of realism," committing fiction to a poetics of
"divergence." As a species of resistance to traditional constructions of reality, self-
reflexive fiction is historically justified: it took shape, according to Federman, in
the sixties and early seventies to fill "the linguistic gap created by the disarticulation of the official discourse in its relation with the individual." The novels written
during these years by Barthelme, Calvino, Coover, Cortázar, Gass, Pynchon,
Vonnegut, challenged the false claims to stability of referential discourse, exposing
its systems of beliefs and symbols. By replacing a conventional mimesis of "content" (stable myths and symbols) with a subversive "mimesis of form" that renders
"concrete and even visual in its language, in its syntax, in its typography and
topology" the differential energy of American experience, this type of fiction
created a disorder in the traditional socialization of reality, disentangling the
discourse of the subject from "official discourse." Other writers associated with
Federman's notion of "surfiction" (Abish, Katz, Hauser, Gins, Major, Reed, Sor-
rentino, Sukenick) departed more radically from the "linear movement and sequential logic" of referential fiction, denouncing its silent agreement with "the
official discourse of the State." Their "critifictions" attacked out of ideological
necessity, rather than formalistic self-indulgence, "the very vehicle that expressed
and represented that [American] reality: discursive language and the traditional
form of the novel" (p. 1155). The novel took on an important ideological function, renewing social imagination, expanding the available modes of narrative and

cultural articulation so as to allow individuals to take creative hold of their own life stories.

Clearly, not all descriptions of self-referentiality are as pointed and political as Federman's reappraisal of innovative fiction. Earlier pronouncements on the subject often emphasized the playful, self-canceling, aesthetic dimension of reflexivity. Innovative writers share with their critics some of the responsibility for their own misrepresentation, often describing their task in formalistic rather than political terms: "The elements of the new fictitious discourse . . . must be digressive from one another—digressive from the element that precedes and the element that follows. Rather than being a stable image of daily life, fiction will be in a perpetual state of redoubling upon itself. It is from itself, from its own substance that the fictitious discourse will proliferate—imitating, repeating, parodying, retracting what it says."[3] In a more philosophic vein, William H. Gass has insisted that the story "is taking place the only place it could take place: on the patient page, in among the steadfast words, the metaphors of mind and imagination."[4] Fictional language "devours" the "real," replacing it with "this unfolding thing of words in front of us, this path the mind will follow in search of a feeling. . . . Nothing is being represented. A thought, instead, is being constructed: a memory" (pp. 81, 83). For Ronald Sukenick even this description of the workings of fiction is "encumbered . . . by undigested leftovers from other theories." By treating fiction as a model of the world, Gass "reintroduces the schizoid split between art and reality. This is basically a subtler kind of imitation in which the continuity between art and experience is broken because art is seen as a mode essentially different from experience."[5] Sukenick's own "digressions on the act of fiction" have called for a more radical version of "nonrepresentational" fiction whose "main qualities are abstraction, improvisation, and opacity."[6] This referential opacity "should direct our attention to the surface of a work, and such techniques as graphics and typographical variation, calling the reader's attention to the technological reality of the book," to "the truth of the page" (p. 212).

Critics of postmodernism have protested that this reorientation toward the technological-articulatory reality of the novel represents a "recoiling" from the moral function of literature. In Alan Wilde's typical description, the "fragmented and randomized surface" of "reflexivist" fiction projects only an authorial self-image concerned "entirely and wholeheartedly with 'writing about writing',"[7] What innovative fiction lacks, in John Aldridge's view, is an unspoiled, Hemingway-type "relationship with the concrete objects": whereas "Hemingway's works can be read as a series of instruction manuals on how to respond and comport one's self in the testing situations of life," the postmodern texts are steeped in an "orthodoxly negativist vision of contemporary experience" and "gratuitous ugliness."[8] For De Villo Sloan postmodernism is "by its nature a decadent form, saved only by its reflective ability to be aware of its decadence."[9]

Relying heavily on Beckett's "model of nonideology," De Villo Sloan asserts that experimental fiction has drifted toward "an increasing self-reflection without the benefit of a useful subject material," reducing "the traditional notion of the human" to "endless chains of metalanguage" (p. 37).

As this brief sampling suggests, such critiques of innovative fiction rely heavily on unexamined, problematic assumptions. Some can be relegated to the category of sanctimonious cliches (Sloan's "traditional," unchanging "notion of the human," Aldridge's "dependable rules of feeling and conduct") that do not withstand a serious examination. Others are more insidious and deeply embedded in the critical discourse, requiring a closer analysis—which is what I intend to undertake here. One such assumption positions Beckett at the "nonideological" pole of the self-reflexive tradition, as chief proponent of an "aesthetics of failure"[10] whose "heroic absurdity" Hassan has celebrated as exemplary of an austere male denial of matter, world, and historical tradition:[11]

> Beckett redefines originality as a flight from originality, imagination as an escape from amplitude, language as silence. In the anxiety of genius, Beckett does not attempt to surpass Joyce; he "negates" him by his own example. . . . The quest for total verbal consciousness in Joyce, the quest for a minimal verbal consciousness in Beckett—both express a postmodern will to dematerialize the world, to turn it into a gnostic reality, a fantasy.[12]

In the next section of my paper I will challenge this linear-oppositional view of Beckett as a relentless negativist, rereading him through the work of an exemplary post-Beckettian innovator, Raymond Federman.[13] Beckett should not be simply viewed as the antithesis of Joyce: a reductionist, substituting a thematic and linguistic minimalism for Joyce's quest for total verbal consciousness. In Kristeva's words, Beckett's "derisory and infernal testimony" reaffirms the capacity of writing to "blaze a trail amidst the unnamable," to envision potentialities amidst impossibilities.[14] His "art in a closed field" (Hugh Kenner) has, paradoxically, stimulated the "open field" narration of radical innovators from Coover and Pynchon to the surfictionists; just as it has inspired the quieter "literature of replenishment" of a metafictionist like John Barth.

In the remainder of the present section, I want to address another problematic assumption that has prevented us from a stronger sociocultural valorization of narrative innovation. Critics of postmodernism want fiction to seriously address the contemporary crisis, yet remain free of epistemological and structural reflection. Rather than dally in endless interrogation, the novel should—in Charles Newman's view—become again an effective "storytelling machine," reinforcing "the positive socializing function of literature."[15] The novelist's awareness of the manipulative side of his narrative métier should not interfere with his task of imposing order on reality: "What we finally want from literature is neither amusement, nor edification, but the demonstration of real authority which is not to be confused with sincerity, and of an understanding which is not gratuitous" (pp. 97, 173). Behind such dubious, unconditional endorsements of narrative authority lies a nostalgic model of narration as a successful totalizing machine; the same model that prompted Fredric Jameson's more refined critique of postmodernism as a weakened modernist aesthetic, unwittingly reinforcing "the logic of consumer capitalism."[16] Innovative fiction has been alternatively described as overly pluralistic and destabilizing, "a vehicle for disparate voices" and narcissistic self-explorations (Charles Newman); or as politically quietist and entrenched, its critical edge blunted by a tendency to put all narrative and thought categories under erasure.

Paradoxically, radical theorists like Jameson who have raised the latter point, have themselves contributed to this blunting of fiction's critical edge. Of late, Jameson's work has focused almost exclusively on forms of art that give support to his deterministic model of postmodernism as "symptomatic" of (complicit with) the socioeconomics of late capitalism: video "in its twin manifestations as commercial television and . . . 'video art',"[17] postmodern architecture and photography, nonpolitical "conceptual" art, or the new wave science fiction ("cyberpunk") described as "the supreme *literary* expression if not of postmodernism, then of late capitalism itself" (p. 419n1), a symptom of an "ultimate historicist breakdown" (p. 231). While Jameson continues to theorize about the need for a more reflective art of "cognitive mapping," the examples he cares to provide remain politically ambivalent, reinforcing his reproductive model: the fiction of that "epic poet of the disappearance of the American radical past," E. L. Doctorow (p. 24), pseudohistorical nostalgia film, the "cognitive mapping" of John Portman's Westin Bonaventure Hotel in Los Angeles, or Frank Gehry's Santa Monica house, Hans Haacke's conceptual art installations, science fiction texts by Philip K. Dick and J. G. Ballard.[18] At best, these works "undo postmodernism homeopathically by the methods of postmodernism," which for Jameson are mostly pastiche, metafictional fabulation, and parody.[19] As such, they do not yet constitute a politically significant "counterdiscourse." On the other hand, Jameson ignores entirely or mentions only in passing more radical forms of postmodern reformulation: political metafiction, surfiction, L=A=N=G=U=A=G=E poetry, feminist literature, and art. For example, he hastily dismisses the "autoreferential fabulations of the short-lived Anglo-American 'new novel'," without challenging the conventional formalistic view of their work (which he himself applies to the French *nouveau roman*). By rendering alternative forms of fiction and art invisible through his exclusivist vision, Jameson contributes even further to the marginalization of politically significant experimentation. One is tempted to say with Lyotard that behind "the diverse invitations to suspend artistic experimentation, there is an identical call for order, a desire for unity, for identity, for security, or popularity. . . . Artists and writers must be brought back into the bosom of the community, or at least, if the latter is considered to be ill, they must be assigned the task of healing it."[20]

The contemporary debates about postmodern experimentation perpetuate, in René Girard's view, our guilty, agonistic consciousness about artistic "progress" that has traditionally opposed innovation to imitation. As Girard explains, the "negative view of innovation is inseparable from a conception of the spiritual and intellectual life dominated by stable imitation. Being the source of eternal truth, of eternal beauty, of eternal goodness, the models should never change. Only when these transcendental models are toppled, can innovation acquire a positive meaning."[21] Imitation and innovation are regarded as largely incompatible, caught in a psychodrama that pits a quasitheological fear of heretical change against a "terroristic" promotion of innovation for the sake of creating *ruptures épistémologiques*. The "tendency to define 'innovation' in more and more 'radical' and anti-mimetic terms, . . . reflects a surrender of modern intelligence to this mimetic pressure [to exacerbate the competitive spirit], a collective embrace of self-deception" (p. 16). But just as pernicious as this "mimetic rivalry unleashed by the abandonment of transcendental models," is the anti-innovative resentment that blocks, according to Girard, "external" and "internal" mediation." Both are manifestations of a conflictive mentality that does not see imitation and innovation as continuous and complementary (p. 14). The prerequisite for "real innovation is a minimal respect for the past, and a mastery of its achievements, i.e., *mimesis*. To expect novelty to cleanse itself of imitation is to expect a plant to grow with its roots up in the air" (p. 19). Successful innovation challenges tradition from inside, mediating as well as transforming it.

Girard's concept of innovation may appear limited and cautious, excluding radical shifts as "meaningless agitation" (pp. 18–19). But it presents us with the possibility of moving beyond a constraining dualism of terms (mimesis/innovation, formalism/realism). However, we will have to expand his framework to be able to account for more radical forms of postmodernism (surfiction, feminist narration, postcolonial writing, the "L=A=N=G=U=A=G=E" poetry) that pit realism against self-reflection, assuming an "adversarial"/revisionistic relation to both. The current critical terminology often stands in the way of a comprehensive understanding of postmodern innovation. Used all too often to explain recent forms of art, terms such as "metafiction," "metapoetery," "antinarrative," "pure fiction," "parody," "pastiche," have reduced postmodernism to an "either-or" logic that opposes deconstruction to articulation and self-reflection to "true" mimesis. This must appear particularly ironic to those innovative projects (the postmodern fantastic of Calvino, Kundera, García Márquez, Morrison; self-reflexive feminist fiction and film; "borderline," multicultural literature; the oppositional poetics of the "L=A=N=G=U=A=G=E" poets, the textualist/dialogic techniques of East European experimenters, etc.) which have struggled to get outside this binary logic, refusing both a naive experiential stance, and nihilistic self-deconstruction. The oppositional poetics proposed by the L=A=N=G=U=A=G=E poets has radicalized not only syntax, but also poetry's "stance toward reality," using language experimentation to reempower individual and public discourse. Self-referential techniques are used here both to challenge the common assumptions about "transparent" reality and "unmediated communication"; and to remove/reshape "the distance between writing and experience," fact and fiction, public and private.[22] Self-referentiality engages the poetic text in a "politics . . . of both the Sign & Social Context," in a hermeneutics of art and of the social sphere.[23] In similar ways, the disruptive-reformulative strategies employed in surfiction or feminist narration seek to radicalize fiction's rapport with reality, opening the self-contained "system of language up to experience beyond language."[24] Steve Katz's stories in *Moving Parts* (1977) may look like experiments in "pure writing," lively improvisations with "the quality of music, riffs and jams,"[25] but a closer examination will find them concerned with narrative frames and mental systems that form "a cataract of dogma over your perceptions of things as they are."[26] At the same time, these stories suggest ways in which fiction can rewrite reality, establishing "uncontrollable and mysterious resonance[s]" with experience: "Art prepares the bed of contingencies from which reality sprouts, ripens, and is harvested."[27]

The important point that innovative novelists have been making is that the self-critical focus on fiction's traditional frames and tasks is a *sine qua non* condition for a creative response to reality:

> What I'm interested in is exploring the potential of storytelling. I think storytelling, more than the novels as such, serves a function in human intercourse. And I want to stretch the bounds of the potential of storytelling, which always has to be refitted to the times, reexamined, reinvented. In other words, the structure of the exchange has to be reimagined.[28]

The important task of redefining the novel as a cultural object includes both a self-referential focus on the writing situation ("a writer sitting there writing the page"), and a related focus on the ideological function of the novel as a vehicle for cultural exchange. In this double definition, innovation means much more than "playing with the mechanics of and approaches to storytelling."

Criticism has been more willing of late to revise its descriptive concepts to better account for the experiential and the ideological-rhetorical aspects of innovation. The narratological analyses of postmodern fiction published over the last decade have made clearer the connection between a writer's struggle to rearticulate her "life story," and her critique of the dominant modes of narrative/cultural articulation. For example, Larry McCaffery included under the label of metafiction both "a type of fiction which either directly examines its own constructions as it proceeds, or which comments about the forms and language of previous figures"; and a more general category of "books which examine how all fictional systems operate, their methodology, appeal and dangers of being dogmatized."[29] Similarly, in Linda Hutcheon's view, "metafiction is less a departure from the mimetic novelistic tradition than a reworking of it. It is simplistic to say, as reviewers did for years, that this kind of fiction is sterile, that it has nothing to do with 'life.' . . . Instead I would say that this 'vital' link is reforged, on a new level: on that of the imaginative process (of storytelling), instead of on that of the product (the story told)."[30] The kinds of questions that innovative fiction is concerned with, "bearing on the ontology of the literary text itself or on the ontology of the world it projects,"[31] tip over—by Brian McHale's admission— into the area of cultural ideology, reflecting on fiction's contribution to the social construction of reality. Therefore, in his recently published *Constructing Postmodernism* (1992), McHale felt compelled to correct the formalistic approach of his earlier book on *Postmodern Fiction* (1987), with a constructivist, theory-conscious approach. In lieu of the all-inclusive inventory of structural features and corpus of texts offered in the previous book, he now "proposes . . . a plurality of constructions [of postmodernism] that, while not necessarily mutually contradictory, are not fully integrated, or perhaps even integrable, either."[32] These "constructions" valorize differently the conflicting ideological choices of postmodernism (ontological construction vs. political destabilizing, recycling vs. transgression, centering microworlds vs. living in the "zone"/loop, paranoid reading vs. antiparanoia), drawing attention to the role that the critic's own theoretical and ideological preferences have in framing new versions of the "postmodern story." One could argue that, for all his commendable effort to engage the ideologies of postmodernism, McHale remains a formalist at heart: he still constructs for us "multiple, overlapping and intersecting inventories" of topoi and texts. The important difference, however, is that this time his repertoires and paradigms are ideologically aware, conceived in the postmodern spirit of provisional, experimental thinking. McHale's attempt at "telling postmodernist stories otherwise" unfolds like a contrapuntal discourse, valorizing not only alternative corpora of texts (from late modern, through innovative postmodern, to "post-cyber-modern-punkism"), but also alternative (mis)readings of the same text.

A more consistent effort to valorize the ideological thrust of postmodernism can be found in Linda Hutcheon's *The Politics of Postmodernism* (1989), a book that argues that self-reflection is inextricably bound up with a critique of power and domination. In her discussion of feminist photography or of Terry Eagleton's *Saints and Scholars* (1987), Hutcheon finds self-reflexivity compatible with a politically significant artistic stance interested in denaturalizing and revising the culture's power systems. She credits Eagleton with a "return to history and politics through, not despite, metafictional self-consciousness and parodic intertextuality."[33] But some of the concepts she continues to use (metafiction, parody, pastiche, intertextual appropriation) weaken her effort to redefine postmodernism. Within her framework that emphasizes a parodic reappropriation of "forms of the past to speak to a society from within the values and history of that society, while still questioning it," it is difficult to talk about political postmodernism. Hutcheon's preferred examples are "quietist," self-controverting: feminist photography and not experimental feminist film, the historical metafiction of E. L. Doctorow, Christa Wolf, John Fowles, Julio Cortázar, and not surfiction, feminist narrative, or the political metafiction of Robert Coover and Thomas Pynchon, which upset the dominant cultural narratives more profoundly.

Even when revised, many of the concepts associated with self-referentiality continue to create evaluative problems. A term like "metafiction" is essentially a misnomer, positing a problematic locus outside and above the fictional process, whence an effective critique of narrative models can be attempted. Such a theoretically ambiguous term encourages fuzzy and whimsical applications, like those in Robert Boyers's retrospective of the "Avant-Garde." What defines a "serious avant-garde"[34] for Boyers is the type of anticonsumerist, self-referential opacity he finds in Abish's novel, *How German Is*. But this type of effective "autocritique" is then assigned rather arbitrarily to some writers and refused to others: Gass's *Willie Masters' Lonesome Wife* is acknowledged as a valid language exploration that mocks the "idiot ejaculations and glib spontaneities of would-be vanguardists like Jack Kerouac" (p. 719), or the "bloodless aestheticism" of surfiction. Barthelme is called an intrepid explorer of the dreck of contemporary culture, but one who "cost[s] us nothing," making identification with his cultural parodies too easy for the reader (p. 743). Unqualified praise is on the other hand bestowed on Guy Davenport's "allusive, learned, precise, languorous" prose (p. 744), and on Steven Millhauser's ironic "autocritique" that harks back to "modernist masters like Mann and Kafka," rather than follow the "self-proclaimed avant-garde in the United States."

We need to trade our ambiguous formalistic-ontological labels for stronger sociocultural concepts that can better account for the "double-coded politics" of postmodern reflexivity.[35] For example, the twofold focus on narrative *revision* and cultural *rewriting* that I have proposed,[36] calls attention to the sociocultural reformulation that goes on in self-reflexive art, replacing a more limited understanding of postmodern innovation as mere subversion; but it also acknowledges the self-problematized nature of the postmodern revisioning, its conflicting impulses. Antireferential postmodernism does not simply make the referent opaque or problematic, nor is it merely content to denounce realism theoretically, while retaining its power. The disruptive strategies employed in surfiction discredit

realistic representation, exploiting its errors of focus, judgment, and interpretation. At the same time, they allow alternative modes of narrative articulation to
emerge: "subversively personal, . . . unruly [and] unpredictable,"[37] emphasizing
"tissue-like connections" in lieu of traditional symbolic structures. Disarticulation
and recreation are the two complementary sides of this project. When Federman,
Hauser, Major, Reed, or Sukenick break away from a controlling story, derailing
narration with self-referential digressions, they assert their imaginative need to
unwrite/rewrite an already existing autobiographical scenario: this upsets fiction's
"discourse system of recuperation,"[38] preventing it from following predictable
story lines. In similar ways, feminist self-reflection has been engaged in a critique
of androcentric representation, but this has involved more than a deconstructive
subversion: rather than scrap traditional epistemologies, feminist theory and literature have contributed significantly to their reformulation, creating new narrative
structures (fluid, anti-authoritarian, collaborative) within which feminine subjects
may play liberated, imaginative roles. Surfiction and feminist narration share with
other recent projects (postcolonial literature, L=A=N=G=U=A=G=E poetry, postmodern film) a revisionistic type of "experiential thinking" that seeks to "undercut
official versions of reality in favor of our individual sense experience."[39] To inter-
pret their work as narrowly self-referential is to miss its ideological potential for
both "de-toxifying"[40] and changing the dominant systems of meaning and value.

BECKETT AND THE POSTMODERN NOVEL

> *All good storytellers go to BETHICKETT on the way to Heaven*
> *& that is why perhaps they are so long in reaching their*
> *destination.*
>
> —Raymond Federman, *Take It or Leave It* (1976)

> *Watt could not accept them for what they perhaps were, the*
> *simple games time plays with space, now with these toys, and*
> *now with those, but was obliged because of his peculiar*
> *character, to enquire into what they meant, oh, not into what*
> *they really meant, his character was not so peculiar as all that,*
> *but into what they might be induced to mean, with the help of*
> *a little patience, a little ingenuity.*
>
> —Samuel Beckett, *Watt* (1953/1959)

Federman's reassessment of self-reflexive fiction in *The Columbia Literary History
of the United States,* and others that have been published since, appropriately

rehistoricize innovative fiction, inscribing literary aesthetics within the framework of a cultural politics that both asserts and problematizes the sociocultural value of narrative experimentation. But they continue to hesitate between two theoretical descriptions of innovation: one explains the novelist's task in deconstructive terms, as a "purification" of language by "rendering [it] seemingly irrational, illogical, incoherent, and even meaningless";[41] the other emphasizes the culturally relevant task of reformulation, arguing that "the techniques of parody, irony, introspection, and self-reflexiveness directly challenge the oppressive forces of social and literary authorities" (p. 1156). The first evaluation tends to confine postmodern fiction to a "disruptive complicity" with its medium, to a "negative aesthetics" identified with Beckett, cited as "the ultimate model for most serious fiction written during the 1960s and 1970s" (p. 1157).[42] The second evaluation credits innovative fiction with a rearticulative capacity: its role is not simply to "neutralize the fiasco of reality and the imposture of history," but also to create a space for the affirmation of the repressed, imaginative qualities of experience.

At the origin of this theoretical hesitation between two concepts of innovation is a dissociative model of narration in which deconstruction and rearticulation, improvisation and analysis, are often at odds. Criticism has dissociated these two sides of the postmodern project even further, attributing innovative postmodernism a negative, self-ironic poetics that puts major categories of thought and narration *sous rature* ("under erasure"). Derived from a simplified understanding of Derridean deconstruction and of Michel Foucault's and J.-F. Lyotard's critique of the falsely universalizing discourses of modernity,[43] this critical view has usually emphasized the divisiveness and incompleteness of postmodern narration. Even some of the recent efforts to repoliticize postmodernism stop short of bridging this gap, distinguishing the self-problematized, ironic representational discourse of "historical metafiction" from what Linda Hutcheon calls the "anti-representational late modernism" of Beckett, the *Tel Quel* novelists, and American surfiction. Historical metafiction illustrates for her a mode of "post-modern de-naturalizing—the simultaneous inscribing and subverting of the conventions of narrative"; in this type of work "there is no dissolution or repudiation of representation; but there is a problematizing of it."[44] By contrast, the deconstructive texts of American surfiction and the French *Tel Quel* are seen as "extensions of modernist notions of autonomy and auto-referentiality," lacking sociohistorical grounding (p. 27).

This emphatic division undermines, in my view, Hutcheon's political revalorization of postmodern innovation, excluding from it the radical disruptions of traditional mimesis in surfiction and feminist narrative or film, and emphasizing instead a more indecisive denaturalization of representation in historical metafiction and feminist photography. What I would like to argue is that the deconstruction of traditional models of representation is a precondition for a new cultural articulation, that this type of reformulative critique does not have to turn fiction into a pile of dehistoricized fragments, but that it can sustain the re-historicizing effort of which Linda Hutcheon speaks. I intend to illustrate this with Federman's work, which has from the very beginning negotiated the difficult problem of historical narration in a postholocaust and postrealist world. I will contend that Federman's linguistically aware, self-controverting narratives can be read as examples of what Brian McHale has called a "revisionistic historical novel,"[45] and that, even though his brand of narrative revisionism has drawn primarily on Beckett rather than on Sartre, it is not any less committed as a result. Federman's literature redefines narrative commitment for us, rereading Beckett through more imaginative lenses than those customarily applied to him by criticism.

The programmatic essay Federman added to the 1981 edition of his *Surfic-tion* collection distinguished between two forms of ideological commitment, one referential, the other self-referential:

> Much of contemporary fiction does not relate the reader directly to the external world (reality), nor does it provide the reader with a sense of lived experience (truth), but instead, contemporary fiction dwells on the circum-stances of its own possibilities, on the conventions of narrative, and on the openness of language to multiple meanings, to contradiction, irony, paradox.[46]

After quoting Sartre's concept of committed literature, Federman argues that contemporary literature must confront its own crisis of knowledge and language before it can deal with the historical crisis evoked by Sartre. The writer should reorient his efforts towards clearing fiction of its traditional, mimetic definitions, promoting a literature "that refuses to represent the world or express the inner-self of man. . . . What replaces knowledge . . . about the world and about man, is the act of searching—researching even—within fiction itself for the meaning of what it means to write fiction" (pp. 299–300). Interestingly, the non-mimetic epis-temology that Federman seems to outline here conjoins a critical-deconstructive with a reformulative task. On the one hand, fiction foregrounds the culture's epistemological crisis with a vengeance: "The new novel seeks to avoid knowledge deliberately, particularly the kind of knowledge that is received, approved, deter-mined by conventions. . . . The new novel affirms its own autonomy by exposing its own lies: it tells false stories, inauthentic stories; it abolishes absolute knowledge and what passes for reality" (p. 300). But the novel is not content to function only as a version of the "LIAR'S PARADOX" (p. 308), giving the "lie" to the rest of culture. It also draws on its reflexive potential, the "searching . . . within the fiction itself for the meaning of what it means to write fiction" (p. 300). This latter function is more committed to a transformative agenda, translating Sartre's concept of political commitment as "linguistic freedom—a freedom of speech, . . . a freedom to be able to say everything, in any possible way. This freedom to explore the possibilities of saying and writing everything is . . . as crucial and as subversive as what Sartre proposed some thirty years ago" (p. 305). Fiction seeks a "reassessment of the world, of its objects, of its people, but without imposing upon them a pre-established signification"; its effort is to "reinstate things, the world, and man in their proper place—in a [new truth]. That, in my opinion, is also a form of literary commitment" (p. 306).

Federman's entire poetics revolves around this impulse to "reinstate" things in a new truth. This impulse creates an unstilled oscillation between disarticulation/rearticulation, saying and unsaying in narration. Like Beckett, Federman proclaims the "impossibility of saying the world," but mainly in order to raise the stakes of narrative articulation and uncover within it "the incredible possibility that everything can be said now, everything is on the verge of being said ANEW" (p. 306). To use Federman's own metaphor, his fiction has deliberately chosen this challenging route, going to "BETHICKETT on [its] way to Heaven"; and the traces of its imaginative detour through the only author whose work Federman has never stopped reading and studying are numerous. As Melvin J. Friedman has suggested, "one can liken Federman's critical apprenticeship as Beckett commentator to Beckett's early critical gestures toward Joyce and Proust."[47] Federman's works, from his Beckett study (*Journey to Chaos: Samuel Beckett's Early Fiction,* 1965), to most every narrative he has published so far, abound in fond gestures and dialogic nods toward Beckett, his predecessor in the teetering land of exile, existential chaos, and cultural disruption. Like Beckett, Federman's novels blur distinctions between criticism and fiction, encoding and decoding of texts. "In short, the early Beckett of *Murphy, More Pricks than Kicks,* and *Echo's Bones and Other Precipitates* has left its stamp on this critifiction phase of Federman's work. . . . The later Beckett, with his spare, accentless prose, clearly helped form the brief, unparagraphed, unpunctuated, bilingual *The Voice in the Closet/La Voix dans le cabinet de débarras.*"[48] The imaginative pla(y)giarism of Beckett continues in Federman's two most political novels to date, *The Twofold Vibration* and *To Whom It May Concern,* which use the talents of their protagonists, great "thieves of language" both of them, to rewrite personal and collective history.

The important fact here is that Beckett has provided Federman with more than a few titles or linguistic and thematic echoes. Beckett, I would argue, has offered Federman ways to mediate the two sides of his postmodern project, deconstruction and rearticulation, saying and unsaying. This may not fit our conventional view of Beckett as the champion of a "poetics of impossibility" and cancellation. However, Beckett's struggle with impossible obstacles (an irrational, arbitrary universe, a diverse and yet impotent language, a broken-down process of signification replaced by silence or noise, decentered voices/selves that cannot guarantee narrative order), does not have to be understood narrowly, as a voiding of the narrative process, but rather in Lyotard's sense of a postmodern presentation of the "unpresentable," a putting forward of the "unpresentable in presentation itself."[49] This entails the cooperation of two contradictory narrative perspectives:

> The emphasis can be placed on the powerlessness of the faculty of presenta-
> tion, on the nostalgia for presence felt by the human subject, on the obscure
> and futile will which inhabits him in spite of everything. The emphasis can
> be placed, rather, on the power of the faculty to conceive, on its "inhu-
> manity" so to speak . . . , since it is not the business of our understanding
> whether or not human sensibility or imagination can match what it con-
> ceives. (p. 80)

The first perspective "denies itself the solace of good forms, the consensus of a taste which would make it possible to share collectively the nostalgia of the unattainable" (p. 81). Its purpose is to "perpetually flush . . . out artifices of presentation which make it possible to subordinate thought to the gaze and to turn it away from the unrepresentable" (p. 79). The second approach, however, activates "the power of the faculty to conceive," reinventing the preestablished rules and familiar categories of thought, seeking a new realization: both in the sense of a *mise en oeuvre*, and a new *mise en scène* of reality (p. 82). Beckett's fiction, in my view, bears out Lyotard's description, exemplifying an ongoing process of narrative (de)realization, rather than a mere "aesthetics of failure." In the sequence *Molloy* (1950), *Malone Dies* (1951), and *The Unnamable* (1952), the narrators of each subsequent novel claim to have authored the previous ones, opening up these narratives (and, indeed, Beckett's entire fiction) to alternative, competing enunciations. Revision and cancellation work to increase—rather than decrease—Beckett's "freedom of ontological improvisation, . . . constructing, revising, deconstructing, abolishing and reconstructing"[50] a repertoire of possibilities in a "closed field." Though Beckett's trilogy and the narratives following it (the experimental *Texts for Nothing*, 1954; *How It Is*, 1961; *Company*, 1980), could be described as deathbed or "posthumous discourses,"[51] their rhetoric remains largely unsettled, not only deconstructive, but also transformative/revisionistic. Beckett's plays may be said to work in similar ways: under the guise of an austere, "deprived" aesthetics,[52] they often manage to sketch an alternative semiotic, skeptical and ironic but also productive, turning the paucity of aesthetic attributes into a complex rhetorical and psychological performance. As David Hayman has argued,

> From the beginning, though not quite so transparently, Beckett seems to
> have aimed at achieving expressive wealth through the progressive im-

poverishment of his means. . . . Beckett's procedures can be likened and contrasted to those of Matisse, who produced his drawings by a process of elimination, cutting back to the expressive minimal line. In Beckett's case the line itself is attacked, though haunting vestiges of the trappings of discarded conventions remain.[53]

Described alternatively as "phenomenological reductions"[54] and formalist restrictions, Beckett's "decreative" procedures "systematically disempower the tools that it employs," putting "in question all aspects of narrative validity" (Hayman, p. 113). But while Beckett undermines the macrostructural level of the "action," replacing what he scornfully called the "penny-a-line vulgarity of a literature of [realistic] notations," with whimsical juxtapositions of "events," he allows a different type of self-generated linguistic action to emerge at the microtextual level (p. 115). Elements of a ludic, preverbal imaginary often infuse the repressive level of the symbolic, creating imaginative breaches within it. As Beckett explained in a letter to his German friend, Axel Kaun, the goal of today's writer is to "bore one hole after another in [language], until what lurks within it—be it something or nothing—begins to seep through."[55] Usually, what seeps through is a "literature of the unword," an incipient interior discourse projected on the "sky of my skull"; or a wordless play of essentialized images as in Beckett's later "visual poems" written for television, *Quad I* and *Quad II*.[56] But even these ritual pieces, exploiting permutations of body movement, color, and sound on a square surface (in *Quad I*, four hooded figures in light blue, yellow, orange, red and white, shuffle across a square field in various combinations, avoiding collision both with the center and with each other; in *Quad II*, the permutations are performed only by a blue and a white figure, and their movements are considerably slower), have cultural relevance: the "quad" suggests either a carceral space (Tom Bishop), or a self-regulating dynamic system that sets bodies on a collision course, without consummating their conflict. The political suggestiveness is even stronger in two other televised plays, *Catastrophe,* dedicated to Vaclav Havel, and *What Where*. Described as plays on intimidation, they can also be seen as subtle critiques of symbolic language, denouncing both its political authoritarianism (language is used in both plays for interrogation, persecution, or intimidation), and its metaphysical failures (the unrelenting question-answer pattern in *What Where* underscores the uncertainty of enunciation, the questionable status of everything said). Beckett's problematization of symbolic language thus takes two different routes, only one of which leads to language deconstruction (the characteristic drive for "lessness"). The other route provokes the rhetorical mechanisms of language, emphasizing the psychodrama of signification. As Dina Sherzer put it, language remains for Beckett a perfect medium "which enables him to create tension. . . . Solitary, desperate, sick individuals who might deplore the lack of value of words and even attack words with animosity, the characters of his plays and the narrators of his novels sustain themselves by talking, writing, addressing or answering other characters, or merely monologuing or listening to an inner voice which empties a flow of words on empty stages. Language keeps them going."[57]

This deconstructive and regenerative process becomes even clearer in Federman's reuse of some of Beckett's "illusion-breaking" devices against what he himself calls the "fairy tale" of realism. The narratological significance of these procedures is well established in Federman criticism;[58] but unlike Brooke-Rose, who basically believes that "the famous renewal in some American postmodernism is achieved entirely through anti-illusionistic devices, self-reflexive 'strategies' and topoi, by now pretty fatigued" (p. 217), I will argue that Federman's fiction has always counterbalanced disruption with complex revisionistic procedures that reconfigure narration, opening it up to a "renewed and renewing content." As explained by Federman in his programmatic essays, these procedures (derived mostly from Beckett) take a narrative already attached to a particular linguistic and ontological order, and "unwrite/rewrite" it: destabilizing its oral or visual spaces, relocating it into another order (*displacement*); removing and complicating the established meaning of words by "double exposure" or the mixing of voices/ languages/media (*cancellation*); decomposing the formal structure and syntax of texts through oral or visual dislocation (*pulverization*); repeating text by oral and visual overlapping, causing variation and distortion in it (*repetition*); pluralizing seemingly static texts through plagiarizing (*revision*).[59] Federman's early essays focused on the ontological significance of this intertextual splitting and drifting in narrative, allowing one to "pla(y)giarize one's life: voices within voices." More recently, Federman has emphasized the ideological value of these transformative strategies particularly in narratives that have as their main object a critical rereading of history.

Federman has thus found a more complex (and balanced) use for Beckett's antirealistic procedures. Described as "stor[ies] that cancel [themselves] as they go," his novels shun the extremes of typographical disruption ("concrete prose"), and realistic logorrhea, moving tentatively ahead, through trial and error, assertion and retraction. Errors play an important part in Federman's process of narration: in *Take It or Leave It*, an initial "little error" perpetrated by his army captain prevents "Frenchy" from undertaking his grand quest across America. Both his journey and his retelling of it are blocked, detoured. Echoing Beckett's *Molloy*, where the journey and its narration end in a ditch, Federman's story takes its hero to the edge of a natural and symbolic precipice. By only a hairbreadth, the protagonist misses self-cancellation, the final "error." But that makes the whole difference: the Beckettian motif of cancellation through error is converted into a more benign (and democratic) acceptance of error as constitutive of the narrative process. Federman's candid heroes and "second-hand" narrators outlive their errors of judgment, interpretation, and language that decry their effort to rationalize life. They survive them minimally, content to operate in a circular, comic type of "story" that guarantees no advancement, but still allows the old man in *The Twofold Vibration* (an offspin of Beckett's *Malone Dies*), to outsmart his own death, reliving life in his own fictional recreations.

Another example of how Federman reemploys Beckett to expand his own theory and practice of fiction can be found in his twin concepts of narrative "recitation" and "self-translation." The process of narration goes in Federman's novels by the name of "recitation," a term borrowed from Beckett that designates a self-conscious, histrionic activity that combines memorization with invention, oral performance with a preexisting script, production with reproduction. The essential question posed by Federman's fiction is whether this type of narrative recitation can recapture the living circumstantiality of the world, or whether it is condemned to remain a mere simulacrum. Obviously, there is no simple, unequivocal answer to this question. Narration encircles tentatively, in countless "re-translations," an "original" story that is itself but an imperfect "translation" of an elusive truth. Federman's fiction makes this vertigo of *translation* immediately apparent: his books have French versions or pages with bilingual columns of text, his narrative persona is a "schizotype" who "humps two languages at the same time"; narration becomes a "big crossing" of texts for the "mad acrobat of fiction" who seeks enlightenment in "the mere accumulation of facts," signs, and languages (*Take It or Leave It*, p. 199—my pagination).

In a recent "lecture/demonstration" on the theme of bilingualism, Federman has constructed an ingenious literary epistemology (and personal myth) around the notion of self-translation. Autobiographically, the author is "a voice within a voice" that "constantly plays hide and seek with itself," a "bilingual being, a double-headed mumbler, and as such also a bicultural being."[60] Federman's narrative poetics also relies heavily on "self-translating" (p. 2), in both a literal and a metaphoric sense. Self-translating has conflicting effects: on the one hand, it "results in a LOSS, a weakening and even betrayal of one's original work" (p. 7). The intersecting voices (languages) threaten to displace and swallow each other. On the other hand, translation offers the writer an invaluable second chance for expanding his work through "transcreation," "correcting the errors of the original text" (pp. 6–7, 8–9). In terms that recall the deconstructive philosophy of translation developed by Jacques Derrida and Paul de Man in their respective commentaries on Walter Benjamin,[61] Federman defines translation as a supplementing and corrective act, enriching both the "original," and the "ambivalent (ambidextrous) psyche" of the writer (p. 3). Any single narration remains incomplete, suspended in its own "ignorance": but while de Man conceived of this aporetic "blindness" as insurmountable, Federman suggests that narration can move forward, toward partial "light" and "knowledge" by multiplying its languages, voices, versions. The perfect example of this can be found in Beckett's "twin-texts" (whether French/English or English/French) [which] are not to be read in sequence, are not to be read as translations or substitutes for one another, they are complementary to one another" (p. 5).[62] But what Federman has pursued in his own bilingual narratives is something less-than-perfect—and therefore more tensional, dialogic—that reflects his divided literary biography: while his characteristic protagonist remains "a Frenchman in exile," his fiction always has an "implied reader, or rather an explicit, active and omnipresent interlocutor in the text . . . [who] is of the English language" (p. 11). This creates a never-settled tension in reading/writing as both Federman's narrators and we, readers, try to negotiate the "walls of antithesis" (French/English, voice and "mute language," pretext/text/ postscript).[63] Federman's more recent novels have reinforced this dialogic understanding of narration as an interplay of incomplete articulations, but they have also made explicit the political significance of their concern with historical rearticulation.

Federman's fiction—like that of Beckett, his acknowledged master in the art of discontinuity and survival—has been about the "perception of chaos, the survey of chaos, the immersion into chaos."[64] A historical chaos, primarily, which could only be broached through the endless preparations, evasions, and detours of the postholocaust writer: "It is as if the experience of the Holocaust is more than language can comprehend or communicate—except, perhaps, by a denial of language."[65] But this denial was always followed by a reconstructive effort. Confronted with what Philippe Sollers has called an "experience of limits,"[66] that is, radical events (World War II, the Holocaust, exile and transplantation on the New Continent) that have tested the boundaries of personal and cultural narratives, Federman's fiction has pushed narration to the edge, rupturing the traditional frameworks set up by epistemological and social discourse, in order to accommodate a more honest approach to history. This has conferred an often explicit political dimension upon his work, not unlike that with which Beckett's prophetic explorations of ideological and existential terror have been credited particularly in Eastern Europe.[67]

The theoretical justification for this revisionistic narrative process is stated clearly in Federman's most recent novel, *To Whom It May Concern* (see epigraph to previous section). Refusing the prepackaged stories of his culture "which provide a chain of terminal satisfactions from predictable beginnings to foreshadowed endings,"[68] the Federman narrator places the genre of the novel under "the sign of Saturn, the planet of detours and delays" (p. 19): "to get on with the story one must avoid precision. One must digress. Skip around. Improvise. Leave blank what cannot be filled in. Offer multiple choices. Deviate from the facts, from the where and the when, in order to reach the truth" (p. 104). By avoiding the "tricks and gimmicks" of specificity, the autobiographical narrator tries to keep at bay the "imposture of realism, that ugly beast that stands . . . ready to leap in the moment you begin scribbling your fiction" (p. 106). The history that Federman retells is too brittle and complex to withstand the "banality of realism" behind which always lurks "a catastrophe or a bad joke" (p. 107). Historical "reality" in Federman's view is unreliable, unfolding as a series of betrayals and substitutions: the spot in Paris where the apartment building of a number of Holocaust victims once stood, has been usurped by an art museum that stands there as a "scandalous substitution. The immorality of history replaced by the playfulness of modern art" (p. 107). That is why "it is essential to avoid the specificity of time and place, even at the risk of skirting allegory. History is a joke whose punch line is always messed up in advance" (pp. 107–8). There isn't much to say about a historical fiasco and scandalous disappearance like that of Federman's own family in the gas chambers. The chapter that ponders "the correctness or incorrectness of the unforgivable enormity" is only half a page long, interrupted by blankness and silence (pp. 99–100). This "absolute erasure" can only be represented as a sequence of Xs ("X-X-X-X").

Since recent history is to Federman a "story of erasures," "why not erase all traces of pretense, and have a story that empties itself of references" (p. 168)? The proposition is tempting, but it has never been pursued by Federman or his narrators: what they try to erase is not the historical sequence of events and substitutions, but its narrative (mis)representations. Federman's narrators would probably agree with André Bleikasten that "history" is always already "historio-*graphy*":

> a *mise en mots,* according to communicable linguistic and rhetorical codes; a *mise en scène,* in accordance with representational procedures that are like-wise codified; and a *mise en intrigue* (*mythos,* in Aristotle's sense, or "emplot-ment," to borrow Hayden White's term). . . . All recounting carries forth a fiction, is transformed into fiction by the word that engenders it. But all narrative, even a fairy tale, is also a denied fiction: upon hearing it or reading it, *one must believe it.* There is no narration that does not reflect the fall-acious promise of truth.[69]

"Living" history is continually distorted by our systems of representation and the "ARROGANCE OF STORY-TELLING" (*The Twofold Vibration,* p. 169). Therefore, the approach Federman's narrators pursue is more modest, acknowl-edging that their narrative reconstructions are neither privileged nor complete, needing the cooperation of a sympathetic audience "concerned with what is told here, or cannot be told" (p. 168). The history these narratives rehearse in their "indecision and formlessness" is "exploratory or better yet extemporaneous," approaching self and humanity "from a potential point of view, preremembering the future rather than remembering the past" (pp. 1–2).

Federman's revisionistic narrative strategy, his hesitation between articulation and silence, *said* and *unsaid,* has a biographical explanation as well. There are at least three ruptures in Federman's personal "history" that the writer has tried to come to terms with, in repeated narrative versions, "straddling two languages, two continents and two lives, two cultures also" (*Take It or Leave It,* p. 100—my pagination). The first—and most forbidding—involves Federman's "primary" experience, his survival as a child from the Nazi genocide, stashed in a closet by his mother. The second rupture concerns Federman's later "exilic" leap across the Atlantic, from native France to the New World; the third, his wanderings through another "kind of void . . . America." A positive quest is involved in Federman's treatment of each traumatic gap in his autobiography: the search for a meaningful, morally justifiable way out of the "primordial closet" that claimed Federman's immediate family; an exile's pursuit of the elusive "terre mater–Ameri–Eldorado," a foreigner's emotional quest for integration ("penistration") of America. All three quest plots are dramatic and "tellable": they can be easily translated into "stories." Even the "unthinkable" event of the genocide can induce narration along predictable lines:

> Genocide is . . . a [precision] machinery which fabricates death on a large scale. Though we are disturbed, troubled, outraged, horrified by the final product (the final solution!) of genocide, when talking or writing about it, it is usually the machine, the mechanism which becomes the central topic of our discourse rather than the tragic fate of the victims. Somehow genocide always seems to displace language from end-product to process, from content to form. . . . Whether it is to destroy a family, a tribe, a race, or a whole nation of people, genocide functions like a gigantic machine which once set in motion cannot stop its work.[70]

It is this very machinery of deception, the "piece of chocolate to take away your fear," the triumphant "mise-en-scène" of disasters, that Federman has resisted in his own writing. Federman's commitment to a deconstructive-recreative response to history has something of the uncompromising integrity of Beckett,[71] even though he has replaced the latter's uncompromising "literary monasticism"[72] with a more accepting, participative attitude that draws on the conflictive energies of contemporary culture. His early novels struggled with versions of the "unnamable," replacing "plot" with a tentative, conditional "story" that allows for surprise and rupture, but also for some narrative development, at least of the circular kind—the "spherical [purgatory that] excludes culmination" that Beckett attributed to *Finnegans Wake.*[73] Federman's own version of narrative purgatory is (with a word purloined from Joyce) a "Bethickett," a Beckett-made thicket (*Take It or Leave It,* p. 176).[74] Federman's early narratives illustrated an aporetic "indecision," moving Beckett-like "by affirmations and negations invalidated as uttered,"[75] making us painfully aware of his struggles to articulate a world of unthinkable events. Federman's more recent narratives have been more willing to speak the unspeakable, striking a "cunning," "irrational balance" (*Double or Nothing,* p. 9) between enunciation and denunciation, disruption and rearticulation. With its "extemporaneous," multivoiced visitation of the scene of the Holocaust, *The Twofold Vibration* upsets our notions of coherent history, but also allows us to experience its contradictory unfolding in the revisionistic space of the text. The anxiety and promise that accompany us in the "borrowed land" of narration is memorably summed up by Federman's Beckettian narrators:

in a way this postponement of the end, this transition from lessness to endlessness, this shift from ultimate to penultimate or even to antepenultimate, seems to adumbrate a greater mystery, a greater horror, too, and that is why perhaps our old man must be expelled from this world, one cannot wander forever in a borrowed land, live a deferred life, but of course I am only speculating here

The Twofold Vibration dramatizes a Beckettian disjunction between discursive worlds, much like the one found by Federman in *Watt,* where three different worlds collide: "the material world (traditional fiction), where seemingly rational characters are confronted with external reality, with facts and tangibles; the Knott world, where the hero (Watt) and other fellow servants struggle to disentangle elements that are as irrational, as illogical, and as evasive as fiction can permit; and the world of insanity, where human and heroic alike are driven when they fail to reconcile the outer with the inner world, or when they fail to understand the Knott world."[76] *Smiles on Washington Square,* on the other hand, emphasizes the comic, conciliatory side of this theme. This book may lack something of the textual complexity and emotional stake involved in Federman's previous narratives, but it outlines an amusing and in many ways credible reconciliation between the alternate sides of the literary process: reality and fiction, experience and story, voice and textuality. The proposed "love story" becomes possible because of the converging force of narration, coalescing several tentative storifications: Federman's frame narratives, but also the stories wished into existence by the two characters. In them, Moinous and especially Sucette perform important narrative functions that supplement Federman's own effort to create a "love story of sorts." They name themselves and interact in the imaginative space of storytelling, inventing their own amorous encounter. The true "encounter" between Moinous and Sucette takes place on *paper,* in a fictional/textual convergence that defines several constantly readjusted relationships: between a *character* (he) and an *embracing text* (she); between an author-within-the-text (Sucette) and a narratee (Moinous) who critiques her story in progress; or between two characters locked in their respective texts, with their parallel narratives meeting only on the imaginary horizon of intertextuality.

Narrative cooperation undergirds also Federman's most recent book, *To Whom It May Concern.* There is first of all cooperation between the author-narrator and his protagonists whose postholocaust story of separation and reunion he tries to recreate. The characters take on part of the burden of shaping and understanding their own life story, imagining alternatives to it, rehashing its basic plot. The scenes are recounted from the overlapping perspectives of the two main characters, Sarah and her visiting cousin, "world traveler and renowned artist" (p. 13), as they anticipate their reunion, one at home in Israel, the other "stranded at the airport of the city [Paris] where it all started" (p. 14). In their individual reminiscing both protagonists "repeat the same words, ask the same questions," whisper "fragments of their story," circling around its mysteries much like the extradiegetic narrator does with their combined stories. Both the narrator and his characters make repeated attempts to complete and understand a "story [that] refused to be spoken" (p. 110), saving it from the "incomprehension" into which it periodically lapses.

The narrative effort is again heroic, reminiscent of *The Twofold Vibration:* what the cousins "are now seeking in this reunion is the meaning of [their] separation [exactly thirty-five years ago]—the meaning of their absence from each other" (p. 40). Their reconciliation with personal and collective history can only take place in narrative form that allows them a cathartic understanding of the collapsed structures of history and the "meaning of an absence" (p. 108). The narrator struggles with his own sense of absence, trying to fill the void created by history, to speak his characters back into meaningful existence. His ambition is to create "a stereophonic effect" in the linear discourse of history: "If only one could inscribe simultaneously in the same sentence different moments of the story. . . . That's how it feels right now inside my skull. Voices within voices entangled within their own fleeting garrulousness" (pp. 76–77). His stereophonic narrative invokes an ideal narratee: a fellow writer to whom letters containing ideas, queries, fragments of the projected narrative are addressed periodically. The writing of this self-dubbed "wintry book" becomes a joint enterprise, a project for both of them to do and undo. *To Whom It May Concern* gives new meaning to Federman's theme of "leaning": the leaning now is no longer "against the wind," but rather on a fellow writer-reader, whose presumed responses—even when evasive—support the work of "carving, the molding, the scratching away, the erasing" that a narrative performs on history. Of course, the name of that fellow writer-rereader is ultimately Sam, Federman's true intertextual voice.

Notes

1. The epigraph is quoted in Raymond Federman, "The Writer as Self-Translator," in *Beckett Translating/Translating Beckett*, ed. Alan Warren Friedman, Charles Rossman, and Dina Sherzer (University Park and London: The Pennsylvania State University Press, 1987), p. 15.

2. Federman, "Self-Reflexive Fiction," in *Columbia Literary History of the United States*, ed. Emory Elliott (New York: Columbia University Press, 1988), p. 1145.

3. Raymond Federman, "Surfiction—Four Propositions in Form of an Introduction," in *Surfiction: Fiction Now . . . and Tomorrow*, ed. Federman, 2nd ed., enlarged (Chicago: Swallow Press, 1981), p. 11.

4. William H. Gass, *Habitations of the Word: Essays by William H. Gass* (New York: Simon & Schuster, 1985), p. 78.

5. Ronald Sukenick, *In Form: Digressions on the Act of Fiction* (Carbondale and Edwardsville: Southern Illinois University Press, 1985), p. 23.

6. Sukenick, "The New Tradition," *Partisan Review* 39 (1972): 580–88; rpt. in *In Form*, p. 211.

7. Alan Wilde, *Middle Grounds: Studies in Contemporary American Fiction* (Philadelphia: University of Pennsylvania Press, 1987), pp. 18, 20, 48.

8. John W. Aldridge, *The American Novel and the Way We Live Now* (New York and Oxford: Oxford University Press, 1983), p. 150.

9. De Villo Sloan, "The Decline of American Postmodernism," *SubStance* 16.3 (1987): 37.

10. Hugh Kenner, *Samuel Beckett* (Berkeley: University of California Press, 1968), pp. 33–34 and elsewhere. Taking his cue from Beckett's 1957 comment on Joyce ("The more Joyce knew the more he could. He's tending toward omniscience and omnipotence as an artist. I'm working with impotence, ignorance. I don't think impotence has been exploited in the past."), Kenner inaugurates the classic distinction between Beckett as a "clown" of fictional impossibility and Joyce as an "acrobat" of fictional possibility: while the latter exploits his narrative ability, the former thematizes "his own inability to walk a tightrope. . . . He does not *imitate* the acrobat; it is plain that he could not; he offers us, directly, his personal incapacity, an intricate art form."

11. Ihab Hassan, *The Dismemberment of Orpheus: Toward a Postmodern Literature* (New York: Oxford University Press, 1982), p. 213. In "The Literature of Silence, (*The Postmodern Turn: Essays in Postmodern Theory and Culture* [Columbus: Ohio State Univer-

sity Press, 1987], pp. 3–22), Hassan likewise praised Beckett's radical irony that decreates both literature (pushing it toward antiliterature) and reality.

12. Ihab Hassan, "Joyce, Beckett, and the Postmodern Imagination," *TriQuarterly* 34 (1975): 185, 196. Elsewhere in this article, Hassan turns the Joyce-Beckett opposition into an overarching myth of (post)modernism: "Joyce and Beckett represent two ways of the imagination in our century. Joyce and Beckett, two Irishmen. They divide the world between them, divide the Logos, the world's body. One, in high arrogance, invents language anew, and makes over the universe in parts of speech. The other, in deep humility, restores to words their primal emptiness, and mimes his solitary way into the dark. Between them they stretch the mind's tether until it begins to snap" (p. 183).

13. For a similar reexamination of the Joyce-Beckett-postmodernism relation, see Breon Mitchell, "Samuel Beckett and the Postmodernism Controversy," in *Exploring Postmodernism*, ed. Matei Calinescu and Dowe Fokkema (Amsterdam and Philadelphia: John Benjamins, 1987), pp. 109–22.

14. Julia Kristeva, "Postmodernism," in *Bucknell Review: Romanticism, Modernism, Postmodernism*, ed. Harry R. Garvin (Lewisburgh, Pa.: Bucknell University Press, 1980), p. 141.

15. Charles Newman, *The Post-Modern Aura: The Act of Fiction in an Age of Inflation* (Evanston, Ill.: Northwestern University Press, 1985), pp. 5–6.

16. Fredric Jameson, "Postmodernism and Consumer Society," in *The Anti-Aesthetic: Essays on Postmodern Culture*, ed. Hal Foster (Port Townsend, Wash.: Bay Press, 1983), pp. 124–25. Terry Eagleton similarly deplores the "dissolution" of recent art "into the prevailing forms of commodity production." "Capitalism, Modernism and Postmodernism," *New Left Review* 144 (1985): 60.

17. Fredric Jameson, *Postmodernism, or, the Cultural Logic of Late Capitalism* (Durham, N.C.: Duke University Press, 1991), p. 69.

18. For a good critique of Jameson's theoretical bias and narrow choice of exemplifications, see Brian McHale, *Constructing Postmodernism* (London and New York: Routledge, 1992), pp. 141, 158–59, 177; McHale, "Postmodernism or the Anxiety of Master Narratives," *Diacritics* 22.1 (Spring 1992): 17–33; Curtis White, "Jameson Out of Touch?" *American Book Review* 15.1 (December–January 1993): 21, 30. David Shumway questions Jameson's use of John Portman's Bonaventure Hotel as an example of postmodernism, rather than of late-modernism as Jencks and others have suggested; see "Jameson/Hermeneutics/Postmodernism," in *Postmodernism/Jameson/Critique*, ed. Douglas Kellner (Washington, D.C.: Maisonneuve, 1989), pp. 172–202.

19. Anders Stephanson, "Regarding Postmodernism: A Conversation with Fredric Jameson," in *Postmodernism/Jameson/Critique*, ed. Kellner, p. 59.

20. Jean-François Lyotard, "Answering the Question: What Is Postmodernism?," trans. Régis Durand; rpt. in *The Postmodern Condition: A Report on Knowledge*, trans. G. Bennington and B. Massumi (Minneapolis: University of Minnesota Press, 1984), p. 74.

21. René Girard, "Innovation and Repetition," *SubStance* 19.2–3 (1990): 11.

22. Erica Hunt, "Notes for an Oppositional Poetics," in *The Politics of Poetic Form: Poetry and Public Policy,* ed. Charles Bernstein (New York: Roof Books, the Segue Foundation, 1990), p. 199.

23. Bruce Andrews, "Poetry as Explanation, Poetry as Praxis," in Bernstein, *The Politics of Poetic Form,* p. 28.

24. Sukenick, *In Form,* p. 11.

25. Jerome Klinkowitz, *The Life of Fiction* (Urbana and Chicago: University of Illinois Press, 1977), p. 166.

26. Katz interviewed by LeClair and McCaffery, in *Anything Can Happen: Interviews with Contemporary American Novelists,* ed. Tom LeClair and Larry McCaffery (Urbana and Chicago: University of Illinois Press, 1983), p. 226.

27. Steve Katz, *Moving Parts* (New York: Fiction Collective, 1977), p. 75.

28. Katz interviewed by LeClair and McCaffery, in *Anything Can Happen,* pp. 121, 131.

29. Larry McCaffery, *The Metafictional Muse: The Works of Coover, Gass and Barthelme* (Pittsburgh: University of Pittsburgh Press, 1982), p. 16.

30. Linda Hutcheon, *Narcissistic Narrative: The Metafictional Paradox* (Waterloo, Ontario: Wilfred Laurier University Press, 1980), pp. 5, 3.

31. Brian McHale, *Postmodernist Fiction* (New York and London: Methuen, 1987), p. 10.

32. McHale, *Constructing Postmodernism,* pp. 2–3.

33. Linda Hutcheon, *The Politics of Postmodernism* (London and New York: Routledge, 1989), p. 61.

34. Robert Boyers, "The Avant-Garde," in *The Columbia History of the American Novel,* ed. Emory Elliott (New York: Columbia University Press, 1991), p. 738.

35. Hutcheon, *The Politics of Postmodernism,* p. 101.

36. Marcel Cornis-Pope, "Postmodernism Beyond Self-Reflection: Radical Mimesis in Recent Fiction," in *Mimesis, Semiosis and Power,* ed. Ronald Bogue (Philadelphia and Amsterdam: John Benjamins Publication Company, 1991), pp. 127–55. See also "Narrative Innovation and Cultural Rewriting: The Pynchon-Morrison-Sukenick Connection," in *Narrative and Culture,* ed. Janice Carlisle and Daniel Schwarz (Athens: University of Georgia Press, 1993).

37. Sukenick, *In Form,* p. 33.

38. Raymond Federman, *The Voice in the Closet/La Voix dans le cabinet de débarras* (Madison, Wis.: Coda Press, 1979), p. 15 (my pagination).

39. Sukenick, *In Form,* p. 67.

40. Hutcheon, *The Politics of Postmodernism,* p. 153.

41. Federman, "Self-Reflexive Fiction," p. 1156.

42. In Federman's retrospective narrative, Beckett's death in 1989 marks the final

point of postmodernism itself, whose culmination coincided with its own demise, presaged by its "epistemological and ontological doubt conveyed through disjoined formal structures." See "Before Postmodernism and After" (manuscript), pp. 1, 9.

43. See Michel Foucault, *The Order of Things: An Archaeology of the Human Sciences* (New York: Vintage, 1973/1966), particularly chs. 2, 3, and 5; Jean-François Lyotard, *The Postmodern Condition: A Report on Knowledge,* trans. Geoff Bennington and Brian Massumi (Minneapolis: University of Minnesota Press, 1984).

44. Hutcheon, *The Politics of Postmodernism,* pp. 49, 50.

45. McHale, *Postmodern Fiction,* p. 90.

46. Federman, "Fiction Today or the Pursuit of Non-Knowledge," in *Surfiction: Fiction Now . . . and Tomorrow,* p. 292.

47. Melvin J. Friedman, "Making the Best of Two Worlds: Raymond Federman, Beckett, and the University," in *The American Writer and the University,* ed. Ben Siegel (Newark: University of Delaware Press, 1989), p. 137.

48. Friedman, "Making the Best of Two Worlds," pp. 138.

49. Lyotard, *The Postmodern Condition,* p. 81.

50. See McHale, *Postmodernist Fiction,* pp. 12–13.

51. Ibid., p. 230.

52. See, for example, *Samuel Beckett: Farago of Silence and Words* (London: Hutchinson University Library, 1971), pp. 132–48; Steve Connor, *Samuel Beckett, Presence and Repetition in Beckett's Theater* (New York and Oxford: Basil Blackwell, 1988), pp. 115–18; David Hayman, "Beckett: Impoverishing the Means—Empowering the Matter," in *Beckett Translating/Translating Beckett,* ed. Friedman, Rossman, Sherzer, pp. 109–19.

53. Hayman, "Beckett: Impoverishing the Means—Empowering the Matter," p. 109.

54. S. E. Gontarsi, *The Intent of Undoing in Samuel Beckett's Dramatic Texts* (Bloomington: Indiana University Press, 1985), pp. 2–3 and passim.

55. Samuel Beckett, *Disjecta: Miscellaneous Writings and a Dramatic Fragment,* ed. Ruby Cohn (New York: Grove Press, 1984), p. 171.

56. See Martin Esslin, "A Poetry of Moving Images," in *Beckett Translating/ Translating Beckett,* ed. Friedman, Rossman, Sherzer, pp. 65–76; Tom Bishop, "Beckett Transposing, Beckett Transposed: Plays on Television," ibid., pp. 172–73.

57. Dina Sherzer, "Words about Words: Beckett and Language," in *Beckett Translating/Translating Beckett,* ed. Friedman, Rossman, Sherzer, pp. 53–54.

58. For a discussion of disruptive devices such as self-controverting narrators, improvised or "borrowed" characters, metaleptic switches between story planes, narrative "erasure," self-conscious literalization, see McHale, *Postmodern Fiction,* pp. 123–24, 186–87, 201–4, 212–13 (all exemplifications are from Federman's work); also, Brooke-Rose, *Stories, Theories and Things,* chapter 14, "Illusions of Anti-Realism."

59. Federman, "Federman: Voices within Voices," in *Performance in Postmodern*

Culture, ed. Michel Benamou and Charles Caramello (Milwaukee, Wis.: Center for Twentieth-Century Studies/Madison, Wis.: Coda Press, 1977), pp. 159–61.

60. Federman, "Federman: A Voice within a Voice" (in manuscript), p. 1. An earlier version of this aesthetics of bilingualism and self-translating can be found in Federman, "The Writer as Self-Translator," *Beckett Translating/Translating Beckett,* ed. Friedman, Rossman, Sherzer, pp. 7–16.

61. Jacques Derrida, "Des Tours de Babel," in *Difference in Translation,* ed. Joseph F. Graham (Ithaca: Cornell University Press, 1985), pp. 209–48; English trans., pp. 165–207. Paul de Man, "Conclusions: Walter Benjamin's 'The Task of the Translator,' " in *The Resistance to Theory* (Minneapolis: University of Minnesota Press, 1986), pp. 73–105.

62. See also Federman, "The Writer as Self-Translator," pp. 9, 11–12, 15. Brian T. Fitch ("The Relationship between *Compagnie* and *Company:* One Work, Two Texts, Two Fictive Universes," in *Beckett Translating/Translating Beckett,* ed. Friedman, Rossman, and Sherzer, pp. 25–35) offers a good exemplification of the complexity of textual and narrative transformations (verbal tenses, narrative information, narrative voice) involved in two Beckett texts. "Many aspects of the constituent parts of the universe of *Company* are either modified or absent in *Compagnie*" (p. 27). The French version can be seen as a "kind of paring down or a process of reduction" in relation to the English text, outlining the "*quintessential* universe of *Company/Compagnie*" (p. 28). In this sense, despite obvious modifications, the French text does not contradict the English one, but rather complements it. Their coexistence does not produce a simple incremental order, but rather "something *other* than such a sum total. We have seen, for example, that the two fictive universes do not entertain what might be called an incremental relationship with one another so that they could be added together to form a whole more complete than either of them, for, in the process of adding them together, irreconcilable elements remain." (p. 32)

63. Charles Caramello, "On Styles of Postmodern Writing," in *Performance in Postmodern Culture,* ed. Benamou and Caramello, p. 230.

64. Walter A. Strauss, review of Raymond Federman, *Journey to Chaos: Samuel Beckett's Early Fiction, The Modern Language Journal* 50.7 (November 1966): 505.

65. Ronald Sukenick, "Refugee from the Holocaust," *The New York Times Book Review* (October 21, 1972): 40. Federman himself includes, among other plausible theories about the genesis of postmodernism, the idea that "postmodernism as a literary notion was invented to deal with the Holocaust. The prewar split between form and content was incapable of dealing with the moral crisis provoked by the Holocaust, and therefore writers like Beckett, Abish, Sukenick, Federman, Kosinski, and many others, invented Postmodernism to search among the dead, to dig into the communal grave, in order to reanimate wasted blood and wasted tears . . . or perhaps simply in order *to create something more interesting than death*" ("Before Postmodernism and After," p. 28).

66. Philippe Sollers, *Writing and the Experience of Limits,* trans. Philip Barnard with David Hayman (New York: Columbia University Press, 1983), pp. 185–207. The title

essay first appeared in English in *Surfiction. Fiction Now . . . and Tomorrow,* ed. Federman, trans. Christine Grahl, pp. 59–74.

67. On this issue, see Rosette Lamont, "Crossing the Iron Curtain: Political Parables," in *Beckett Translating/Translating Beckett,* ed. Friedman, Rossman, and Sherzer, pp. 77–84. Lamont writes: "Beckett is not a political writer, but history has stamped him with its pain." (p. 79) Emerging "from his personal pain, from his apprehension of human suffering" (p. 81), his work often has some understated political implications; these suggestions are more emphatic in *Catastrophe,* written in honor of the jailed Vaclav Havel (1982), and *What Where* (1983).

68. Raymond Federman, *To Whom It May Concern: A Novel* (Boulder, Normal, Brooklyn: Fiction Collective Two, 1990), p. 86.

69. André Bleikasten, "Roman vrai, vrai roman ou l'indestructible récit," *Revue française d'études américaines* 31 (January 1987): 9.

70. Federman, "The Art of Genocide," *The American Book Review* 8 (1986): 1.

71. By Federman's admission, he has always heeded the advice of his friend, Sam: "Raymond, whatever you write never compromise, and if you plan to write for money or for fame, do something else." Federman, "Samuel Beckett, The Gift of Words," *Fiction International* 19.1 (Fall 1990): 180.

72. Irving Howe, "The Idea of the Modern," in *Literary Modernism,* ed. Irving Howe (Greenwich, Conn.: Fawcett Publications, 1967), p. 26. In addition to Hassan's celebration of Beckett as the (post)modern epitome of heroic male denial as opposed to the "female" acquiescence of matter, world, and historical tradition (*The Dismemberment of Orpheus,* p. 213), one could cite Adorno's description of Beckett's work as exemplary for art's capacity to produce a "negative knowledge of the actual world." See Ernst Bloch et al., *Aesthetics and Politics* (London and New York: Verso, 1977), p. 160.

73. Samuel Beckett, "Dante . . . Bruno . Vico . . Joyce," in *transition* 16–17 (1929): 242–53; rpt. in *Our Egzamination Round His Factification for Incamination of "Work in Progress"* (New York: New Directions, 1962), pp. 21–22.

74. The story of these various purloinings and adaptations, as retold by Federman in a January 9, 1993 letter to me, is suggestive of his favorite theme of "playgiarism":

> As you know Joyce used [abused] a lot of people to whom he would dictate the text when he was blind, and young Beckett was one of them. One day, in the middle of the dictation someone knocked on the door of the room where Joyce and Beckett were working. Joyce said "come in" in the middle of whatever he was then dictating and young Beckett who was concentrating on what he was doing wrote "come in" in the middle of the text. The next day, when Beckett was reading to Joyce what he had been dictating the previous day, and he read "come in," Joyce asked what is this "come in"? Beckett told him, that's what you said, and so Joyce not only decided to leave that "come in" in the text, but then added this passage (p. 112) about Beckett lost in the thicket of Joycean words. This is the passage:

You is feeling like you was lost in the bush, boy? You say: It is a pulling sample jungle of woods. You almost shout out: Bethicket me for my stump of a beech if I have the poultriest notions what the farest he all means.

I am sure you know all that, but just in case, I wanted to inform you as to how that statement in *Take It or Leave It* originated. But there is also another source to it, because, as you know, all good *playgiarists* [and I think of myself as one of the best] know how to camouflage their sources. On page 84 of Ihab Hassan's *Paracriticisms* [which is, of course, a monstrous work of playgiarism inspired by Federman's leap-frog technique] one reads:

> What can I possibly add to this subject, except perhaps to suggest that all good structuralists go to *Finnegans Wake* on their way to heaven.

75. Federman, "Before Postmodernism and After," p. 26.

76. Federman, *Journey to Chaos: Samuel Beckett's Early Fiction* (Berkeley: University of California Press, 1965), p. 97.

6

LOST IN THE MALL

Beckett, Federman, Space

Brian McHale

I

A funny thing happened to Sam Beckett on his way to the shopping mall: he ran into Ray Federman coming the other way, and . . .

II

Here are three short prose fictions—anonymous for now, stripped of identity markers: titles, authors, publication dates (let's just say, later twentieth century), proper nouns, other specifics. Call them Texts A, B, and C. Let me describe for you the worlds of these three texts in the most general terms.

Text A thrusts us without preamble into a strange and enigmatic world, a bounded, self-enclosed universe, one that is somehow all interior, lacking an "outside." It is a mechanical, not a natural, environment—a vast machine, in some sense. Moreover, the mechanical character of the environment seems to have contaminated the social relations of the machine's human inhabitants, whose strictly regimented interactions are described with ethnographic detachment. Finally, the mechanical universe of this text, in common with all the machines and systems of our own universe, is threatened by entropy: it is irresistibly running down.

Text B, on the other hand, thrusts us without preamble into a strange and enigmatic world, a bounded, self-enclosed universe, one that is somehow all interior, lacking an "outside." It is a mechanical, not a natural, environment—a vast machine, and so on.

As for Text C, it thrusts us without preamble into a strange and enigmatic world, and so on.

Evidently there is a good case to be made for regarding these three texts as different realizations of, or variations on, the same chronotope (in the sense of Bakhtin, 1981). Call it, for now, the "microworld" chronotope. Of course, they

112

are not *identical* realizations of it, except at this very general level of description. For one thing, the unfolding of Texts A and B is driven by more or less conventional plots, while Text C is plotless. Specifically, A and B develop according to the dynamics of an *epistemological* plot, the progressive discovery on the protagonist's part of the true nature of the microworld into which he has been born. This epistemological quest is accompanied, in Text A, by conventional adventure episodes, while adventure is minimal in B, and nonexistent in C. In Text C, indeed, there is no epistemological gain at all from beginning to end, and the microworld's true nature, its purpose (if any), what lies outside it, all remain unknown: "For in the cylinder alone are certitudes to be found and without nothing but mystery."

The universe of Text A, though not really a "universe," does prove to be both sublimely vast and thrillingly complex and labyrinthine, a honeycomb space of levels and compartments—ideally suited for adventuring. Worlds B and C, by contrast, are derisorily shrunken and cramped. The world of Text B barely accommodates a population of fourteen, and is compact enough to be parked in an aircraft hangar. As for the world of C, its dimensions and inventory are very precisely specified: a cylinder, 50 meters around by 16 meters high, its surface, "solid rubber or suchlike," featureless apart from certain niches, arranged in irregular groups of five in the upper half of cylinder wall; bare of furnishings except for ladders used by the inhabitants to ascend to the niches; the inhabitants themselves, some two hundred in number, all naked, most in constant motion, following certain fixed patterns of behavior; the whole interior space subject to a regular "twofold vibration" or oscillation in temperature and illumination.

Finally, only Text A finishes on a positive, upbeat note, with the protagonist acting decisively to reverse the downward entropic spiral in which his world is caught, thus opening the way for further adventures (sequels would follow). Entropy triumphs in Texts B and C, however—bathetically in B, as the project that sustains the text's microworld is threatened with closure for lack of government funding; with a desolate dying fall in C, as the world lapses into terminal silence, darkness, motionlessness.

You will already have recognized, no doubt, that Text C is Samuel Beckett's *The Lost Ones* (1972; French version, *Le Depeupleur*, 1971). You may also have guessed that Texts A and B are science fiction stories. Specifically, Text A is "Universe" by Robert Heinlein, first published in *Astounding Science Fiction* in 1941, while Text B is "Thirteen for Centaurus" by J. G. Ballard, first published a quarter of a century later, and collected in a volume of Ballard's stories in 1974.

The enigmas of Heinlein's initial premise are cleared up when the "universe" of his title is revealed to be an immense starship, designed to ferry colonists to distant worlds on a voyage originally expected to last several generations. All knowledge of the original mission having been lost generations ago, in the aftermath of a catastrophic mutiny, the space-travellers have come to believe that their microworld is coextensive with the universe, until Heinlein's hero shows them otherwise, restarts the long-dormant engines, and sets the expedition back on course for Proxima Centauri. Heinlein's story is thus a "straight" realization of the science-fiction topos of "worlds in flight," while Ballard (typically for him) subjects the conventional topos to ironic revisions and bathetic reductions of scale.[1] In his version, the supposed multigeneration voyage to the stars is actually an earthbound laboratory experiment. The "spacecraft" is a nonfunctional mockup of one, and the crew, deceived about the true nature of their mission, are little better than laboratory rats—all but one of their number, that is, who divines the truth of their situation, and uses his knowledge to turn the tables on the experimenters.

The question, of course, is not why these two science-fiction stories have so much in common—their respective realizations of the same science-fiction topos is explanation enough—but what Beckett is doing in this "low" company. Although the publication dates allow for it, it is hard to imagine that Beckett could have been aware of these particular stories, let alone that he sought deliberately to work a further variation on this particular topos. Indeed, it is hard to imagine Beckett paying any attention to science fiction at all—unless, perhaps, the "cylinder" of *The Lost Ones* bears the trace of some more or less remote memory of H. G. Wells's *The War of the Worlds*.[2] So the identity, at some general level of description, of Beckett's realization of the microworld chronotope with these two science-fiction realizations must be explained differently, perhaps in terms of very deep shared roots.

Roots, for instance, in Dante, who is often cited (by those anxious about science fiction's pedigree) as a precursor of science-fiction world-building, and who not only exerts a demonstrable influence on many details of *The Lost Ones,* but is actually mentioned by name in a text otherwise utterly devoid of proper nouns.[3] Or roots, deeper still, in Plato's myth of the cave (in the *Republic*), which perhaps underwrites the epistemological dynamics of Heinlein's and Ballard's versions, and which undergoes an ironic reversal in Beckett's version, where the truth of the world of light outside the cave is forever inaccessible to the cave-dwellers: "For in the cylinder alone are certitudes to be found and without nothing but mystery."

But perhaps such roots are *too* deep to have much explanatory power. After all, not only Beckett and postwar science fiction writers, but the whole of the rest of so-called Western culture as well, share roots in Dante and Plato. So tracing these versions of microworld back to some ultimate double origin in Dante and Plato, to which *everything else* in Western culture can also (directly or indirectly) be traced, hardly explains the apparent convergence among *these particular* texts.

I would like to propose an alternative explanation, in terms not of genealogies and shared origins but of reverse chronology and *post factum* influence. In full consciousness of the paradox, I would like to propose that Beckett's affiliation with science fiction has come into being *after the fact;* that Beckett's writing never had any connection with science fiction before (before, say, 1982), but that it has one now. I'm proposing that Beckett's *The Lost Ones* has been "retrofitted," in effect, as a science fiction story and the realization of a science fiction topos (call it "microworld," call it "world in flight"). Moreover, this retrofitting has been accomplished by *another text.* The text I have in mind is Raymond Federman's novel *The Twofold Vibration.*

III

Here are three more prose fictions (no need for anonymity this time): Alan Lightman's *Einstein's Dreams* (1993), Paul Auster's *In the Country of Last Things* (1987), and Federman's *The Twofold Vibration* (1982). They have little in common, except for their "hypertextual" relation to Beckett's *The Lost Ones.*[4]

Lightman's text, in the chapter headed "14 May 1905", rewrites the final phase of life in Beckett's cylinder, when the last one of its inhabitants who is still mobile finally freezes into immobility, and terminal darkness, stillness, and cold descend. Auster's text reinscribes Beckett's taxonomy of behaviors observed among the cylinder-dwellers: where Beckett distinguishes among searchers, the temporarily sedentary, the permanently sedentary, the "vanquished," climbers of ladders, and watchers of climbers, Auster has Runners, Leapers, clients of the Euthanasia Clinics, members of the Assassination Club, and miscellaneous scavengers.[5] In both cases, the source material from Beckett has not been directly appropriated, cut-and-pasted, but rather *transcoded* in terms of another text, genre, or set of conventions, as if translated from the original "Beckettese" into some other dialect.[6] In Lightman's case, this other text is Italo Calvino's *Invisible Cities,* the primary model for Lightman's own text, and the basis for the "dialect" ("Calvinoese"?) into which all the raw materials of *Einstein's Dreams* have been systematically transposed.[7] As for *In the Country of Last Things,* here the secondary code is that of the genre of dystopian fiction, and the elements of Beckett's world are transcoded into the terms of conventional dystopian cities.[8]

The Twofold Vibration differs from these other texts in at least one important respect, in that it alludes explicitly to its source in Beckett, whereas Lightman and Auster leave the Beckett connection to be inferred. Federman's novel advertises its hypertextual affiliation with *The Lost Ones* in its title, its epigraph, and its penultimate sentence, all three echoing a key sentence from Beckett: "But the persistence of the twofold vibration suggests that in this old abode all is not yet quite for the best."[9] Apart from such direct allusions, however, Beckett's hypertextual presence registers most strongly in the represented spaces of Federman's world.

The space of Beckett's cylinder reappears in *The Twofold Vibration* in the form of a "hall of departure" at Federman's spaceport of the future, where undesirables are marshalled prior to boarding rocket transports for deportation to off-world colonies:

> the hall . . . was lit by bright yellow disks in the ceiling, the entire room, even the floor and ceiling, was made of shiny gray metal and, except for the huge doors opened to the spaceship positioned just outside the hall, there was not a single seam in the structure . . . which meant that when the giant doors were shut the hall was totally airproof, waterproof, and presumably soundproof as well . . . the place was so gigantic, so incredibly big that twenty-five Arcs de Triomphe could easily fit inside that great hall of departure.[10]

Many of the details here seem to have been derived directly from *The Lost Ones*. The milling crowds, the coercive but invisible social authority exercised over them, the cavernous space, the yellow light, the seamless gray surface, the controlled climate, and so on—all strongly recall Beckett's space. But if the hall of departures is transparently a version of Beckett's cylinder, it also refers to conventional, indeed hackneyed, science-fiction enclosure types, as indicated by the "futuristic" materials ("shiny gray metal"), by the breathless hyperbole and gigantism of the entire description ("so incredibly big that twenty-five Arcs de Triomphe could easily fit inside"), and of course by the iconic spaceship poised so conspicuously just outside. Here, then, we have a kind of double exposure, Beckett's space superimposed on an imagined enclosure straight out of the science-fiction repertoire.

In other words, Federman transcodes elements of Beckett's world—the interior space of the cylinder, the spatial disposition of its inhabitants, its "twofold vibration" of light and temperature, and so on—in terms of conventional science-fiction topoi of spaceflight: spaceports, space colonies, huge rocket transports, and the like. This transcoding of Beckett in conventional science-fiction terms is precisely how Federman's text retrofits *The Lost Ones* as science fiction: science fiction after the fact.

IV

This seems an ironic conclusion to draw, in view of Federman's disclaimer, in the opening pages of *The Twofold Vibration*, of any intention to write science fiction: "what do you mean science-fiction, not at all" (p. 1). He proceeds to rattle off, rapid-fire, a catalogue of conventional science fiction motifs of precisely the kind that I have just identified in his representation of the spaceport, but these are motifs that he claims to have repudiated:[11]

no futuristic crap, I mean pseudoscientific bullshit, space warfare, fake theories of probabilities, unsolvable equations, strange creatures from other planets, ludicrous busybodies with pointed ears, wings instead of arms or wheels instead of legs . . . no gadgetry, no crass emotionless robots . . . no none of that infantilism, at least within reason, no invasions of earth by superbrains, spaceship battles in the galaxies, worlds that collide, nothing spuriously progressive or regressive in this story, nothing prophetic or moralistic either. (pp. 1–2)

It is possible, of course, that Federman is bluffing here, or even trying to mislead us about the real extent of his indebtedness to science fiction conventions; or that he is *pretending* to try to mislead us, in a game of double irony in which he knows that we know that he knows. . . . But what if one took his disclaimer seriously? For what reason would a writer who has no use for the conventions of science fiction nevertheless resort to spaceflight motifs?

Federman himself supplies the answer, albeit cryptically. What use is science fiction if one repudiates its futuristic pretensions and its extrapolations, which is to say, most of its motif repertoire? It is, he writes,

a question of more space, room to expand forward and backward, a matter of distanciation if you wish, room to turn imagination loose on the spot and shift perspectives unexpectedly. (p. 1)

In one sense, of course, Federman is merely laying claim to science fiction's greater imaginative latitude (figurative "space"). But I want to stress a second, literal sense of this formulation: it is all "a question of space," literally a vehicle for exploring spatial representations, an opportunity to reflect on the implications of representing space (and of represented spaces). Here Federman's sense of science fiction's potential converges with recent science fiction theory, in particular with Jameson's argument that science fiction's special contribution is its sustained resourcefulness in seeking to appropriate the category of space for the imagination. If space is the dominant of postmodern culture,[12] then the science-fiction genre is intrinsically and precociously postmodern, in ways which Federman seems to have grasped. Moreover, its privileged relation to the spatial allows it to serve as a tool for reflecting on the "postmodern condition."

In other words, the science-fiction motif repertoire functions for Federman as part of a kind of "spatial code." This code organizes and semanticizes representations of space dispersed throughout *The Twofold Vibration,* producing a coherent system of spatial/semantic associations, analogies, and antitheses. Thus, the spaceport-terminal space stands in opposition to the claustrophobic "antechamber of waiting," also called, ominously enough, the "final closet" (p. 66), where the novel's protagonist is sequestered until his turn comes to join the crowd of deportees in the hall of departure. This antechamber, in turn, is explicitly associated with the "closet" of Federman's autobiographical myth, the enclosed space in which, according to the story that recurs repeatedly throughout his oeuvre, Federman as a child hid to evade deportation to the Nazi death camps, but also the private space of consciousness, of inwardness, from which Federman emerges as a self-aware writer.[13]

This spatial opposition between the hyperbolic hall of departure, on the one hand, and the claustrophobic antechamber of waiting and its analogues, on the other, is in a sense "resolved" in a third space: the space of Dachau, or rather the Dachau *museum*, which Federman's protagonist visits in a flashback episode. Dachau is clearly associated with the closet space, not only because it was to Dachau or its equivalent that the child Federman escaped being deported when he hid in the closet, but also because of the analogy established here between the "final closet" and the gas chambers of the Nazi death camps (see pp. 145–46). On the other hand, Dachau is also associated with the hall of departure, for the "space colonies" of Federman's future dystopia are suspected of being death camps, and "deportation" of being merely a transparent euphemism for genocide (as in the Nazis' sinister fiction that the Jews were merely being "relocated" to "resettlement camps" in the East).

Moreover, the Dachau museum and the hall of departure share certain spatial qualities, at least according to Federman's account. His description insistently emphasizes the "emptiness" of Dachau, in every sense, including the literal, physical sense. Dachau, Federman's protagonist reports, is today a "vast empty space" (p. 97), with only two or three buildings left standing; there is "nothing much to see, except for the huge space where the barracks once were." Entering the Dachau museum proper, he experiences a desire "to get to the core of this thing" (p. 99); ironically, at the core of the museum, itself the core of Dachau, he finds only another void, "a large empty space" (p. 101). At the end of one's tour of the museum,

> you find nothing, a void, an emptiness . . . this whole machine has led to this, to this vacuum, the whole Nazi machine has produced nothing, nothing but an absence, it was invented to fabricate death. (p. 101)

This void enclosure at the center of the Dachau death factory seems to mirror the void enclosure of the hall of departure after it has emptied of its crowds of deportees. Like the former, the latter too is described in terms of spatial qualities of emptiness, cavernousness, and absence—metonyms of death.

Federman uses this coded spatial system—the hall of departure opposed to the antechamber of waiting, the latter analogized to the closet, all three affiliated with the space of Dachau—to produce a kind of implicit discourse of architectural criticism. Or rather, since he is less interested in architecture as such than in architecture *as symptom,* he uses spatial code to mount an implicit critique of modernity itself. In this, he is preceded by such memorable novelistic critiques of contemporary built space as Brigid Brophy's *In Transit* (1969) and J. G. Ballard's *High Rise* (1975).

We can decode Federman's spatial critique of modernity by interpreting the represented spaces of his text in terms of familiar modernist building-types, and then following the lines of affiliation his text traces among these types. The obvious place to start is the hall of departure. If the intertextual referents of this space are, as we have seen, Beckett's cylinder and certain science fiction enclosures, its *extra*-textual referents include all those "microworld" spaces and "great places within"[13] that are so characteristic, for better or worse, of our late-modernist built environment: vast terminal-buildings of hub airports, enclosed shopping malls, soaring hotel atriums, and all the hybrids among these types—terminals that are also shopping malls (such as the new Greater Pittsburgh International Airport, USAir's hub), malls that are also hotels (such as the Westin Bonaventure, as described by Jameson; see below), and so on. Spaces of commerce, circulation, and transit, sealed off from the outside world, such enclosures are vast yet inconspicuous when viewed from a distance. Like Beckett's cylinder, they *lack exteriors,* in effect; they are meant to be experienced *from within,* not from without. (The Westin Bonaventure is rendered "invisible," in a sense, by its reflective outer surface; Pittsburgh International is, implausibly for so large a structure, hard to spot from the air, utterly nondescript from the ground, and in any case experienced by travelers in transit through the hub exclusively as an interior space.)

Familiar spaces—comforting, almost. Yet recall that, by the logic of Federman's spatial code, the "great space within" of the spaceport terminal is also associated with the terminal void of Dachau. What could shopping malls possibly have in common with death camps? Federman's appalling juxtaposition serves to jog our historical memory. The International Style of architecture, we recall—the style disseminated by Le Corbusier, the Bauhaus, Walter Gropius, Mies van der Rohe, and others—was inspired by the fresh "modern" forms and the functionalist ideology of industrial architecture.[15] Thus the modernist movement in architecture at its very inception succumbed to the glamour (what Jameson calls the "technological sublime") of the machine and the assembly-line factory, with their mystique of efficiency and quintessential modernity. That fascination with the factory system and its characteristic architectural forms persists, albeit covertly, right down to the present day, encoded in the building types and the modernist aesthetic ideology of much contemporary architecture, notably including the architecture of shopping malls, air terminals, and the like.

But that same factory system and that same mystique of mechanical efficiency also underwrote the Nazi death factories at Dachau and elsewhere. If the Nazi genocide could be said to have had an "aesthetic" motive (appalling thought), its underlying principles were akin to those of modernist architecture: clean, efficient lines, clarity of form, transparency of function, the kind of "purity" that has no tolerance for ethnic "contaminants." It is this aspect of the Holocaust, its affiliation with the modern factory system and machine aesthetics, that Federman exposes when he has the protagonist of *The Twofold Vibration* compare the museum at Dachau to the Ford Motor Company Museum in Dearborn.

Bizarre or irresponsible or merely tasteless though it may at first appear, this coupling of Dachau and Dearborn makes a telling historical point. For after all the Nazi death camps merely applied to the ends of mass murder the industrial assembly-line methods first pioneered at Ford: without Dearborn, no Dachau. The only difference, according to Federman's protagonist, is that at the end of the Dearborn tour one enters a "large well lit room" where the latest product of the Ford Motor Co. ("the new Thunderbird or LTD") is displayed; while, at end of the Dachau tour—nothing; the void; the same void (according to the spatial logic of this text) that one finds at the heart of the spaceport of the future, or at the heart of Beckett's cylinder, and (by extension) at the heart of all the shopping malls and air terminals and atrium hotels, all the "great places within," of the contemporary built environment. Some machines are machines for living (as Le Corbusier called his International Style houses); some are machines for shopping; some are machines for killing ("depeupleurs"); all are implicated in each other, and in our unhappy late-modernity.

V

By inserting the fictional space of *The Lost Ones* among the coded spaces of *The Twofold Vibration,* Federman implicates Beckett's text in his own spatial critique of modernity.

It is, of course, nothing new to suggest an affiliation between the worlds of Beckett's fictions and the concentration-camp world; this has been a commonplace of Beckett criticism since Adorno first gave the idea currency.[16] What *is* new, however, is the implication that the space of this particular Beckett fiction models *both* the death-camp space *and also,* by a kind of double-exposure, the shopping-mall space of commerce and circulation.

We can safely assume, I think, that Samuel Beckett never directly experienced a contemporary shopping mall. Nevertheless, Federman's recontextualization of Beckett in *The Twofold Vibration* calls our attention to ways in which Beckett seems weirdly to have anticipated a certain critique of shopping-mall space and the shopping-mall experience.

Striking parallels suggest themselves between *The Lost Ones* and Fredric Jameson's celebrated account of getting lost (or losing himself?) in John Portman's Westin Bonaventure Hotel on Bunker Hill, Los Angeles.[17] Consider, first of all, Jameson's account of the Westin Bonaventure's isolation from the city outside, its constitution of itself as a self-contained world, a "microworld." This isolation is attributable in part to the obscurity and insignificance of the building's entrances, as if the space inside aspired not to be accessible to the city outside, in part to its reflective glass skin, which turns the surface of the Westin Bonaventure complex into a mirror of everything around it, thereby "achiev[ing] a peculiar and placeless dissociation of the Bonaventure from its neighborhood."[18] Recall, in this connection, the central mystery of the cylinder in *The Lost Ones:* it has no outside, as far as anyone knows; it comprises an interior space with no exterior, or no knowable exterior: "In the cylinder alone are certitudes to be found and without nothing but mystery."[19]

It is this quality of isolation that allows such "great places within" to function as microworlds, as miniature scale-models of, or even *alternatives to,* the world outside. The Westin Bonaventure, writes Jameson, "does not want to be a part of the city but rather its equivalent and replacement or substitute."[20] Mike Davis, otherwise a dissenter from Jameson's analysis, concurs for once. "Most of the new downtown centres" such as Portman's Westin Bonaventure complex, he writes, "might as well have been built on the third moon of Jupiter. Their fundamental logic is that of a claustrophobic space colony attempting to miniaturize nature within itself."[21] A claustrophobic space colony like, one presumes, those in Heinlein's "Universe" or Ballard's "Thirteen for Centaurus"—or *The Lost Ones.*

Consider, secondly, the experience of space that according to Jameson, afflicts visitors to the Bonaventure hotel atrium. His description is memorable:

> a constant busyness [elsewhere characterized as "milling confusion"] gives the feeling that emptiness is here absolutely packed, that it is an element within which you yourself are immersed, without any of that distance that formerly enabled the perception of perspective or volume. You are in this hyperspace up to your eyes and your body.[22]

"Constant busyness," "milling confusion," "packed emptiness": these formulations are readily transferable to the behavior of Beckett's cylinder-dwellers, or to the throng crowding Federman's hall of departure.

However, for even a closer analogue, compare Beckett's curious description of the quality of *light* in the cylinder:

> this light is further unusual in that far from evincing one or more visible or hidden sources it appears to emanate from all sides and to permeate the

entire space as though this were uniformly luminous down to its least particle of ambient air. To the point that the ladders themselves seem rather to shed than to receive light with this slight reserve that light is not the word. No other shadows then than those cast by bodies pressing on one another willfully or from necessity as when for example on a breast to prevent its being lit or on some private part the hand descends with vanished palm. Whereas the skin of a climber alone on his ladder or in the depths of a tunnel glistens all over with the same red-yellow glister and even some of its folds and recesses in so far as the air enters in.[23]

"Light is not the word": here (and not for the only time) the flattened, instruction-manual prose of Beckett's text[24] skips or lurches, slips sideways, and loses its descriptive footing. If "light is not the word," then what *is* the word? Perhaps "space"—or, as Jameson would have it, "hyperspace." Light inside the cylinder does not behave like light but rather like a kind of congealed space, space become material substance, filling or coating other objects; precisely the sort of "emptiness" that "packs" the Bonaventure atrium, in which (according to Jameson) one is "immersed" up to the eyes and the body.

Consider, finally, the behavior of the inhabitants of Beckett's enclosure—their continuous ascent and descent of the ladders, their restless circulation as they search the crowd for—what or whom? For their "lost ones," presumably, whom they never find or whom, having found them, they proceed to lose again; or, to speak more abstractly, for the objects of their desire, constantly lost and found and lost again, replaced and renewed. What are these people, then, if not quintessential shoppers? What is this text if not a supremely alienated ("ethnographic") description of their behavior? And what, finally, is this cylinder-enclosure if not a kind of minimalist shopping mall in which the lost ones circulate endlessly, subject to the twofold vibration until the lights go out once and for all?

Notes

The material in this chapter has had a longish and somewhat checkered career. It appeared first as a paper delivered at the conference "Engagement and Indifference: Beckett and the Political," organized by Henry Sussman at SUNY/Buffalo in April 1993. Next it resurfaced as part of a paper presented at the Synopsis No. 5 conference "Models/Schemas/Frames—A New Umbrella?" held at the Porter Institute for Poetics and Semiotics, Tel Aviv University, in May–June 1994. I am grateful to the organizers of both these conferences, and those who listened to and discussed my presentations, for helping me to get it right (or at least, less wrong) the third time.

1. The *locus classicus* for this topos is James Blish's sequence of novels collectively entitled *Cities in Flight* (1955–62, some of the material having originally appeared as short stories as early as 1950). Ballard's ironic revision of the "worlds in flight" *topos* exemplifies the strong tendency of science-fiction writing to reflect critically on its own models, even to deconstruct them. That tendency yields an ironic chronotope of its own, that of the derelict or decaying space-station or space-colony in, for example, Bruce Sterling and William Gibson's "Red Star, Winter Orbit" (1983), Lewis Shiner's *Frontera* (1984), and John Shirley's *Eclipse* (1985).

2. If so, it could only be a memory of the *word* "cylinder," since nothing else in Beckett's text bears the least resemblance to Wells's invasion-from-Mars novel. Recall, in particular, that the "cylinders" that bear the Martian invaders to Earth in Wells's "scientific romance" are never described from the inside, but only seen from without, while Beckett's cylinder is *only* experienced from within and seems altogether to *lack* an outside.

3. Of the four kinds of activity to be distinguished among the cylinder's inhabitants, the fourth is that of "those who do not search or non-searchers sitting for the most part against the wall in the attitude which wrung from Dante one of his rare wan smiles" (Beckett *The Lost Ones,* in *Six Residua* [London: John Calder, 1978], 58). The allusion appears to be to Dante's encounter in Purgatory with Belacqua (*Purgatorio* iv, 121–22), a character whose name Beckett had earlier appropriated for the protagonist of the stories in *More Pricks Than Kicks*. Belacqua's posture (squatting, his head between his knees) is ascribed in *The Lost Ones* to the motionless woman who serves for orientation, the cylinder's "north" (p. 76). Other gestures, postures and even phrases also seem to echo the *Commedia*.

I am indebted to Enzo Neppi for these details, as well as for reminding me of the relevance of Plato's myth of the cave.

4. The term "hypertext," as used in this context, is Gérard Genette's, and the general theoretical perspective I am adopting here derives from Genette (*Palimpsestes* [Paris: Seuil, 1982]) and Riffaterre (*Semiotics of Poetry* [Bloomington: Indiana University Press, 1978]). Genette's and Riffaterre's theories of hypertextuality/intertextuality are not identical (as Genette himself makes clear, *Palimpsestes,* pp. 8–9), but they are compatible and do overlap to some degree. In any case, I have not followed either of them with rigorous fidelity.

I am indebted to Gerald Prince for pointing me in Genette's direction.

5. *In the Country of Last Things* is not the only one of Auster's texts in which he reinscribes Beckett, of course. For instance, *Moon Palace* (1989) rewrites the "pseudo-couple" Hamm and Clov of *Endgame,* while the second half of *The Music of Chance* (1990) reimagines the situation of *Waiting for Godot;* and there are more general echoes of Beckett throughout the *New York Trilogy* and elsewhere in Auster's corpus.

6. For Genette, hypertextuality is always a relation between two texts, the source-text ("hypotext") and the hypertext into which it is reinscribed. Nowhere does he mention the possibility of mediation by a third text (or genre, set of conventions, etc.) that would serve as a secondary code for re- or trans-coding the hypotext—a kind of "filter" through

which the hypotext passes before its reinscription in the hypertext. Riffaterre has more to say about such cases, though he does not treat them as constituting a distinct category of intertextual relations. Nevertheless, both Genette and Riffaterre mention examples that fit my model of transcoding, including Stoppard's *Rosencrantz and Guildenstern Are Dead* (Genette), in which *Hamlet* is transcoded in terms of *Waiting for Godot,* and Alfred Jarry's "The Passion of Jesus Considered as an Uphill Race" (Riffaterre), in which the Gospel accounts are transcoded in terms of sports-journalism discourse; compare also J. G. Ballard's "The Assassination of John Fitzgerald Kennedy Considered as Downhill Motor Race," from *The Atrocity Exhibition* (1969).

7. In fact, the intertextual relations here are even more complex, for Lightman first recodes *Invisible Cities,* transposing the frame-tale (Marco Polo's dialogues with Kublai Khan become a series of "interludes" involving the dreamer Einstein and his friend Besso) and, more importantly, systematically recasting Calvino's thematics of *space* as a thematics of *time.* It is into the terms of this recoded model, where spatial thematics have become temporal thematics, that the Beckett material is translated.

8. Auster alerts us to the relevance of this genre through his epigraph from Hawthorne, in which the latter mentions "the famous City of Destruction." This sends us back beyond Hawthorne to Bunyan and even earlier avatars of the City of Destruction, such as Dante's infernal city of Dis; but it also sends us forward to more recent exemplars, including the dystopian cities of Wyndham Lewis's *Human Age* trilogy, Samuel Delany's *Dhalgren,* Alasdair Gray's *Lanark,* and recent science-fiction films (*Blade Runner, Robocop*), among many others.

9. Samuel Beckett, *The Lost Ones,* in *Six Residua* (London: John Calder, 1978), p. 78.

10. Raymond Federman, *The Twofold Vibration* (Bloomington: Indiana University Press, 1982), p. 167.

11. Compare the notorious negative catalogue, compiled by Henry James in his monograph on Hawthorne (1879), in which he lists everything that is missing from American culture, for lack of which the American novelist is placed at such a disadvantage relative to his European counterparts: "No State, in the European sense of the word. . . . No sovereign, no court, no personal loyalty, no aristocracy, no church, no clergy, no army, no diplomatic service, no country gentlemen, no palaces, no castles, nor manors, nor old country-houses, nor parsonages, nor thatched cottages nor ivied ruins . . . no literature, no novels, no museums, no pictures," and so on. Henry James, *Hawthorne,* in *Henry James: Essays on Literature, American Writers, English Writers,* ed. Leon Edel and Mark Wilson (New York: Library of America, 1984), pp. 351–52.

12. Jameson argues this in *Postmodernism, or, The Cultural Logic of Late Capitalism* (Durham, N.C.: Duke University Press, 1991), pp. 154–60, 364–76.

13. The definitive version of Federman's "closet experience" is to be found in *The Voice in the Closet* (1979), originally designed to appear as an inset within *The Twofold Vibration* but ultimately published as an independent, free-standing text.

14. Robert A. M. Stern, *Pride of Place: Building the American Dream* (Boston: Houghton Mifflin/New York: American Heritage, 1986), pp. 215–49.

15. For a recent account, see Reyner Banham, *A Concrete Atlantis: U.S. Industrial Building and European Modern Architecture* (Cambridge, Mass.: MIT Press, 1986).

16. According to Deirdre Bair's biography (*Samuel Beckett* [New York: Harcourt, Brace, Jovanovich, 1978], p. 508), the study window of Beckett's Paris apartment, in the last decades of his life, overlooked the exercise yard of the Sante prison. Could the highly regimented behaviors of the cylinder-dwellers of *The Lost Ones* incorporate observations of prisoners' behavior in the exercise yard? If so, then any resemblance to the concentration camp world would be far from coincidental—would, in fact, amount to a kind of "family resemblance."

17. "Postmodernism, or, The Cultural Logic of Late Capitalism," *New Left Review* 146 (July–August 1984): 53–94; rpt. in *Postmodernism*. For an argument that Jameson's disorientation in the Westin Bonaventure is in fact gendered—an acculturated male response to a commercial space conventionally reserved for women—see Judith Goldstein, "The Female Aesthetic Community," *Poetics Today* 14.1 (Spring 1993): 143–63.

18. Jameson, *Postmodernism*, p. 42.

19. Beckett, *The Lost Ones*, p. 70.

20. Jameson, *Postmodernism*, p. 40.

21. Mike Davis, "Urban Renaissance and the Spirit of Postmodernism," in *Postmodernism and Its Discontents: Theories, Practices*, ed. E. Ann Kaplan (London: Verso, 1988), p. 86.

22. Jameson, *Postmodernism*, p. 43.

23. Beckett, *The Lost Ones*, p. 69.

24. David Porush, *The Soft Machine: Cybernetic Fiction* (New York and London: Methuen, 1985), p. 162.

7

THE SAME OLD HAG

Gender and (In)Difference in Samuel Beckett's Trilogy

AnJanette Brush

Bodies don't matter, but hers went something like this. . . .

—Samuel Beckett, *More Pricks Than Kicks*

To problematize the matter of bodies may entail an initial loss of epistemological certainty, but a loss of certainty is not the same as political nihilism. On the contrary, such a loss may well indicate a significant and promising shift in political thinking. This unsettling of "matter" can be understood as initiating new possibilities, new ways for bodies to matter.

—Judith Butler, *Bodies That Matter*

Samuel Beckett's play *Waiting for Godot,* according to its author, "strove at all cost to avoid definition";[1] according to many of his critics, such striving on Beckett's part represents an attempt at transcending the limits of language and moving beyond the limits of self. The concept of a certain liberation of identity in Beckett's writing—albeit a very anxious sort of liberation—is reflected in the comments of Linda Ben-Zvi: "Besides being there, Beckett's characters share other characteristics. Despite their physical presence, they are uncertain of themselves. They often answer to several names, trying them on as they try on hats, searching for a fixed self."[2] The search for coherence of identity is something Beckett's narratives and "characters" expound as they ultimately avoid, simultaneously thriving strangely on and disgusted by their ever-increasing physical and narrative fragmentation. The uncertainty and experimentation sometimes adopts a humorous tone— something as insignificant(ly arbitrary) as donning an article of clothing—or it

126

can be in fact quite unsettling, even perhaps violent. And it has instigated a wide-ranging variety of critical conversations about the nature, purpose, and function-ing of Beckett's unconventional narrators of the modernist void.

"So much for the plans and organization of man."[3]

In all three novels of Beckett's trilogy—*Molloy, Malone Dies, The Unnamable*—names shift, dislocating identity, relationships, and understanding of a reasonable "character." The result is a series of conflated, unreliable, and often incoherent narrators, suffering from physical deterioration, faulty memories, narrators for whom even the present is grasped only problematically, only partially. These instances of contradiction, negation, nonsense, and ironic ridiculousness in Beck-ett's figures and their various undertakings can be seen as indicative of a collapse of logic, or more specifically for some Beckett scholars, as "an indictment of Western logic."[4] Certainly the reader of Beckett is witnessing a true disdain for ordering, for conventional methods of organizing narrative and identity, when he/she con-fronts a scene such as that of Molloy sorting his stones in the first novel of Beckett's *Trilogy*. In this instance the narrator obsessively, fruitlessly, ridiculously devises schemes for rotating among his pockets sixteen stones—stones kept by Molloy to be sucked—in order to achieve their most even and general circulation, taking this task to the extent of considering sewing in an extra pocket. Similarly, in his observations of "dancing" bees late in the story, the same narrator attributes possible, elaborate, and ultimately meaningless explanations for relating the bees' hum to their patterns of movement:

> But there was to be considered not only the figure and the hum, but also the height at which the figure was executed. And I acquired the conviction that the selfsame figure, accompanied by the selfsame hum, did not mean at all the same thing at twelve feet from the ground as it did at six. For the bees did not dance at any level, haphazard, but there were three or four levels, always the same, at which they danced. And if I were to tell you what these levels were, and what the relations between them, for I had measured them with care, you would not believe me.[5]

In such disregard for conventional systematicity—and in the accompanying gestures toward molding new, paradoxically pointless meanings—lies the trilogy's political possibilities. With respect to character or identity, this could very well be a liberatory politics, as it is precisely out of and away from the confining logic of metanarratives that various "postmodern" subjects desire—and need—to move. As contemporary theoretical sensitivities call for the multiplication of sites of subjectivity, for the creation of varying and contestatory rather than normative identifications, Samuel Beckett's collapsing figures might be considered exemplary of just such processes. For if it is in naming and arranging that a "truth" and its accompanying limits and constrictions are produced, then the void at the end of the trilogy that is *The Unnamable,* in both name and product, is the reverse of such processes of definition.

It is their lack of distinguishing marks and their failure to fit categorization that sets Molloy and Malone and Mahood, if not exactly *free,* then adrift. Although the trilogy's narrating character is increasingly confined, restricted, jarred and effectively entombed over the course of the three novels, that which often leads to the hailing of the author as a revolutionary are the narrative breaks with distinctions marking self and other, presence and absence, and past and present: "My life, my life, now I speak of it as of something over, now as of a joke which still goes on, and it is neither, for at the same time it is over and it goes on, and is there any tense for that?"[6] As Ben-Zvi writes of the effects of Beckett's disruptions: "Thus, the individual failures of characters are not anomalies; they become part of the human struggle to transcend the limits of language and the limits of self."[7] Exemplifying this effort to transcend language's limits, obviously, is the trilogy's sliding nomenclature. Molloy is followed by a similar-sounding series of successors—Moran, then Malone, McMann, and Mahood—further undermining any sense of stability. Apparently it might not matter who is who in the trilogy. Through landscapes apparently exceeding the categorization of identity and its attributes move Molloy and Malone, figures perhaps caught in what Michel Foucault, in his deliberations on the nature of a hermaphrodite's existence, termed the happy limbo of a nonidentity.[8] But just as these characters, though frequently portrayed with humor, would probably not be what most readers could readily label happy, their positions are also more significantly complicated than they are uncontaminated.

In addition to aspects of naming, a perceived move in the novels of the trilogy beyond typical male/female categorizations is also often cited as a displacement of standard divisions of identity and identification. Carol Helmstetter Cantrell, for example, writes that in Molloy's generalizing eyes all gender distinctions collapse.[9] And in the same volume exploring the issue of gender and the Beckettian world—*Women in Beckett: Performance and Critical Perspectives*—Angela Moorjani praises *Molloy* and *Ill Seen Ill Said* for "subverting the mythic network imprisoning female and male."[10] This move leads her to an interesting consideration of the ideas of Hélène Cixous together with Beckett's dis-ordering. Moorjani looks to Cixous on rendering all conceptualization null and void in an effort to transcend the binarisms of mind/body, male/female, culture/nature, and so on. And, turning to Cixous and Catherine Clément's *The Newly Born Woman,* one in fact finds an evocative equation of an emptiness—perhaps such as that shaped by the undefined quality of the trilogy's characters—with a substantial degree of freedom:

> the country of writing ought to be a no where into which we can fly in a tarantella of rage and desire, a place beyond "vileness and compromise" where the part of ourselves that longs to be free, to be an "it" uncontaminated by angel or witch (or by sorceress or hysteric) can write itself, can dream, can invent new worlds.[11]

So the text that is more or less "androgynous" potentially represents an immediate "no where," a beyond into which "we" (here, women) can escape. The potential of "the country of writing" is that of an uncontaminated locus to be used for creation of something "new." Its potential clearly seen by some as being realized in texts like the trilogy, which invent alternative, fragmented identities to inhabit these new worlds—though Beckett's worlds, of course, are anything but "beyond" their own particular "vileness."

> Does all of this mean, then, that the better programme for feminism now would be—to minimise "women"? To cope with the oscillations by so downplaying the category that insisting on either differences or identities would become equally untenable?[12]

It is overly simplistic to consider freedom in/from [gendered] identity as a simple matter of treating all subjects as supposedly equal—or perhaps in the case of Beckett's trilogy, treating them all equally poorly. While the question of gender and identity in Beckett might not be most productively focused on accusations of misogyny—accusations reductively displaced by focusing instead on a more general misanthropy—neither should it be unproblematically assumed that a neutrality is involved with an erasure of gender distinctions. Rather, an inquiry should be made into what aspects of identity are maintained even as it appears to be falling apart, what these mechanics of identity might mean for the figure of "woman" and for that of "man." Minimizing the differences structured by traditional characterization is not inherently revolutionary, but rather is even capable of producing discourses not necessarily so unfamiliar, so subversive and transcendent as might be initially assumed.

The processes constitutive of the Beckettian dismantling of identity's logic as displayed in the trilogy—what could be called the mechanics of identity—are complex and multilayered, as are their results. The ambiguity, indifference, and occasional hostility surrounding women in *Molloy* must therefore be examined carefully before conclusions about gender "transcendence"—conclusions about male and female as liberated from their norms—can be drawn. Instances presented by *Molloy* for the examination of gendered roles include the presence of the figure Lousse, the remembrance of the maternal, and the reminiscence of other lovers presumably—apparently—female. What is initially striking in these accounts of the women populating Molloy's existence is that—not unlike Molloy himself—they are the sites of plural confusions; often, as mentioned above, barely distinguishable from one another: "And there are days, like this evening, when my memory confuses them and I am tempted to think of them as one and the same old hag, flattened and crazed by life."[13] And of course, much to his dismay, Molloy's blurring of these female figures extends to the very limits of taboo and shame: "And God forgive me, to tell you the horrible truth, my mother's image sometimes mingles with theirs, which is literally unendurable, like being crucified, I don't know why and I don't want to."[14] But is this lack of differentiation in any way a freeing or elevating of the figure of "woman," serving to dismantle her position as one in opposition to "man"? In fact, whether or not this particular problematization of gender is indicative of a promising shift in thinking about traditional categories, a freeing from that "mythic network imprisoning male and female" is perhaps not so easily answered as might be assumed.

The question demands a more thorough look at possibilities for negotiating gender roles. In the arena of gender, sexuality, and identities fixed within or with respect to these, Judith Butler is one theorist looking for innovative discursive options. Butler, in *Gender Trouble,* argued that gender identity discourse is intrinsic to the fictions of heterosexual coherence, and that feminists need to learn to produce narrative legitimacy for a whole array of noncoherent genders.[15] Gender identity discourse insists on the nonreducibility, even the antagonistic relation, of coherent women and men. The task at hand, then, is in fact to essentially "disqualify" the analytic categories, like sex or nature, that lead to univocity. This move would expose the illusion of an interior organizing gender core and produce a field of gender difference open to resignification. Butler's ideas concerning the "naturalness" of gender and her reconsidering of presumptions about sexuality have been extensively employed. The question—especially with respect to work such as Beckett's—becomes whether or not Butler's conceptualizations can be considered to simply imply that *any* subject gendered noncoherently, *any* character seemingly without a stable "core identity" and its corresponding fiction(s) is somehow indicative of the properly "feminist" identity, or rather, nonidentity. Is Molloy's extended dissolution, and the ways in which it provides for him to relate to other (gendered) characters, somehow a gender-negating/negotiating move?

The wavering character/voice in Beckett's trilogy, the "I" slipping in and out of the narrating position, is certainly an identity under attack, under an attack on many of identity's facets, from sexuality to physical presence to history and name. The "hero(es)" of these three Beckett narratives deteriorate from book to book, faster and faster; he—Molloy, Malone, Mahood, Worm—loses the use of his limbs, first gradually and then at a rapid pace, as the extensions of his body diminish as well, from bicycle to crutch to stick. Finally, the reader of the trilogy learns that, no longer able to even drag himself about, the final manifestation of this voice in *The Unnamable* finds himself restrained or jailed in a room, a shrinking one at that, in which his senses gradually abandon him. As Alain Robbe-Grillet writes of these barely-there Beckettian characters:

> Thus all these creatures which have paraded past us served only to deceive us; they occupied the sentences of the novel in place of the ineffable being who still refuses to appear there, the man incapable of recuperating his own existence, the one who never manages to be present.[16]

In Beckett's trilogy, we see this nonapparent man involved in failed or incomplete events, acts, and relationships; these are only ambiguous sites of what Butler terms masculine self-elaboration, the definitive occupying of a standardized "male" position. Also ambiguous is any intersex interaction, interaction that is frequently read as not significant enough for the evolution of one "type" of gendered figure or the marginalization of another. For example, the almost-affair with Lousse early in the trilogy, in *Molloy,* seems at most ambivalent. Molloy and Lousse meet only when the bicycle-riding Molloy accidentally runs over and kills Lousse's dog, a pet for whom he becomes a virtual substitute. He returns with Lousse to her home, staying on with her as a result of his own great passivity:

> And suddenly overcome by a great weariness, in spite of the dying day when I always felt most alive, I threw the bicycle back in the bush and lay down on the ground, on the grass, careless of the dew, I never feared the dew. It was then that Lousse, taking advantage of my weakness, squatted down beside me and began to make me propositions, to which I must confess I listened, absent-mindedly, I had nothing else to do, I could do nothing else, and doubtless she had poisoned my beer with something intended to mollify me, to mollify Molloy, with the result that I was nothing ore than a lump of melting wax, so to speak. And from these propositions, which she enunciated slowly and distinctly, repeating each clause several times, I finally elicited the following, or gist. I could not prevent her from having a weakness for me, neither could she. I would live in her home, as though it were my own.[17]

Though Lousse assumes the more active role in their pseudorelationship, in fact spying on and inspecting him after this initial, questionable seduction, both Lousse and Molloy are alternately the weaker figure or the controlling: she seduces, even poisons him, but only because he "had nothing else to do." He in fact sees her "but little" during the term of his stay, and can do nothing about the odd forces of attraction operating between them. Lousse's presence, her sex, her gender, her "love"—as one must somehow here speak of it—seem in the end of slight or no consequence as these are portrayed with respect to the narrator. He claims "I had nothing to lose, I would have made love to a goat to know what love was,"[18] and "I would have preferred it seems to me an orifice less arid and roomy, that would have given me a higher opinion of love it seems to me."[19] He even allows himself to wonder "if she was not a man rather or at least an androgyne. She had a somewhat hairy face, or am I imagining it, in the interests of the narrative?"[20] It does seem, in the end, rather unclear what or whom this tenuous hero thinks he desires or has. What is clear, on the other hand, is that the status of Lousse as a "woman," as a female body and biological woman, here fail to matter to him. Instead, the figure of this woman is conflated with much that has apparently little to do with her, an unsurprising process on the part of Molloy, who has already confessed to being tempted to think of all women as "one and the same old hag."

The episode with Lousse, whom Molloy first calls Loy, Mrs. Lousse, or Sophie is, together with the reminiscences of Molloy's affair with a certain Ruth inspired by it, one of the most prolonged [hetero]"sexual" encounters of the trilogy. In Cantrell's consideration of this scene, she points out that the forest out of which Molloy emerges represents "nature" and Lousse's house represents "culture," in a reversal of "the more usual association of man with culture and women with nature."[21] The problem, according to Cantrell, is that Beckett's text stops short of the would-be associated recognition of Lousse's achievement as a maker of culture, thereby selling this particular woman short of an entirely active role. Rather than something respected and worthwhile, Lousse's culture remains artifice, unnatural, as evidenced by *Molloy*'s general hostility toward women. Cantrell convincingly shows how this hostility operates for the purposes of Molloy's overall detachment—from self, body, world, family. But to illustrate this she must still rely on predictable dualisms, such as a nature/culture dichotomy drawn along gender lines, as well as on stereotypical gender roles, such as that of caretaker:

> Just as the novel excised and renamed her ["the woman reader's"] reproductive system, so it castigates and then eliminates the work of care which the sexual division of labor has assigned to her—care of the body, of the shelter, of the children. Somewhat to her surprise she finds that each monologue dwells at length on a rejection or inversion of this kind of care.[22]

In what is an otherwise rather reductive and generalizing analysis of "the woman reader" and "her" expectations, as well as in an unquestioning use of "the" sexual division of labor, Cantrell calls attention to an interesting and important point about the signification of gender in *Molloy*. She sees, in fact, how an implicit claim to the universal and normative is shaped for the narrator Molloy, a claim structured by the treatment of Lousse and her domain as typically, predictably feminine—"pink and transparent and adorned with ribands and lace"[23]—and as a place where Molloy clearly does not belong. Regardless of whether it represents nature or culture, male or female, caretaking or providing, the process of exclusion—along gendered lines—occurs here, displaying a dualistic hierarchy, one relying on the oppositions of male/female and inside/outside.

Molloy, of course, leaves Lousse; her home is clearly not his, her realm not fit for him to occupy for long. He is thoroughly indifferent to Lousse ("The poor woman, I saw her so little, so little looked at her"[24]), just as he was indifferent to the woman of a previous encounter, referred to with uncertainty as Ruth: "She went by the peaceful name of Ruth I think, but I can't say for certain. Perhaps the name was Edith."[25] Potentially productive for the creating of gender complexity is Beckett's use of this figure's relationship to Molloy to hint at androgyny, in gestures that clearly fuel the positive responses to his "liberatory" handling of gender roles. In remembering Edith/Ruth, one of the women he had "rubbed up against," Molloy notes that she had "a hole between her legs, oh not the bunghole I always imagined, but a slit."[26] Before too many lines pass, however, after she has bent over and he has wondered about true love, Molloy begins to wonder what kind of being this woman might be:

> She too was an eminently flat woman and she moved with short stiff steps, leaning on an ebony stick. Perhaps she too was a man, yet another of them. But in that case surely our testicles would have collided, while we writhed. Perhaps she held hers tight in her hand, on purpose to avoid it. She favoured voluminous tempestuous shifts and petticoats and other undergarments whose names I forget.[27]

Her stick is curiously reminiscent of Molloy's own artificial appendages. But the fact that testicles can be said to be "hers," that "she" can hold "hers tight in her hand," brings to mind the cross-gendering evident in Butler's quoting of a woman who "likes her boys to be girls."

What is interesting also is that these multiple confusions/blurrings take place only with the figure of *her*—she might be a man, while men are never potentially women in disguise. There is no such extended wondering about Molloy's having female genitalia, just a brief wondering about a knee that is clitoris-like. One could approach a consideration of Molloy, Mallone, the sometime "I" of these narratives, as exhibiting Butler's "heterosexual coherence." He is at the very least—or perhaps at most—a "he," and readable as such throughout much of the trilogy. He speaks of his specific body parts, their functions, and the occasional admitted sexual activity, if not pleasure. In *Molloy:*

> . . . when your frantic member casts about for a rubbing place . . .[28]

> She had a hole between her legs, oh not the bunghole I had always imagined, but a slit, and in this I put, or rather she put, my so-called virile member.[29]

> For waking again towards dawn, this time in consequence of a natural need, and with a mild erection.[30]

And in *Malone Dies:*

> Now my sex, I mean the tube itself, and in particular the nozzle, from which when I was yet a virgin clouts and gouts of sperm came streaming and splashing up into my face, a continuous flow, while it lasted, and which must still drip a little piss from time to time.[31]

Butler writes that such activities and pleasures are said to reside in certain body parts or organs, and such descriptions "correspond to a body which has already been constructed or naturalized as gender-specific."[32] In other words, some parts of the body become conceivable locations of pleasure precisely because they correspond to a normative ideal of a gender-specific body. Molloy's indifference toward, or confusion about, his sexual partner is potentially—and for some writers, definitely—exemplary of the refusal to become or to remain a "gendered" man or a woman, a refusal that is

> an eminently political insistence on emerging from the nightmare of the all-too-real, imaginary narrative of sex and race. Finally and ironically, the political and explanatory power of the "social" category of gender depends upon historicizing the categories of sex, flesh, body, biology, race, and nature in such a way that the binary, universalizing opposition that spawned the concept of the sex/gender system . . . implodes.[33]

But the gender confusion, the refusal, remains on the side of the female figure. This hero Molloy, Mallone, Mahood, Worm, with a rapidly deteriorating body that is sex-specific, with the partial but pertinent physical attributes of a man, performs this reasonably pathetic body as one constructed gender-specifically. One would certainly be hard-pressed to find evidence of a coherent character "Molloy," but whether or not that which Adrienne Rich was first to term "compulsory heterosexuality"[34] is also missing is questionable. It is clear that Beckett has shaped a tremendously fragmented figure in Molloy—one split between mind and body, ambivalence and action. It is not quite as clear, however, whether his radical indifference to his sexual partners somehow signifies more than the fact that they all are nevertheless women, that these are in fact heterosexual encounters, encounters between a man whose voice is shifting and a woman whose name he shifts himself.

> Consider gender, for instance, as a corporeal style, an "act," as it were, which is both intentional and performative, where "performative" suggests a dramatic and contingent construction of meaning.[35]

The arguments expounded in Butler's *Gender Trouble* maintain that the loss of gender norms would have the effect of proliferating gender configurations, destabilizing substantive identity, and depriving the naturalizing narratives of compulsory heterosexuality of their central protagonists: "man" and "woman."[36] Butler has written that "Categories of true sex, discrete gender, and specific sexuality have constituted the stable point of reference for a great deal of feminist theory and politics."[37] She naturally resists the stability of any "truth" of sex, as well as the move toward defining or redefining "man" and "woman," following Foucault's notion of identity and sexuality as effects of institutions, practices, discourses with multiple and diffuse points of origin. And as a result, Butler, along with other Foucauldian feminists, has been accused of elucidating a feminism without women, a feminism that asks whether feminist politics "can do without a 'subject' in the category of women."[38] But when one looks more closely and carefully at the terms of her argument, it should be discovered that there is a very real possibility of articulating a position somewhere *between* the eradicating or erasing of a subject defined by gender difference and the establishing of a "truth" of women and of men. It is a position that retains a certain specificity, as is revealed in Butler's development of the notion of performativity. Early in *Gender Trouble,* she introduces this notion, writing that

> *gender* is not a noun, but neither is it a set of free-floating attributes, for we have seen that the substantive effect of gender is performatively produced and compelled by the regulatory practices of gender coherence. Hence, within the inherited discourse of the metaphysics of substance, gender proves to be performative—that is, constituting the identity it is purported to be.[39]

It is upon this introduction of "performativity" that Butler is frequently misunderstood or oversimplified, considered to be advocating a certain arbitrariness about or simple choice in the matter of gender identity. In fact, her rethinking of gender categories is more complicated than a mere blurring of the typical male/female distinctions, and more specific than rendering "all conceptualization null and void." The "inner truth" of gender might be a fabrication, a discursive act, but Butler makes clear that it is not one without constraint. Writing after *Gender Trouble,* she clarifies the point that what has been understood as the performativity of gender is "neither free play nor theatrical self-presentation," and is "far from the exercise of an unconstrained voluntarism."[40] While Beckett's characters might be seen as freely and randomly trying on identities as they might try on a hat, Butler's gender performativity—her "styles of the flesh"—are historicized, contingent, and operating under constraint.[41] These are styles that are "never fully self-styled, for styles have a history, and those histories condition and limit the possibilities." And the negotiating of these possibilities becomes a matter of strategy and survival:

> because gender is a project which has cultural survival as its end, the term strategy better suggests the situation of duress under which gender performance always and variously occurs. Hence, as a strategy of survival within compulsory systems, gender is a performance with clearly punitive consequences.[42]

Butler's gender performativity and identity as *historicized* and *contextualized* complicate what Beckett's gender-interested critics are reading in the abstractness of the works. Attention to this abstractness should neither be a means for sidestepping issues of gender, nor should it be read as automatically indicative of some new, subversive, and idealistic sexuality. That gender, following Butler, is something performed both under coercion and as a strategy for surviving suggests that its realm is not that of the random play or free-for-all. So in the terms of *Gender Trouble's* debate, the notion of the simply noncoherent gender as opposed to the simply compulsory heterosexuality must necessarily be complicated. The question calls for the consideration and introduction of complexity through specificity, rather than the allowing of voluntaristic disordering to indicate a "postgender" world. Despite the exhaustive dismantling of the logic of identity, in Molloy's increasing emptiness one still finds meaning. The fragmented characters of the void are not so fragmentary as to exemplify an indictment of *all* logic or ordering. As Beckett moves from the dismissive "But what matter bodies?" to decide "here's hers anyway," we see that his dismantling of identity is, in fact, not always an indifferent process. Molloy's indifference grows into disdain for women, and the story narrated across the trilogy remains distinctly that of this character as he is developed in relation to others. His mother, Lousse, and Ruth provide narrative space for him to examine his foibles and frustrations, to lose himself in a language of exile, solitude, and death. The use of all of these characters as variously unsteady marks for sexuality and subjectivity does not, however, result in equanimity in the production of desire and definition. The differences indicate that gender in these earlier works of Beckett had yet to transcend certain predictable limitations, that bodies in the trilogy do matter in significant and specific ways even in their subcertain states.

Notes

1. Linda Ben-Zvi, ed., *Women in Beckett: Performance and Critical Perspectives* (Urbana: Un iversity of Illinois Press, 1990), p. 142.

2. Ibid., p. 140.

3. Linda Ben-Zvi, *Samuel Beckett* (Boston: Twayne Publishers, 1986), p. 85.

4. Ibid.

5. Samuel Beckett, *Three Novels by Samuel Beckett: Molloy, Malone Dies, The Unnamable* (New York: Grove Press, 1958), p. 169.

6. Ibid., p. 36.

7. Ben-Zvi, *Samuel Beckett*, p. 83.

8. See Herculine Barbin, *Herculine Barbin, dite Alexina B. / présenté par Michel Foucault* (Paris: Gallimard, 1978).

9. Carol Helmstetter Cantrell, "Cartesian Man and the Woman Reader," in *Women in Beckett: Performance and Critical Perspectives* (Urbana: University of Illinois Press, 1990), p. 123.

10. Angela B. Moorjani, "The Magna Mater Myth in Beckett's Fiction: Subtext and Subversion," in *Women in Beckett: Performance and Critical Perspectives* (Urbana: University of Illinois Press, 1990), p. 139.

11. Hélène Cixous and Catherine Clément, *The Newly Born Woman*, trans. Betsy Wing (Minneapolis: The University of Minnesota Press, 1991), p. xviii.

12. Denise Riley, *Am I That Name? Feminism and the Category of Women in History* (Minneapolis: The University of Minnesota Press, 1989), p. 112.

13. Beckett, *Three Novels*, p. 59.

14. Ibid.

15. See Judith Butler, *Gender Trouble: Feminism and the Subversion of Identity* (New York: Routledge, Chapman and Hall, 1990), esp. chapter 1, "Subjects of Sex/Gender/Desire."

16. Alain Robbe-Grillet, *For a New Novel: Essay on Fiction* (New York: Grove Press, 1965), p. xx.

17. Beckett, *Three Novels*, p. 47.

18. Ibid., p. 57.

19. Ibid., p. 58.

20. Ibid., p. 56.

21. Cantrell, "Cartesian Man," p. 128.

22. Ibid., p. 126.

23. Beckett, *Three Novels*, p. 44.

24. Ibid., p. 56.

25. Ibid.

26. Ibid.

27. Ibid., p. 57.

28. Ibid., p. 58.

29. Ibid., p. 56.

30. Ibid., p. 139.

31. Ibid., p. 235.

32. Butler, *Gender Trouble*, p. 70.

33. Donna J. Haraway, *Simians, Cyborgs, and Women: The Reinvention of Nature* (New York: Routledge, Chapman and Hall, 1991), p. 148.

34. See Adrienne Rich, *Compulsory Heterosexuality and Lesbian Existence* (Denver, Colo.: Antelope Publications, 1982), first published in *Signs* 5.4 (1980).

35. Butler, *Gender Trouble*, p. 139.

36. Ibid., p. 146.

37. Ibid., p. 128.

38. Ibid., p. 142.

39. Ibid., p. 25.

40. Judith Butler, *Bodies That Matter: On the Discursive Limits of "Sex"* (New York: Routledge, Chapman and Hall, 1991), pp. 93–95.

41. Butler, *Gender Trouble*, p. 139.

42. Ibid.

8

WHAT REMAINS?

Christopher Devenney

For it's the end gives meaning to the words.

—Samuel Beckett, *Texts for Nothing*

We always find something, eh Didi, to give us the impression we exist?

—Samuel Beckett, *Waiting for Godot*

It is true that one of the greatest difficulties involved in approaching the writings of Samuel Beckett arises from the repeated assaults his texts enact upon themselves, upon their own progress and self-generation, and thus also upon the contexts and resources of traditional literature. The storyteller's art is not Beckett's, and to the extent that his early writings—including the novels *Murphy* and *Watt,* and then later the first-person monologues of *Molloy* and *Malone Dies,* and to a lesser extent *The Unnamable*—unfold around various masks and faces, characters, narratives (of a sort), and plots it is only as a preliminary step intended ultimately to dispel precisely these. But for what? Toward what end? Because they have run their course, and exist now at best as relics of a cultural, artistic, and philosophic ethos of a false humanity. Because now, after the texts of Nietzsche and Wittgenstein, not to mention Proust and Woolf, how can we continue to speak seriously of a stable self, a fixed and inert stratum of *res cogitans* that somehow grounds and stabilizes both the self and the world from a place apart from the movements and instances of language and grammar? Or, in more literary terms, isn't it clear by now that there are only slight differences between what is referred to as literary character and the Cartesian *ego cogito ergo sum?*

From the very beginning of Beckett's career as a writer, long before the stories or the novels of the trilogy were begun, it was clear that it would be impossible to simply continue in the vein of English (and Irish) letters already set forth. In a letter written in German to Axel Kaun in 1937 and published in 1983 as "The German Letter of 1937" he asserted:

> it is indeed becoming more and more difficult, even senseless, for me to write an official English. And more and more my own language appears to me like a veil that must be torn apart in order to get at the things (or the Nothingness) behind it. Grammar and style. To me they seem to have become as irrelevant as a Victorian bathing suit or the imperturbability of a true gentleman. . . . Is there any reason why that terrible materiality of the word surface should not be capable of being dissolved?[1]

There are a number of questions raised here; for instance, what exactly would constitute an "official English" for an Irish writer such as Beckett? What is the veil that his own language—whatever that is—appears as which "must be torn apart"? What does it conceal? Despite the appearance of a program of an "assault against words," as it is said elsewhere in the letter, and the tearing asunder of the "veil" of language, phrases that intimate a certain program of writing outwardly sympathetic to the various assaults mounted by avant-garde writers of the early twentieth-century, the references to "grammar and style"—"to me they seem to have become as irrelevant as a Victorian bathing suit or the imperturbability of a true gentleman"—reflect a different direction. Initially, the references to grammar and style indicate an unmistakable impulse on Beckett's part to distance himself from the practitioners of what he had referred to in his essay on Joyce ten years earlier as the "architects of literary stylistics"—in other words, the forebears of the literary styles that make up, and continue the progress of literary culture in the British and Irish contexts. Undoubtedly he has Joyce in mind, but also writers such as Keats, or Tennyson, Swift, Sterne, Coleridge, and so on. In the late 1960s Beckett commented to the critic Richard Coe that he was afraid of English: "you couldn't help writing poetry in it."[2] Marjorie Perloff adds that "this is not . . . a facetious remark . . . English for Beckett is, after all the language of his childhood, more specifically, the canonical language of 'English literature' as taught to a school boy at the Portora Royal School" where he would undoubtedly have been indoctrinated into the long and weighty stream of British tradition from Shakespeare and Milton, to Keats, Tennyson, and Arnold.[3]

But it was not just from the English style that Beckett sought refuge, but rather style in general, in any guise or form. "Let us hope the time will come," he states in the letter, "thank God that in certain circles it has already come, when language is most efficiently used where it is most efficiently misused." What is meant here by misuse, though, is left purposely ambiguous; apart from declaring that "with such a program . . . the latest work of Joyce has nothing whatsoever to do" his only reference is to Stein: "perhaps the logographs of Gertrude Stein are nearer to what I have in mind. At least the texture of language has become porous" (D, 172). But with Stein, at least in Beckett's view, the endeavor has unfolded by accident; she remains, he claims, "in love with her vehicle." Strangely, though, as Beckett offers no examples of what he means by "misuse," the efficient misuse of language that he refers to seems to have a double meaning; on the one hand "misuse" may in fact be language's so-termed correct usage according to grammatical and conventional strictures; while on the other hand, and more typically, the efficient use of language as its "misuse" appears to be meant as a conscious disarticulation of correct usage that he, along with a select number of other writers, has begun to enact in his writing. In either case, inasmuch as style is always to one degree or another a mode or form of accommodation, even consolation that completes, however artificially, the distance that separates a consciousness from the world of things and experience, it is something that must be avoided. Though it may be a departure from realist conventions and more traditional practices of the novel, the religion of style as practiced by a Flaubert—"I value style first and above all, and then Truth"[4]—is to be resisted as much as any other, whether that be the word-apotheosis of a Joyce, or the logographs of a Stein.

But Beckett appears to go even farther than this: "As we cannot eliminate language all at once," he adds, "we should at least leave nothing undone that might contribute to its falling into disrepute. To bore one hole after another in it, until what lurks behind—be it something or nothing—begins to seep through. I cannot imagine a higher goal for a writer today" (D, 172). This goal, which Beckett views as the highest goal for a writer today, is meant in the most extreme sense; ultimately, it is aimed not simply against the strictures and conventions of literary or ordinary language. In the letter Beckett asks Kaun if he minds his errors in German, and then says "from time to time I have the consolation . . . of sinning will-nilly against a foreign language, as I should love to do with full knowledge and intent against *my own*—and as I shall do" (D, 173). Again, though, what Beckett means by "my own" language remains unclear. Conventionally, it would mean his own English. But the fact that Beckett ultimately opted to write in French, only later rewriting his texts in English, suggests that what he has in mind is a full-scale assault not only against English but also against *his own* language, against that language wherein the integrity of a (or *the*) self is at once established and maintained. It is to be an assault against what Beckett termed in his monograph on Proust in 1931 "the great deadening of habit."[5]

Habit, like style, is what sutures a kind of tenuous rapport with the world as it is given in language through the tonality and grace of speech, rhyme, and meter. Style in general, styles of expression, styles of speech are all indexes of habit, of habituation, and habitation, which underwrites the very habits of thought, of speaking, of writing, and of reading within which we live and dwell. These are what must be broken. Though Beckett's point, however discretely, goes farther than this to challenge not only our adherence to a certain aesthetic sensibility, but to challenge our continued cleaving to stable forms of life, to the forms of language that affirm the given and presumed order of reality and being, to the oft-termed real existing conditions that habit perpetuates. Before what Beckett termed "the perpetuum" of reality, human beings enact and reenact according to the change-ability of existence and subjects certain orderings of the world. These orderings, though, are first and foremost orderings both of and *in* language. It is not a matter or question of specific impositions—rightly or wrongly imposed—but rather the habit of imposition as such. It is these habits of expression, habits of thought, of speaking, of reading, and writing that Beckett's writing seeks to unsettle. And it would appear, too, that he has in mind his own habits of expression as much as anyone elses. "Habit," Beckett wrote, "is a compromise effected between the individual and his environment." It is the "guarantee of a dull inviolability. . . . Habit is the ballast that chains the dog to his vomit. Breathing is habit. Life is habit" (pp. 18–19).

℘

It would take Beckett ten years to fully arrive at what was necessary to begin the dissolution of the "terrible materiality of the word surface." This process is what was undertaken in the late 1940s in the turn to French and the writing in quick succession of the texts of the trilogy—*Molloy, Malone meurt,* and *L'Innomable*—as well as the plays *Waiting for Godot* and *Endgame,* and the earlier stories.

Concerning these texts and this period in his work, in the only formal interview he ever gave during his lifetime, Beckett remarked that:

> At the end of my work (*À la fin de mon oeuvre*) there's nothing but dust— the namable. In the last book—*L'Innommable*—there's complete disin- tegration. No "I," no "have," no "being." No nominative, no accusative, no verb. There's no way to go on.[6]

Beckett's remark is a wry illustration of the very circumstance he's describing. He refers to the "end of my work" and then comments, "In the last book— *L'Innomable*—there's complete disintegration"; this would seem to be the end of the matter, but it's not. He continues on and says: "No 'I,' no 'have,' no 'being,'" and so on, "there's no way to go on." Beckett's own words seem to parallel the final despair of the unnamable: "perhaps they have carried me to the threshold of my story, before the door that opens on my story, that would surprise me, if it opens, it will be I, it will be the silence, where I am, I don't know, I'll never know, in the silence you don't know, you must go on, I can't go on, I'll go on."[7]

Who are "they" who have carried the unnamable to the threshold of his story? The various narrators who have preceded? Molloy and Malone, Mahood, Worm, as well as the earlier incarnations of Murphy, and Watt? Speaking of Mahood, his temporary cipher, the unnamable remarks: "Before him there were others, taking themselves for me, it must be a sinecure handed down from generation to generation" (U, 315). He refers to Mahood as well as the others as "vice-existers" (ibid.), essentially occluding access to what must be said, to what or who is actually speaking. But these occlusions, the occlusions of names and masks, are but respites from an even more fundamental occlusion. In a phrase a few lines before the reference to Mahood and the others that at once evokes the scenic beginning of *Waiting for Godot* as well as a parody of Hegel's famous words about the spirit enduring death, winning its truth, the unnamable remarks: "allow me to think of myself as somewhere on a road, moving between a beginning and an end, gaining ground, losing ground, getting lost, but somehow in the long run making headway. *All lies.* I have nothing to do, that is to say nothing in particular. I have to speak, whatever that means. Having nothing to say, no words but the words of others, I have to speak. No one compels me to, there is no one, it's an accident, a fact" (U, 314, emphasis mine). He has nothing here but the "words of others," and the scene or setting of a road, the circumstance of gaining and losing ground, but getting somewhere—"all lies." An accident is indistinguishable from a fact; aptly evoking the circumstance of the Cartesian ego who can simply assert doubt as an absolute rule, the unnamable declares "nothing can lessen what remains to say, I have the ocean to drink, so there's an ocean then" (ibid.). Each effort, each word generated in order to end produces a new obstacle to be overcome: "I have an ocean to drink, so there's an ocean then." In the movement toward the end, toward completion—"with every inane word a little nearer to the last"—the end withdrawals, and the movement toward the end becomes instead the infinite detour of the end.

"You must go on, *I can't go on*, I'll go on." In the interview Beckett goes on to note that in the texts that followed, entitled collectively *Textes pour rien,* there "was an attempt to get out of the attitude of disintegration" but, as he remarks rather tersely, "it failed" (ibid.). In what direction was the attempt to get out of the attitude of disintegration aimed? Was it that Beckett sought initially to avoid disintegration, and wrote on in the hopes of ascending from this circumstance, only to fail over and over? Or was disintegration in some sense always the end or goal, repeated and ever more intense failures the point? Or was there something even more fundamental or essential beyond disintegration that was sought? To look more closely at Beckett's description of the end of his work reveals that the dust is indeed an end—"nothing but dust"—but an end no sooner arrived at than it too is deserted, given up—the namable. But desertion here is neither an abandonment nor a leaving behind, nor finally a passage to a more fundamental realm. Rather, desertion is a matter of something even more essential having to do with the disjunction between words and the absence of the world that the experience of words brings to light. Not just the absence of the world, or a world, but also the absence of language, the fact that in some sense what is being undertaken is a departure from the consolation of a "true" language that is still somehow connected to the world. The "namable" (dust) gives itself over to the immutability of the "unnamable" trace for which there is ultimately no word—"no 'I', no 'have', no 'being'"—in relation to which words and language remarkably perdures nonetheless. And in this we discover the ultimate paradox suffusing Beckett's work; on the one hand, resistant to language, to self-expression and dialectical incorporation, resistance can only be determined in the very language from which escape is sought. But the path of escape is continually obscured by the images, the voices, the figures, the characters and identities, the endless proliferation of shapes, narratives, and narrations, that suggest the outline of a legible and identifiable presence. "It's myself I hear," says the unnamable, "howling behind my dissertation. So not any old thing. Even Mahood's stories are not any old thing, though no less foreign, to what, to that unfamiliar native land of mine, as unfamiliar as that other where men come and go, and feel at home, on tracks they have made themselves" (U, 314). What is there, as Beckett reveals, is something excessive and illegible, not *a* world, unfamiliar behind or apart, but still very much a part of the void that in the Proust-like match-strike of illumination is at once revealed and withdrawn. What remains is a linguistic landscape made barren by the unrelenting process of violation that it has suffered, which remarkably enacts its own violation by remaining nonetheless, by holding to itself. Defenseless, denuded of significance and signification, what remains is interminable, inexhaustible, inevitable.

❧

What Beckett is asking is "do we in fact know the language we speak"? We hear this in the terse opening of *The Unnamable:* "Where now? Who now? When now? Unquestioning. I, say I." The insistence of the questions of "where," "who," and "when," the traditional questions that govern the expectations of narrative and plot are raised, but no sooner raised than they are erased, made irrelevant by the word "unquestioning." But it is not just literary language, the language of plot and narrative that is put into question here; in addition, space (where?), being (who?), and time (when?), in short the philosophical prerequisites to a world, the grounds against which a self would ask of itself "who am I" or "what am I" are eliminated as well. But, as Beckett's opening makes clear, jettisoned or not, something remains, something or someone is doing the jettisoning: "Unquestioning. I, say I." This is Cartesian hyperbolic doubt turned back upon itself, and carried forth to its logical extreme. Let us consider the words again: "Where now? Who now? When now? Unquestioning. I, say I. Unbelieving." Are

these two words, "unquestioning" and "unbelieving," that surround the determinations of the ego meant as adjectives describing the state of the self, of the "I"
who says "I." Or are they meant as transitive verbs enacting a dismantling of the
structures of belief and the logical predicates of the principle of sufficient reason?
Or, lastly, are they simply meant as intransitive verbs characterizing a pure state of
being and self? The answer is most likely all of these. The willed act of "unbelieving" generates the initial doubt against "where," "who," and "when," and leads
further to the active "un-questioning" and "unbelieving." Still, something remains; the "I" of "I, say I." But as a verb this same unquestioning makes of the "I,
say I," a fraud or conceit uttered idly in the face of nothing else left to say.
Nevertheless, "unbelieving," it—who?—continues to speak: "Questions, hypotheses, call them that. Keep going, going on, call that going, call that on," all in a
vain search for "me," for "I," or "who" or "what"?

The illusion of the unnamable's beginning from which the movement toward an end is begun is perfected in one of Beckett's late texts, *Worstward Ho*. The
artifice is demonstrated as a singular and perhaps inevitable motivation to begin in
order to end: "On. Say on. Be said on. Somehow on. Till nohow on."[8] Here, the
voice (by this point in his career Beckett had long since abandoned the image of
character), noting that it stands in proximity to an unreachable void, remarks
enigmatically, "It stands. See in the dim void how at last it stands. . . . A place.
Where none" (NO, 92). But seeing cannot see, and saying cannot say what stands
in the dimness of the void, the place where none. What hope there is to become
this place, this place "where none," this desert which is the place of place, the
absolute itself is, after twenty-seven pages of the most unsparing prose, dashed:
"Such last state. Latest state. Till somehow less in vain. Worse in vain. All gnawing
to be naught. Never to be naught" (NO, 115).

The only language here is one of hypothesis, an imagined language, or the
image of a language. The images of beginning—"On. Say on. Be said on. Somehow on. Till nohow on."—and ending—"Such last state"—are given in their
expected places, their grounding registers intact. But the last state, as the text
indicates, is in fact not the last—"all gnawing to be naught"—not the end, but
only "such" last state, as if to suggest not the last but only the latest state, barely
discernible in fact from the state of the beginning which, at its time or position,
was itself quite possibly the "latest state."

Still, we are inclined to make things easier on ourselves, and presume here a
movement, a "progression," albeit a negative progression toward a certain purity of
expression and sight. But the situation is quite different than this. "Never to be
naught" because the situation, as he will write in the dramatic work *A Piece of
Monologue*, may simply be that "Birth was the death of him. Again. Words are few.
Dying too," and then, several lines later, "Dying on. No more no less. No less. Less
to die. Ever less."[9] Indeed, the paralysis implied by the speaker's indecision—"no

more no less"—is palpable until he declares definitively "no less," as if to say that dying is always less, "ever less," though never final. To be born in this sense without an end that can be said or conceived is already to be dead, and writing, which may begin as an attempt to fill in this space that is void and lacking, only draws out the definitiveness of this incomplete void and voiding space. Such, as the title of one of Beckett's most uncompromising prose works suggests, may indeed be *how it is.*

∞

Beckett's art is an art that aspires to be ever less, in the extreme to be nothing—"only just almost never"—an art of zero. Virtually all of his works unfold by way of bewildering processes of formation and de-formation, serial self-cancellation, affirmations deprived of content—"all I say cancels out"—assertion and contradiction, willed impoverishment, all in a quest for perfect stasis, impotence, nothing. In Raymond Federman's words, from one book to the next Beckett's writing reveals "a deliberate process of disintegration" that "reduces form and content, setting and characters, to a system whereby composition takes place during decomposition."[10] This is indeed correct, but the deliberateness of this movement or progress is paradoxically a deliberate movement toward incompletion, apart from what could be called in any traditional or *meaningful* sense progress or development. In Blanchot's phrase, Beckett's writing is an "experiment without results, yet continuing with increasing purity from book to book."[11] This purity for which Beckett's writing continually strives, though, while it may indeed increase can never be completed or realized fully; what could it mean to purely arrive at no result or end? Things can be vanquished only so far. This is well known, though just as well known is this: this is impossible. A hundred or so pages bound together and set beneath the heading of a title, filled with words and sentences, spare or not, can never be nothing. It must all, in the end, be something.

Beckett, though, was always aware of this. The assault against words, and the repudiation of grammar and style, as it is described in the 1937 letter, takes the following form: "Let us therefore act like that mad (?) mathematician who used a different principle of measurement at each step of his calculation" (D, 173). This is indeed an *undeveloping,* one designed to never end or arrive, as the principles of measurement can be altered, changed, reconceived and figured differently *ad infinitum.* Later, in the "Texts for Nothing," Beckett will suggest a similar paradox: "all you have to do is say you said nothing and so say nothing again."[12] The point to both of these statements, remarkable, even astonishing as it may seem, is that even when saying nothing it must all in the end be something, if only because it was said in the first place, and the only recourse is to say nothing, and then say it again, and again, because nothing, inanity can always be transformed into something. In *Waiting for Godot* Didi remarks "this is all becoming really insignificant," to which Gogo responds, "Not enough."

If there is any sort of systematic undoing or undeveloping in Beckett's writing, it is one that proceeds through the dilemmas proposed in the Cartesian splitting of the subject and object where the subjective will assumes a preeminance, exceeding even the fundamental grounds of self-knowledge, the *cogito,* such that doubt is indeed absolute. Am I speaking? It appears that *I* am, but *am I?* On what ground or basis may I declare that *I am* speaking. At best, it appears that *I am* a hunch, a bet, and not altogether a good one. This is the register of the unnamable, that for which there is no name, no pronoun, no verb, no case. In short the howling silence of a self and mind cut adrift, permitted to assume its absolute prerogatives of willful annihilation up to and including the point of itself. And still something remains.

In the "Texts for Nothing," we read: "How many hours to go, before the next silence, they are not hours, it will not be silence, how many hours still, before the next silence? Ah to know for sure, to know that this thing has no end, this thing, this thing, this farrago of silence and words, of silence that is not silence and barely murmured words. Or to know it's life still, a form of life, ordained to end, as others ended and will end, till life ends, in all its forms. Words, mine was never more than that, than this pell-mell babel of silence and words, my viewless form described as ended, or to come, or still in progress, depending on the words" (CSP, 125). Who is this one who says "mine," who says my life was never more than "words," who says the hours were not hours, the silences were not silence, but only their facsimiles? How even could one answer this question? Only with yet another word—him, or her, or I, or me, or someone, or *something.* Perhaps it's just life— life speaking, as if it, or this could—but then what is this if not also just a word? Here is the unsurpassable "attitude" of disintegration; but this realization—if it can even be termed this—still doesn't make for any sort of progression. There are always more, or new, or different words, or forms and formations of words, forms of life. The *attitude* of disintegration is indeed inescapable, but that's of little consequence. In *Waiting for Godot* Estragon quips, "We are incapable of keeping silent," to which Vladimir immediately responds: "You're right, we're inexhaustible."[13] And with one certain affirmation, an entire world and existence can be deduced. After asserting his inability to control his bowels—"I can't help it, gas escapes from my fundament on the least pretext" (M, 30)—Molloy takes up a count of exactly how many times per day he farts. The number at first appears excessive—"Three hundred and fifteen farts in nineteen hours" (ibid.)—but after some division it comes down to a mere "four farts every fifteen minutes," which he concludes is less than one every four minutes. "Extraordinary how mathematics help you to know yourself" (ibid.).

What Beckett is alluding to here and throughout is the strange temptation toward order and stability that always underlies the disintegrative attitude. Another system, another regime based upon different premises and axioms, is always possible—indeed all-too-possible. In *How It Is,* for example, we see a more ominous recognition of the inevitable recourse to forms of regularity and conformity in an otherwise chaotic and disintegrating world:

> at the instant I reach Pim another reaches Bem we are regulated thus our justice wills it thus fifty thousand couples again at the same instant the same everywhere with the same space between them it's mathematical it's our justice in this muck where all is identical our ways and way of fairing right leg right arm push pull.[14]

And throughout this austere, often decrepit tale of a voice with a body crawling, panting, murmuring across an endless mudflat toward his other, Pim, there are references to "dear figures," ratios of order, calculation, measurement; impostions that refer as much to the otherworldly scene itself as to the tripartite division of the text: "dear figures when all fails a few figures to wind up with part one before Pim the golden age the good moments" and then "sudden swerve therefore left it's preferable forty-five degrees and two yards straight line such is the force of habit then right angle and straight ahead four yards dear figures then left right angle and beeline four yards then right right angle so on till Pim" (H, 47). It's dizzying. You follow it!

Such attentions to order and measure, though, are constantly repeated, here in *How It Is,* and in the other *residua,* "All Strange Away," "Imagination Dead Imagine," "Ping," *The Lost Ones.* Indeed, in these as well as the other later writings, the settings become increasingly strange and barren. We have departed the solipsistic confines of a self-contradicting "I," and its various locales—bed chambers, urns, jars, and so on—for ever more denuded and barren spaces: skulls, cylindrical enclosures mathematical in design, bare rooms, endless mudflats, unlocatable darkness in which silence becomes perfect company. What Beckett's minimal, and ultimately nonrepresentational settings in these later texts effect is a sharply drawn distinction between, on the one hand, a kind of minimal, but unrelenting presence, and on the other hand, an absence intimated, but never realized as such, between the regimes of order that make up the textual spaces and the world, the something up there. This is what is developed, intensified, extended to its most extreme. But it is ultimately the brute fact of the settings themselves, language-spaces as such, apart from any reference places or a world beyond or outside, that reveals the language as a space of absence. A place, to be certain, but a place that is no place inasmuch as it relentlessly signifies nothing other than itself and its own inexhaustibility, admitting of ever-more strange, but precise regimes of order. The increasing focus or turn inward in these writings, a turn that would seem to be the only viable alternative toward something sure and certain over against the realization that the external world and settings of conventional fiction are merely artifice, is in fact no less illusory than the external world of places and things. These inner worlds or domains—even when their dimensions are explicitly reported as in *The Lost Ones,* "inside a flattened cylinder fifty metres round and sixteen high for harmony"—are never truly accessible, they can never be reached or fully adumbrated. The measurements, precise though they may be, are only, as Beckett's text says, "for harmony."

But the same "harmony" extends to the figure or figures of the speaking self, I, or "I." Who, to paraphrase the question Maurice Blanchot asked in the late 1940s in reference to *The Unnamable,* is this I who says at the outset of *How It Is* "how it was I quote before Pim with Pim after Pim how it is three parts I say it as I hear it" (H, 7)? We don't know. We can't know. We'll never know. Apart from a reference to "voice once without quaqua on all sides then in me" (H, 7), there is no intimation anywhere of an identity that is separate from the movement of quotation that underwrites the entire text—"how it was I quote." But the source of the quotation, the original or originating voice now being quoted—"I say it as I hear it"—is absent as well, and if it is a narrative of recollection or memory, it is one without a genuine or reliable source, be it elsewhere or in the narrating voice: "what about it my memory we're talking of my memory not much that it's getting better that it's getting worse that things are coming back to me nothing is coming back to me but to conclude from that" (H, 15). At best all we can discern here is that the source is *not I.* But then who, or what?

This is an impossible text, without beginning or end save that which is arbitrarily invented. It begins: "How it was I quote before . . ." and so forth; and ends by declaring first that the entirety was false, the entire ordeal of crawling toward Pim, being with Pim, and then leaving Pim to await Bim, the figure for whom the narrator will now perform the same role Pim performed for it was false, it never happened, and then even more remarkably that the entirety could have been read or told in reverse. But within this strange narrative the relationship between the narrator and Pim, the sole object of the narration, is one of tormentor and victim. Finally reached, Pim, in part two, becomes the inert, speechless victim taught to speak by the narrator in a gruesome parody of pedagogy and communicative rationality. What *How It Is* displays is the possibility that orders and regimes are in no need whatsoever of a ground or foundation. A novel can, as it were, simply create itself, however strangely or paradoxically. More chilling, though, the invention of *How It Is* appears to run parallel to the same invention of orders and sequences, schemes of organization and hierarchy that define political reality. An order is always possible, because narrative inventiveness is strangely inexhaustible.

∝

There's no getting past it except by an ever-more attentive vigilance. From a critical standpoint, we do well to take seriously what Beckett said in his essay on Joyce's *Work in Progress,* "Dante . . . Bruno . . . Vico . . . Joyce," namely, that the "danger is in the neatness of identifications" where the reader-critic, involved endlessly in the process of tracing allusions and lines of influence in order to maintain the domesticated sight-lines of reading and understanding, becomes in effect, as William Carlos Williams suggested, a conservator of the past. Beckett says simply: "literary criticism is not book-keeping" (D, 19). The same point is made over and over in the writing; faced with this Nowhere and Nothing, the plight of the reader is addressed explicitly in the set of interpretive instructions offered by the unnamable in the form of the following introductory self-commentary: "What am I to do, what shall I do, what should I do in my situation, how proceed? By aporia pure and simple? Or by affirmations and negations invalidated as uttered, or sooner or later? Generally speaking. There must be other shifts. Otherwise it would be quite hopeless. But it is quite hopeless. I should mention before going any further, any further on, that I say aporia without knowing what it means" (U, 291). But with this said, proceed he does. As does Beckett.

Over the years since Beckett's writing first gained notoriety, a convention of sorts has grown around this predicament that states that Beckett's writing is steeped in a numbing "meaninglessness," leads nowhere, and is politically and ethically irresponsible and thus demands a critique and redressing according to the strictures of Lukàcs's social realism. Another version of this, slightly less polemical, is that his writing reflects a reductive and halting "absurdity" demanding interpretive silence. In both cases, however, these conclusions have been assumed too quickly. To say nothing, or to remain silent in relation to Beckett's writing is in no way to come closer to interpretive or hermeneutic authenticity. And to claim "meaninglessness" as the "meaning," as Martin Esslin realized too late, defeats the very purpose of the claim.

The issue is that if in relation to Beckett's writings there is indeed an inability to say anything, then this inability paradoxically becomes the absolute imperative that we must say. For it has not yet been said. Or, having been said, it must be said again. It bears repeating. This is the lesson of *The Unnamable.* Meaninglessness cannot be asserted as the meaning of Beckett's texts, and silence before them is irresponsible. To speak bluntly, we don't yet deserve this. If this is indeed all meaningless, as so many seem to agree, then as Adorno remarked, it is "not because of the absence of meaning—then they [Beckett's texts] would be irrelevant—but because they debate meaning."[15] This, though, is precisely the point of frustration and confusion, for it would seem that in Beckett's writing the debate is endless, and moreover never undertaken in terms of one specific meaning over against another, never according to the specifics of one or another position. Rather, what is debated here is meaning *as such*, the *ideology of meaning* that proceeds from the basis of *ego cogito ergo sum*, but that in fact, as Beckett shows with an almost obsessive drive, is only the imaginary suturing that links *cogito* with *sum*. If meaninglessness is indeed the end—but it is in no way clear that this is so—then it is, as Adorno again puts it, an "evolved and thereby equally deserved meaninglessness" (AT, 221). And yet, the temptation to silence is immense. The last text of the *residua*, the last but certainly not the end, explicitly suggests this temptation by speaking only of the silence and the time still to come: "Such and much more such the hubbub in his mind so-called till nothing left from deep within but only ever fainter oh to end. No matter how no matter where. Time and grief and self so-called. Oh all to end" (CSP, 265). Such is the temptation of reading—"such and much more such"—and the time still to come, the time of the end, the time of completion is only a vague outline, a promissory note upon which payment may or may not follow. The book to be written on Beckett, despite the volumes already written and published, is still to come. It will always be this way. In the same way that the end, the last is constantly deferred and displaced by the very movement of words that would seek to arrive, to accomplish precisely this end, the book will also always be still to come.

These, in brief, are the reasons given by Beckett to speak, to say, and say again, to continue, if only in order to end, to get a little closer, to finish, to say what remains. What remains? Such is the difficulty of *writing on*, of writing toward, or to, or about the text of Beckett.

The lesson of Beckett, or so it would seem, is that meaning, even in the least conducive occasions and instances, is quite inescapable. And this is not simply an intellectual or an aesthetic issue. When we teach our children to write and develop arguments, to create and punctuate sentences correctly according to grammatical rules and regulae, or when our teachers produce finely developed rhetorical arguments, we affirm, by reproducing, a specific political state of affairs; political in the widest sense of the word in which the commonality of order and coherence are presumed, expectations of habit affirmed, and development proceeds as a natural outcome of the movement of thought as it appears and has appeared in the world. We speak of a "mother tongue," a cultural and cultured language, a language of thought, of reason; though when we repeat and reproduce this "mother tongue," we reproduce what Benjamin called the "habitual expression of its sterility."[16] This is what Beckett's writing is resisting. And yet, while it is possible to assert that the resistance to this ordered and ordering development is political, the actual political implications of this resistance are unclear, and moreover must remain necessarily so. The unnamable puts it thus: "The thing to avoid, I don't know why, is the spirit of system." It would be one thing to avoid or resist the spirit of system on the basis of a certain awareness, a conscious and intended resistance that would in effect be to replace one order with another, but it is an entirely different, and ultimately more challenging matter to avoid system for who knows what reason. And in this, in its resistance to development, a resistance that is actually an outright refusal of that process whereby the continuity of narrative, of developed and developing language according to certain regimes of organization is refused, we find a refusal not only of an intellectual and artistic order, but a political state of affairs as well. The "meanings" that assert themselves in political terms are not immune from this self-same grafting. Politics and the languages of politics are but one and the same; each bespeak a kind of organization, an adaptation in language according to certain rules to conditions and circumstances. The rules, though, are the issue. For they are endlessly adaptable. Molloy can organize himself according to the temporality of his gaseous discharges, or, as the famous stone sucking episode reveals, he can spend his time devising schemes by which to rotate sixteen stones in a circulating movement from his pockets to his mouth—"extraordinary how mathematics help you to know yourself."

A writing—be it fictional or critical—that would proceed according to a presumption of either originality or a seamless grounding within the fabric of a national literature becomes violent, even murderous with respect to the otherness of the world and the experience it seeks to portray. In this scheme or system of valuation each, to return for a moment to the Proust study, "counts for nothing" and are reduced simply to the level of a "notion" (P, 53). The decompositions of conventional reality rendered in Swann's flights of involuntary fantasy actually result in a voluntaristic reuniting, albeit in the imaginative faculty of the now detached and isolated artist. Hence, Beckett's paradoxical proclamation: "The artistic tendency is not expansive, but a contraction. Art is the apotheosis of solitude," where solitude serves to magnify and bring into sharp focus the impossibility of authentic expression (P, 64). "Even on the rare occasions," Beckett continues, "when word and gesture happen to be valid expressions of personality they lose their significance on their passage through the cataract of the personality that is opposed to them. Either we speak and act for ourselves—in which case speech and action are distorted . . . or else we speak and act for others in which we speak and act a lie. . . . We are alone. We cannot know and cannot be known" (P, 64).

જી

This is one implication of Beckett's apothegmatized phrase "imagination dead imagine," to cite one of the later *residua*. The piece begins: "No trace anywhere of life, you say, pah, no difficulty there, imagination not dead yet, yes, dead, good, imagination dead imagine" (CSP, 182). In addition to much else, there is at once a warning and an urging in these words; a warning: beware, "no trace anywhere of life," no trace of the Word, no trace of that animating power out of which develops the belief in content and intrinsic meaning, the unifying transcendent mediation of language and the word; and an urging: go ahead, speak, write, indeed you must, you have no choice. The next sentence makes this explicit: "Islands, waters, azure, verdure, one glimpse and vanished, endlessly, omit" (CSP, 182). An image is forming. That animistic power whereby language annexes and makes over the world in its image is in play. But it vanishes: "one glimpse and vanished." The object or objects—"islands, waters"—and their respective colors are seen, duly noted, and taken over in the artistic vision that isolates and detaches things from their utility in the world in order to make them *useful* for art; then elevated by the fluidity of stylization—"azure, verdure"—through which the objects become image, become art. But this isolation of objects from their quotidian schemes, this solitude is not enough; true seeing, true perception begins only when the object seen has been lost, dissolved completely. Thus far, though, the notions of value and utility are still intact. One reads these words only at the point when the image, the image *qua* image, disappears behind yet another image, that of words, the neutral point where it all becomes nothing revealed. But not forever, not definitively or finally; rather "endlessly." The quest to see is endless. There's no victory. The last words of the passage "endlessly, omit," separated as they are by a comma, give us to see the glimpse and the vanishing both as "endless," and the process of cancellation as similarly "endless." And the two neatly divided impulses, the one toward a kind of linguistic fabulation, the other toward silence and nothingness— "endlessly, omit"—coexist simultaneously.

The impossibility of stopping is even more pronounced in the companion piece to "Imagination Dead Imagine" entitled "Ping." Here a voice utters a series of murmured phrases, vaguely asserting a congruence of shape, form, and sound: "All known all white bare white body fixed," and "Legs joined like sewn heels," "Eyes alone," Head haught," "White ceiling never seen ping of old only just almost never," "ping of old perhaps there," "ping of old only just perhaps a meaning a nature." The disposition here of images—legs, eyes, a ceiling, a head, and so on—produces, or threatens to produce, however faintly, an image of a naked human being alone in a room. However, as the image comes closer to becoming fully realized, and thus closer to establishing itself as a meaning-ful entity, the occurrences of "ping" become more frequent, more insistent. Over against the illusion of fiction, the image of the Word, the sound/concept/word "ping" ceaselessly interrupts the flow and permutations of the utterances to act as a sort of non-sensical commentary upon the flow of the narrative. Sometimes, though, it appears sown into the movement as if it was "something," as if it was a discernible element belonging both to the time and space of the narrative—"ping of old perhaps there" and "ping of old only just perhaps a meaning a nature." But what is, or could be "ping of old"? The answer is arrestingly simple; the text says: "only just perhaps a meaning a nature." The image, as it is unfolded in the story, finally lapses at the precipice of materializing: "traces blurs signs no meaning" and "ping silence over ping" (CSP, 193). Ping is simply ping. No more, though most definitely no less.

"Ping" belongs, however strangely, to a level of language at which, or within which one speaks of fiction. What we may say is that it belongs to the metal-anguage of commentary and criticism that continually breaks and ruptures the surface of fiction; here, though, this metalanguage, emptied of semantic and lexical content, has nevertheless become part of the movement of the fiction itself, taken over to reveal that the language of fiction, of art, was always animated by the secret incorporation of a metalanguage, itself a fiction. The repetitions and varia-tions of phrases throughout the narrative, and the increased insistence of "ping" in relation to the figure or image of this naked human begins to replace the subject, "I," with the object/nonobject "ping." And, in the course of this movement, this progression of diminishment, the language of *ego cogito ergo sum* is being made over into that of *cogitat ergo est,* and the central drama or tension is concerned with the effort to join *ego* with *sum.* Although strictly speaking there is no drama—how could there be?—because there is in fact no character, certainly little or no development in the traditional sense, no place, or setting, no time even, and no plot per se. The ventriloquist has revealed the dummy as a dummy, and now remarkably refuses to speak.

◆

In 1949 Beckett, along with George Duthuit, published a small, enigmatic text entitled *Three Dialogues.* In it, Beckett and his interlocutor discuss a number of different artists, the nature of art, its potency, and its possibilities. What Beckett had to say on the issue of the so-called revolutionaries of modern art is informa-tive. Of them he says:

> Among those whom we call great artists I can think of none whose concern was not predominantly with his expressive possibilities, those of his vehicle, those of humanity . . . they never stirred from the field of the possible, however much they may have enlarged it. The only thing disturbed by the revolutionaries . . . is a certain order on the plane of the feasible. (D, 139, 142)

The concern here with "expressive possibilities" and "humanity" again asserts the view of culture as a force of accumulation, as vehemently "result oriented." Though it adds to this the basically humanist foundation of culture, the notion that humanity is what culture reflects and values, that progress is continuous, and can be drawn in the shape of an inexhaustible human face. What Beckett refers to here as the "domain of the feasible" is a domain where expression is equated with power, the *power-to,* the power to express, the power to express much, or little, or finely, or in the end truly. It is this potency to express toward which Beckett's attentions are directed. To his interlocutor's somewhat bemused question, "What other plane can there be for the maker?" Beckett concedes: "Logically none," but then continues, "yet I speak of an art . . . weary of its puny exploits, weary of pretending to be able, of being able, of doing a little better the same old thing, of going a little further along a dreary road." To the interlocutor's next question, "Preferring what?" Beckett responds, in the oft-quoted phrase: "the expression that there is nothing to express, nothing with which to express, nothing from which to express, no power to express, no desire to express, together with the obligation to express." The interlocutor's response, "but that is a violently extreme and personal point of view," is no doubt correct. Beckett says nothing to this, and the interlocutor concludes that "perhaps that is enough for today."[17]

The apparent contradiction of the imperative to express under the *inderdit* that there is nothing *to* express, is contradictory only if one accepts the conventional but stale premise that art is indeed always and only expressive, that its essence and being, as well as its value, lies in the degree to which it is expressive of a culture, that it be expressive of a subject, expressive of man. But at the same time, as Beckett's interlocutor asks, what else can there be, what other plane is possible? Beckett's answer is as succinct as it is limiting—"logically none." However, the issue here, as elsewhere in Beckett's writing, is not one of logic, nor of success or failure in relation to the precepts of logic, nor of a means to achieve a successful inexpressiveness by evading the habitual repetition of the "expressive possibilities" of art. Such an escape is not possible. Rather, as Beckett also declares in the *Three Dialogues,* what is at stake is the recognition that "to be an artist is to fail, as no other dare fail, that failure is his world and the shrink from it desertion, art and craft, good housekeeping, living" (D, 145). Failure is the essential domain of the artist. And for those who make concessions, firstly with the presumption that there is something rather than nothing to be said, and secondly, and necessarily, with the cultural institutions that endorse such expressions, their lot becomes merely "good housekeeping, living," doing a little better the same old thing. In *Molloy* this same point is made in slightly more ironic terms: "I have never been particularly resolute, I mean given to resolutions, but rather inclined to plunge headlong into the shit. . . . But from this leaning too I derived scant satisfaction and if I have never quite got rid of it it is not for want of trying. The fact is, it seems, that the most you can hope is to be a little less, in the end, the creature you were in the beginning, and the middle" (M, 32).

Given the alternatives, either a complete escape—in which case one would have to remain silent—or an artistic housekeeping enterprise, or the seemingly resigned conclusion to simply hope to be a little less in the end, it would appear that there is little likelihood of any sort of real sundering or separation from contexts. But the issue here seems to be less one of political contestation than one of recognizing the epistemic condition within which political realities are fashioned. They, like identity in general, are impostures of language, inevitable fictions of a cultural imagination that desires to maintain the illusions of its life amidst the endless flow of an insurmountable death. Logically, however, there is no other alternative, no recourse except to concession, "good housekeeping, living."

In all of this there is an intentional contradiction. If what is preferred, as Beckett's epigrammatic remark suggests, is "the expression that there is nothing to express," this preference nonetheless falters at the very limit of expression. There is no possibility of such an expression. None is presumed. Logically, from the grounding perspective wherein the principles of identity and noncontradiction secure the ground from which we speak, no other perspective for the maker of art can be presumed or achieved. And Beckett readily admits this. The failure, then, given the tenet, becomes one of monumental proportion, for failure can never be complete; to fail completely, given that failure is the stated end, would paradoxically be to succeed, to accomplish, to say and thus contribute to the cumulative storehouse that is culture. Thus the oft-quoted phrase from *Company:* "No matter. Try again. Fail again. Fail better."[18]

This is not, as some would have it, a purely cynical, or "apolitical" program. On the contrary, engaged here is a subversive unsettling of the idealist basis of the language of philosophy and the social, historical, aesthetic, and political framework this language both institutes and maintains. Within the cultural context, and in relation to the various debates today surrounding the question of cultural politics, and the politics of culture, Beckett's art must and does appear violent, for it is fundamentally an art of questions, relentless and excessive; it questions itself, challenges its own existence as well as the existence of what is defined as art in general. The word games of *Watt,* or Molloy's desultory wanderings, or the endless bickering of Hamm and Clov, and the various narratives of the *residua,* these are all struggles for survival, struggles to stay afloat, to not be swallowed whole. By what? By death? No. By tedium, by what Rimbaud referred to as the long march, the boredom of meaning, of progress, all of which is worse than death.

Politically, this is an interruption, a cut; more than simply a grotesque perversion in the tidy orderings of things, it becomes a radical intervention that makes order unrecognizable; or, alternatively, all-too-recognizable as an artifice of power and control. What Beckett's writing, in its vigilance and attentiveness proposes are breaks with normality and normalization that hold out the possibility for a different, though necessarily unimaginable kind of form.

What Beckett's writing enacts, though in reverse, is the catastrophe of inexhaustible significance where there is in fact none. And yet what he also reveals is that this catastrophe itself can never be spoken, can never be said, precisely because it is the catastrophe of speech, of the excess of violence that is speech that is silent. This catastrophe, whose name is to be spoken only in silence, as Adorno reminds us, is the ultimate, the last catastrophe, before which everything else is penultimate.[19] But it is last neither because of its temporal position, nor its magnitude, nor because it is the most horrific or unimaginable. It is last precisely because it is also and at the same time first, and thus is that point from which there is no step beyond. The horror consists in this: that its point can only be illuminated in thought, grasped retrospectively, after the fact, and in such a way that only reveals the paucity of thought in relation to the singularity of catastrophe. The point is too sharp, the wound potentially too deep, to be held within the omnivorous movement of thought without at the same time piercing the very limits within which this movement institutes itself. Beckett's writing, at once prophetic and comedic, evokes this limit with a precision virtually matching that of its occasion. We hear it in the first line of the play *Waiting for Godot,* "Nothing to be done." In Vladimir's profound hearing of Estragon's "Nothing to be done," we see the comedy of a human face that cries before the banal struggle to remove a boot. "Nothing to be done."

෧

Beckett's writings are a progress toward night, toward nothing, toward where, as it was said in *Molloy,* "all grows dim." The progress, though, is slow going, interminable in fact. The radicality of these writings consists in their refusal of the search for a common order, for coherence, for meaning-fulness, in their defiance of what is termed the natural movement of thought, and the calculus of utility that is the legacy of Hegelianism within which everything is put to use, within which everything has value and functions on behalf of the ideals of progress, development.

In this regard, consider what Beckett had to say concerning the relationship of his own work to that of Joyce:

> With Joyce the difference is that Joyce is a superb manipulator of material— perhaps the greatest. He was making words do the absolute maximum of work. There isn't a syllable that's superfluous. . . . He's tending toward omniscience and omnipotence as an artist. I'm working with impotence, ignorance. I don't think impotence has been exploited in the past. There

seems to be a kind of aesthetic axiom that expression is achievement—must be an achievement. My little exploration is that whole zone of being that has always been set aside by artists as something unusable—as something by definition incompatible with art.[20]

For the time being, let us pass over the question of how impotence, which has not "been exploited in the past," could in fact be exploited at all (indeed, what might it mean to work with, or *exploit* impotence?). Beckett's remark indicates that his work is concerned with what has been "set aside by artists as something unusable—as something *by definition* incompatible with art." The seemingly slight qualification, "*by definition*," is in fact anything but; for it alludes precisely to the point or points of intersection at which art joins with a certain notion, or *definition* of culture from which it derives its own sense of being and definition, and in a reciprocal imperative becomes one of the principle modes of a culture's own self-validation. What is valuable to a culture are achievements, the sum of measurable, calculable accomplishments that may be taken into the movement of progress in order to ensure a seamless flow of past into present, what Rimbaud scornfully referred to as "the march, the burden, the desert, boredom." Indeed, like Rimbaud—but we could also include here Baudelaire, Mallarmé—Beckett's writing is an attempt, as he himself says, to unleash that within literature and literary experience which alienates it from all forms of culture, and to suggest a line of access to what is outside the defining grasps of a culture or its adherents.

Indeed, virtually from the very beginning, and in everything that comes after, Beckett's writing has been and continues to be a challenge to the scope and range (in the end, we may have to say the ideology) of critical discourse, and the shock of this *oeuvre* consists, at least in part, in the ways in which it defies our long-ingrained habits of reading, habits of thinking, of speaking. It demands a critical language stripped of its proleptic commitments to meaning, and a termination of the long-standing allegiance to the negative progression of history and culture that Western thought has held sacred as the basis of its power and singular access to reality. "If I were in the unenviable position of having to study my work," Beckett remarked in a 1967 letter, "my points of departure would be 'Naught is more real . . .' and the '*Ubi nihil vales . . .*'" (D, 113).

Notes

I wish to thank Henry Sussman and Raymond Federman for commenting upon an earlier draft of this essay. I want also to thank Jennifer Caruso for being the respondent and the members of the Graduate Group in Theory at SUNY Buffalo before whom I presented a shortened version of this essay.

1. *Disjecta,* ed. Ruby Cohn (New York: Grove Press, 1984), p. 173, hereafter referred to in the text as D.

2. Richard Coe, *Samuel Beckett* (New York: Grove Press, 1969), p. 14.

3. Marjorie Perloff, *Poetic License: Essays on Modernist and Postmodern Lyric* (Evanston, Ill.: Northwestern University Press, 1990), pp. 161–62.

4. Gustave Flaubert, letter to Louis Bonenfant, December 12, 1856, in *Correspondance,* ed. Jean Bruneau (Paris: Gallimard, 1980), vol. 2, p. 652.

5. Samuel Beckett, *Proust and Three Dialogues* (London: John Calder, 1965), p. 20. Hereafter cited in the text as P.

6. "An Interview with Beckett," by Israel Shenker, in *Samuel Beckett: The Critical Heritage,* ed. Lawrence Graver and Raymond Federman (London: Routledge, Kegan Paul, 1979), p. 148. Hereafter cited in the text as CH.

7. Samuel Beckett, *Three Novels by Samuel Beckett: Molloy, Malone Dies, The Unnamable,* trans. Samuel Beckett (except for *Molloy,* which was translated in collaboration with Patrick Bowles) (New York: Grove Press, 1958), p. 414. Though the novels were published separately, both in their original French versions and later in their English versions, the English edition has gathered all three of the novels in one volume to which I will refer throughout. However, for the sake of clarity I will refer to the individual novels separately, using the pagination from the collected volume, under the following abbreviations M for *Molloy;* MD for *Malone Dies;* and U for *The Unnamable.*

8. Samuel Beckett, *Worstward Ho* in *Nohow On: Company, Ill Seen Ill Said, Worstward Ho,* ed. S. E. Gontarski (New York: Grove Press, 1996), p. 89. Hereafter referred to in the text as NO.

9. Samuel Beckett, "A Piece of Monologue," in *The Collected Shorter Plays of Samuel Beckett* (New York: Grove Weidenfeld, 1984), pp. 265–66.

10. Raymond Federman, *Journey to Chaos: Samuel Beckett's Early Fiction* (Berkeley: University of California Press, 1965), pp. 3–4.

11. Maurice Blanchot, "Where Now? Who Now?," in *On Contemporary Literature,* ed. Richard Kostelanetz (New York: Avon Books, 1964), p. 249.

12. Samuel Beckett, "Texts For Nothing, 6." in *Samuel Beckett: The Complete Short Prose,* ed. S. E. Gontarski (New York: Grove Press, 1995), p. 124. All references to Beckett's shorter prose will be taken from this volume and will be referred to in the text as CS.

13. Samuel Beckett, *Waiting for Godot* (New York: Grove Press, 1954), p. 40. Hereafter referred to in the text as WG.

14. Samuel Beckett, *How It Is* (New York: Grove Press, 1961), p. 112. Hereafter referred to in the text as HII.

15. Theodor Adorno, *Aesthetic Theory,* trans. C. Lenhardt (London: Routledge & Kegan Paul, 1984), pp. 220–21. Hereafter referred to in the text as AT.

16. Walter Benjamin, "One Way Street," in Walter Benjamin, *Reflections,* trans. Edmund Jephcott (New York: Schocken Books, 1986), p. 61.

17. Samuel Beckett, "Three Dialogues," in Samuel Beckett, *Disjecta: Miscellaneous Writings and a Dramatic Fragment,* ed. Ruby Cohn (London: John Calder, 1983), pp. 142, 139.

18. Samuel Beckett, *Company* in *Nohow On,* pp. 46, 89.

19. Theodor Adorno, *Notes to Literature,* vol. 1, trans. Sherry Weber Nicholsen (New York: Columbia University Press, 1991), p. 249.

20. Quoted in Raymond Federman, "Beckett and the Fiction of Mud," in *On Contemporary Literature,* ed. Richard Kostelanetz (New York: Avon Books, 1964), p. 257, emphasis mine.

9
BECKETT [F]OR NOTHING

Raymond Federman

What form can fiction take when it encounters everywhere nothing but verbal dust?

How can the being of fiction give himself a form, relate himself, if he constantly suppresses himself, if he **blots** out the words, the very words that *made him be possible?*

And yet, *Only the words break the silence.*

Strange paradox: *Blots, words can be blotted and the mad thoughts they invent, the nostalgia for that slime where the Eternal breathed and his son wrote, long after, with divine idiotic finger, at the feet of the adulteress, wipe it out, all you have to do is say you said nothing and so say nothing again.* [**Text 6**]

What will become then of the speaking/writing I, if he blots out, negates, cancels the words that have been him—his life?

That is the question raised by **Texts for Nothing.**

But that question could only be raised after the journey of Molloy, the reincarnation of Malone, the verbal agony of the unnamable.

That is to say after the trilogy was written.

Suddenly, no, at last, long last, I couldn't any more, I couldn't go on. Someone said, You can't stay here. I couldn't stay there and I couldn't go on. [**Text 1**]

Here/There—in the space of writing/speaking—one is far from Murphy's garret in the insane asylum, far from Mr. Knott's house of deception, far from Molloy's room, far from Malone's bed.

Far also from the questions the unnamable posed at the beginning of his verbal journey: *Where now? Who now? When now? Unquestioning. I, say, I.*

But close, very close to the end of **The Unnamable:** *You must go on, I can't go on, I'll go on.*

The text of **The Unnamable** attempted to answer the questions of *Where, When,* and *Who*—time, place, and being—by localizing the narrative voice into a fiction, a *kind of story,* but in the process discovered that the voice could not be named, could not speak itself, that in fact it was being spoken by the words that kept it/him unnamable, even though time and space had been inflicted on him.

. . . yes, they've inflicted the notion of time on me to . . . but it's entirely a matter of voices, no other metaphor is appropriate.

I see me, I see my place, there is nothing to show it, nothing to distinguish it, from all the other places, they are mine, all mine, if I wish, I wish none but mine, there is nothing to mark it, I am there so little, I see it, I feel it round me, it enfolds me, it covers me, if only this voice would stop, for a second . . .

Who are these *They* who inflict time and space but not a name on the unnamable?

First I'll say what I'm not, that's how they taught me to proceed, then what I am, it's already under way, I have only to resume at the point where I let myself be cowed. I am neither, I needn't say, Murphy, nor Watt, nor Mercier, nor—no, I can't even bring myself to name them, nor any of the others whose very names I forget, who told me I was they, who I must have tried to be, under duress, or through fear, or to avoid acknowledging me, not the slightest connexion.

In his search for a place to be, a time to be, in his search for beingness, the unnamable encounters only *silence and words,* nothing else. Silence that negates him. Words that fail to name him, to make him. But the unnamable is not ready to admit, to accept that he is mere *wordness* or *wordlessness.* Therefore, he too, like his predecessors, in order to sustain himself, or give himself the illusion of being, invents fiction, stories, playmates—Mahood, Worm.

And why not, since, as he says, mocking the old cliché: *While there is life there is hope.*

Real or fictitious, life here gives the speaking voice only the illusion of being: *It's a question of voices, of voices to keep me going, in the right manner . . . words pronouncing me alive, since that's how they want me to be . . .*

But whose voices? And which pronouns? . . . *enough of this cursed first person, it is really too red a herring, I'll get out of my depth if I'm not careful. . . . Bah, any old pronoun will do, provided one sees through it. Matter of habit. To be adjusted later.*

In order to speak of **Texts for Nothing** one has to backtrack into **The Unnamable,** which gradually generates **Texts for Nothing.**

The Unnamable: Ultimate effort to BE—to BE somewhere, in time and place. But also ultimate failure to do so. Except in the illusion of storytelling. That's Mankind for you, or rather Mahoodness. To give oneself the illusion of being.

The metamorphosis of the pronoun I into **he** or **we,** or into the dynasty of the couple, doesn't negate the fact that it remains the story of I—*I the teller told.*

An I struggling with a growing ontological awareness of himself as he becomes the words, the very word that I speaks. The very words that I calls his life.

Words, mine was never more than that, than this pell-mell babel of silence and words, my viewless form described as ended, or to come, or still in progress, depending on the words . . . [**Text 6**]

Again one must backtrack into **The Unnamable,** for it is not easy to arrive at the stage of pure word-beingness of **Texts for Nothing.** Or rather the stage of word-shit: *That's right, wordshit, bury me, avalanche, and let there be no more talk of any creature . . .* [**Text 9**]

But in order to depersonify itself, in order to decharacterize itself, in order to become wordless, the I must undergo several transformations:

1. Transformation of the I narrator/hero, writer/written, teller/told into an unnamable being. Therefore, loss of nomination, loss of a name.
2. Transformation of the story. The sustaining process that situates the I in place and time, whether real or imaginary. Therefore, loss of the anecdote, the fable.
3. Transformation of the fictitious word-being into wordshit that subsists only as residua beyond fictitiousness. Therefore, loss of beingness.
4. Transformation of the language of fiction that gave the I the illusion of progress. Reduction of discursive/descriptive language to a verbal delirium that leaves the voice stranded on the edge of the precipice of meaning, leaning against the wind of meaninglessness. A delirium that cannot go on and yet cannot stop going on. Therefore, loss of syntactical order, sense, direction.

Language becomes *A rumor transmissible ad infinitum in either direction* [**How It Is**]

This difficult, almost impossible undertaking, that qualifies itself as a *torture,* consists in seizing Mahoodness beyond all concepts of fiction or fabulation. Beyond the lies of fiction.

No, no souls, or bodies, or birth, or life, or death, you've got to go on without any of that junk, that's all dead with words, with excess of words, they can say nothing else, they say there is nothing else . . . [**Text 10**]

The unnamable puts it this way: *Agreed, agreed, I who am on my way, words bellying out my sails, am also that unthinkable ancestor of whom nothing can be said.*

Being on his way to nothingness, the unnamable cannot render himself present— present to his own being, even though he realizes that one cannot exist outside of one's fictions.

> **The Unnamable:** that miraculous work of fiction reveals that man manifests himself while demonstrating that he cannot be found without his fictions. Or rather without language. The language of fiction can no longer create beingness, as in the old fables of the past, it can only manifest a defect of being, expose the imposture of literature. Paradoxically then, even though there is still language there is no being.
> **Texts for Nothing:** . . . *who is this raving now . . . one who speaks saying, without ceasing to speak, Who's speaking?* And if someone is speaking, who hears him? Is Man/Mahood this being who speaks, but who doesn't know why he speaks? *Why, why this need to speak,* since to speak leads nowhere, fails to create being, *fails better.* Especially since the notion that someone is listening to whoever is speaking is a delusion.

. . . qu'il ne vienne plus nous emmerder avec ces histoires d'objectivité et de choses vues. De toutes les choses que personne n'a jamais vues, ces cascades sont assurément les plus énormes. [**La peinture des van Velde ou le monde et le pantalon**]

The fundamental implication of what can be called subjective literature (from romanticism to realism to Proust, Joyce, Sartre, and Camus) was precisely to assure the identity and continuity of being—of the self.

Even in the so-called realistic/objective novel of the nineteenth century, it was the world, society, reality that was vacillating in relation to the individual—the self of fiction, an I usually disguised as an **He** or a **She.**

For most characters [as they used to be called] of that novel, the world was an object of doubt. The subject doubted the object that made him what he [she as well] was.

The romantic hero [the realist hero, same thing] felt alienated from everything except himself. Always ready to undermine the basis, the grounding of others, but never his or hers.

Though the existentialist hero [antihero?]—Roquentin, Mathieu, Meursault, Clamence, including The Dangling Man of Saul Bellow [that displaced neo-existentialist]—doubts the world, nonetheless he believes in the solidity of his own self, in the freedom of the self, even if it brings him to the edge of despair and nausea.

The romantic/realist/existentialist hero remains Cartesian, and like Descartes he doubts everything in order to arrive at an absolute certitude of his own self, however mediocre, tormented, laughable that self may be.

Think of the Dostoevsky hero, the Balzac hero, and even the Proust sufferer. They all want to assert their being and beingness. Stephen Dedalus, that pompous self-impressed *artiste-en-herbe* goes even further in asserting his being, and his freedom of self, by declaring emphatically: *I will not serve that in which I no longer believe whether it calls itself my home, my fatherland or my church.* Down with the great social institutions that have sustained the self for so long. Let the self go alone . . . *to encounter for the millionth time the reality of experience and to forge in the smithy of* [his] *soul the uncreated conscience of* [his] *race.*

The Beckett creature [what else can it be called?]—whether named Molloy, Malone, The Unnamable, or simply I, generated by Belacqua, Murphy, Watt, Mercier, Camier, and all the others—is the first to negate this assertion of being, the first to doubt and cancel his self. The first to dare go beyond doubt, *as no other dare . . . fail.* As such, **Texts for Nothing** is situated beyond the very idea of fiction, beyond the kind of fiction that managed, even as a system of doubt, to sustain beingness.

The central paradox of these short impossible texts is there in the title if one brackets the **f** of **[f]or**—the paradox of writing texts for nothing, into the void, into the abyss of the white page while writing on, writing on to produce yet more words on the page, to write nothing. There is no way in, and no way out: *I couldn't stay there and I couldn't go on.* But description is nonetheless necessary, even though useless: *I'll describe the place, that's unimportant.*

There is then a description of place—*The top, very flat, of a mountain, no, a hill, but so wild, so wild, enough.* But unimportant.

The unnamable also attempted to describe his location: *This place, if I could describe this place, portray it, I've tried, I feel no place, no place around me, there's no end to me, I don't know what it is, it isn't flesh, it doesn't end, it's like air. . . .*

Flesh . . . air . . . mountain . . . hill . . . doesn't matter, all the same. Change a word in the text, change mountain or hill to flesh or air, the place is different, but that's unimportant.

Change the I to **you** or **he,** the pronoun changes, but that's unimportant. The same goes for time. Being and time are one and the same textual movement here. The being hidden in words, the time of the movement from one word to the next. Both these concepts collapse into words, so that being and time implode to being-as-tense: *At first I only had been there, now I'm still here, soon I won't be here yet.*

Time is tense: *now . . . soon . . . yet . . .* the past *had been,* the present *is,* the future *will be—now soon yet* what kind of temporality is this?

As such, **Texts [f]or Nothing** raises the question of what is a text? What kind of texts are these that reject logical sequential temporality? Are these sacred texts, biblical texts, texts without measure, texts without purpose. If so, then why not simply **For Nothing,** as a title?

Why use the word **text** as part of this nontitle work? Is it to suggest that these texts are without a story, without characters, without plot, without human verisimilitude, without time and place? If so, what are these texts about?

No, not about nothing or nothingness in the philosophical sense. These thirteen **Texts for Nothing** are nothing but themselves. There is no about here. No references to anything outside these texts, except of course, by necessity, to the texts that have generated them—Beckett's previous fiction, now reduced to **Texts [f]or Nothing.**

Nonetheless, one must ask: Who speaks here, and from where? Who says I, here, and what kind of I is it? Certainly no longer a human pretense or substitution.

These thirteen meditations, tales, sessions, break off the chain of the delirious flow of words of the trilogy. They present the insularity of the short, brief text as a sign of the isolation, the detachment, the alienation of the wanderer of the preceding fiction. The speaking voice now functions without support, without any staging, without crutches. Very much like the paint of an abstract expressionist tableau that sustains itself without a subject, without geometry. **Texts for Nothing** are like flares of lightning in the silence of language. Pure acts of farewell, of cancellation, through halts and silences, hesitations and false departures.

These thirteen texts must be read, heard rather, as one text, one sound that stops, starts again, overlaps, cancels out. Only language is heard, nothing else. The sound of language speaking from the other side of fiction—from *the reverse of farness*. [**Text 5**]

This language that speaks in the void, this *excess of words* can no longer create birth or death—that's *the junk* of old fiction. That's the old fable: . . . *that's all dead with words, with excess of words, they can say nothing else, they say there is nothing else, that here it's that and nothing else, but they won't say it eternally, they'll find some other nonsense, no matter what* . . . [**Text 10**]

The writer who holds the pen, the scribe who scribbles with the old quill—*I'm the clerk, I'm the scribe, at the hearings of what cause I know not.* [**Text 5**]—is still present, somewhat, here, but outside the fable, outside the myth, beyond the pretense by which he hoped to create a fiction, invent someone. Or as he puts it: *I am far from that wrangle, I shouldn't bother with it, I need nothing, neither to go on nor to stay where I am* . . . [**Text 1**]

Later he adds: *I'm making progress, it was time, I'll learn to keep my foul mouth shut before I'm done, if nothing foreseen crops up.* [**Text 4**]

While the scribe rants, the voice of fiction, or rather the voice of language watches the hand that is writing it: *Out of the corner of my eye I observe the writing hand, all dimmed and blurred by the ▬▬▬ by the reverse of farness.* [**Text 5**]

Marvelous hesitation this dash ▬▬▬, this rupture that allows the language of these texts to locate itself in its own paradox—*the reverse of farness.*

Strange reversal of roles, crucial, however, to an understanding—hearing?—of these texts. This voice of fiction that speaks from inside the page, this voice locked inside language is telling us that it's all words, only words, the words that come out of this mouth to organize themselves on the paper in order to mean nothing. That voice, and the otherness of that voice—the I who speaks—are at the same time the voice of fiction and the mental voice of the fictioneer—the clerk, the scribe.

I'm not in his head, nowhere in his old body, and yet I'm there, for him I'm there, with him, hence all the confusion. [**Text 4**]

Whereas in the trilogy the text was attempting to establish, to install the writer as the central figure of the text, here in **Texts for Nothing,** the language mocks that figure, because finally it is all ***wordshit.*** Wordshit: language and excrement packaged into one sound.

*Wretched acoustics this evening, the merest s[**crap**]s, literally,* laments the voice from within the page [**Text 6**]. One can barely hear what remains to be said and heard— *ill-said ill-heard ill-recaptured ill-murmured in the mud.* The mud, the muck, the merde, the wordshit, that's what remains now. The last element, the final residence, the ultimate abode of the word-being that looms ahead—the reptilian creature of **How It Is.**

Wordshit, the final production of the writer. While demolishing the kind of fiction that could only function on an intention and a pretension, Beckett denounces the inefficacy of language.

The **Texts for Nothing** are not fallouts, leftovers from the trilogy, as some critics have claimed, but important traces that the Beckettian creature leaves behind—as one leaves one's excrement behind in nature while on an outing—before undergoing yet another mutation.

But there is more to these **Texts for Nothing.** One must be careful not to fall into the trap of a title apparently without ambiguity. **Texts for Nothing** are not for nothing. True, they have nothing, that is to say the word nothing as their subject. **Le rien** of the French title—**Textes pour rien**—but this nothing, this **rien** should be read as a little something. In French **rien, un rien** really means a little something, a minor thing. Nothing here is both the subject and the object of these texts. Or rather, language, the meaninglessness, the nothingness of language is the subject here.

The spectacular research, searching, probing, groping of the preceding fiction has led to this. The unnamable has exhausted himself in search of himself, in search of his own self as language. Here, in **Texts for Nothing,** language is on the verge of becoming the result, the end product, the wordshit—the testimony of the search. After having attempted to designate the being of the protagonist: the wandering of Molloy, the dying of Malone, the speaking and the unspeakability of the unnamable, language now designates itself as **Texts [f]or Nothing.**

Therefore, these thirteen texts are not about nothing, they are about the nothingness of fiction, thus affirming the absoluteness of language, language deprived of fiction. A language without stories, without people: *And yet*—the voice tells us—*I have high hopes, I give you my word, high hopes, that one day I may tell a story, hear a story, yet another, with men, kinds of men as in the days when I played all regardless or nearly, worked and played.* [**Text 6**]

But of course, Beckett cannot, will not tell another story. Once committed to language as pure language, one cannot retreat into storytelling. The rest of us can do that, but Beckett will not do that, cannot do that, as he goes on **Worstward Ho.**

These thirteen meditations on language—language as writing, language as voice—not in a philosophical or linguistic sense, and certainly not as fable, declare words as supreme, and it becomes clear that this supremacy of words has no need of order, that is to say form. Impossible to speak here, as one could for the other Beckett works, of a form, or of a narrative structure. Yes, even form and structure have disappeared from **Texts for Nothing.**

How then, one must wonder, are these texts constituted? How are they made possible as ▬▬ here one must hesitate to find the right word, but there is no other word ▬▬ as fiction? For they are, after all, fiction, and not essays, or philosophical treatises, or whatever. Unclassifiable fiction, and yet fiction, even though the words now lead nowhere, achieve nothing: *The words too, slow, slow, the subject dies before it comes to the verb, words are stopping too. Better off then than when life was babble?* [**Text 2**]

. . . *when life was babble:* babbling, with all its implications and connotations of birth, growth, development towards being, toward character, towards maturity, death, and inevitably toward narrative structure, is no longer necessary here. Here, the text no longer needs to seek growth and form. Here, language does not accumulate upon itself to create a narrative whole that moves toward a resolution, or a final solution. Here, words merely belong to themselves, to their own form-lessness and meaninglessness.

Where am I? . . . who is this clot who doesn't know where to go, who can't stop, who takes himself for me and for whom I take myself, anything at all, the old jangle.

Those evenings then, but what is this evening made of, this evening now that never ends, in whose shadows I'm alone . . . [**Text 11**]

The *where am I?* and especially the word *evening* set up a series of terms that accumulate around *this evening,* that gather like grapes, not to construct a story or an anecdote, but simply to fill the gap of *this evening now*—the writing *session.*

That is the process here. One word sets up a movement of words without direction, without destination, without shape, until there is nothing more to write. Words follow their course so well towards nothingness that ultimately they cancel out: *I recapitulate,* says the I-voice, and then adds, *impossible.*

The words of **Texts for Nothing** postulate a fictitious being that remains neutral and remote, a being who cannot become another, as Molloy, Malone, and even the unnamable became the playmates they invented.

Will they succeed in slipping me into him, the memory and dream of me, into him still living, amn't I there already, wasn't I always there, like a stain of remorse. . . . Pah there are voices everywhere, ears everywhere, one who speaks saying without ceasing to speak, who's speaking?

If the voice can no longer incarnate itself into another body, another character, another self, into fictitious beingness, how can it exist? How can it be? It exists because it is heard—*pah there are voices everywhere, ears everywhere . . .*

In **Malone Dies** spoken language [spoken-ness] becomes written language [written-ness] when Malone corrects himself: *. . . it must be over a week since I said, I shall soon be quite dead at last, etc. Wrong again. That is not what I said, I could swear to it, that is what I wrote.* In so doing Malone escapes his own death as a spoken/speaking protagonist, or rather resurrects himself as the writer of his own undying. Malone does not die, he writes himself out of death, as he emerges backward out of the *great cunt* of existence.

In **Texts for Nothing,** the words are made possible, the words become their own fiction because there is, inscribed in the texts themselves, a listening presence [an implied reader?]—an ear that hears these words.

That is the crucial step that Beckett's fiction will take beyond **Texts for Nothing.** Starting with **How It Is** until the final words, the last testament **Stirrings Still,** language will listen to itself talk in the vacuum of fiction, language will invent a listener for itself in order to hear its own logocentricity.

It is no longer a question of the teller/told dichotomy, or the teller/told juxtaposition or superimposition, it is now the coming together of the speaker and the listener, the verbal and the oral: *fallen in the mud from our mouths innumerable and ascending to where there is an ear . . . an ear to hear even ill these scraps of other scraps of an antique rigmarole* [**How It Is**].

The French say *s'entendre* when they mean to hear oneself, to understand oneself. The existence of one who speaks is made possible because he is heard, or hears himself talk. It's a question of *acoustics* we are told. [**Text 6**]

If in the fiction that led to **Texts for Nothing** it was a question of telling and writing, now it is a question of saying and listening: . . . *so given am I to thinking with my breath. . . . And personally, I hear it said, personally I have no more time to lose . . .* [**Text 7**]

Ultimately, it is the presence of human breath that sustains and coordinates these texts, this oral adventure of words. With **Murphy** and **Watt,** we were in the zone of seeing. With the trilogy, we were in the zone of telling. With **Texts for Nothing,** we enter the zone of listening. Beckett does not write for nothing, he writes for all the senses.

CONTRIBUTORS

AnJanette Brush is a photographer who has taught art at Columbia College, Chicago. She is currently a freelance writer in New York City.

Marcel Cornis-Pope is Professor of English and Critical Theory at Virginia Commonwealth University. His publications include *Anatomy of the White Whale: A Poetics of the American Symbolic Romance* (Bucharest: Univers, 1982) and *Hermeneutic Desire and Critical Rewriting: Narrative Interpretation in the Wake of Poststructuralism* (New York: St. Martins, 1992). He edits *The Comparatist,* journal of the Southern Comparative Literature Association.

Christopher Devenney received his Ph.D. in Comparative Literature at SUNY/Buffalo, and is a Visiting Assistant Professor of English at Haverford College.

Raymond Federman, Melodia Jones Chair, French, SUNY/Buffalo, author of, among many works in a postmodern idiom fusing fiction, theory, discourse, and autobiography, *The Voice in the Closet, The Twofold Vibration,* and *Double or Nothing.* He also contributed the first full-length study of Beckett's fiction in English: *Journey to Chaos: Samuel Beckett's Early Fiction* (Berkeley: University of California Press, 1965).

Carla Locatelli is Professor of English, University of Trent, Italy. She is author of *Unwording the World: Samuel Beckett's Prose Works after the Nobel Prize* (Philadelphia: University of Pennsylvania Press, 1990), a seminal theoretical exploration; also, among many other publications, of *Texts and Contexts: A Cultural History of English and American Literature* (Milan: Signorelli, 1981). For some years, she has edited the proceedings of annual international conferences on pressing theoretical and cultural issues she organizes at Trent.

Brian McHale has made pivotal contributions to the primary field implicated by this volume: *Postmodernist Fiction* (New York: Methuen, 1987) and *Constructing Postmodernism* (London and New York: Routledge, 1992). He is currently a Distinguished Professor of English at West Virginia University.

Christian Prigent is an independent poet and essayist in Le Mans, France.

Gabriele Schwab, Professor of English and Comparative Literature, University of California, Irvine, is the author of two Harvard University Press books

173

on narrative and critical theory. In addition, she has published *The Mirror and the Killer Queen: Otherness in Literary Language* (Bloomington: Indiana University Press, 1996).

HENRY SUSSMAN, Julian Park Chair of Humanities, SUNY/Buffalo, author of a number of critical studies, most recently, *The Aesthetic Contract: Statutes of Art and Intellectual Work in Modernity* (Stanford: Stanford University Press, 1997).

INDEX

175